Linguistic Variation Yearbook

VOLUME 7   2007

General Editor

Jeroen Van Craenenbroeck
Catholic University Brussels

Associate Editor

Johan Rooryck
Leiden University

John Benjamins Publishing Company
Amsterdam/Philadelphia

Linguistic Variation Yearbook

Table of contents

Introduction

Jeroen Van Craenenbroeck and Johan Rooryck

We are pleased to introduce the seventh installment of the *Linguistic Variation Yearbook*. As has become customary by now, the volume contains one fairly programmatic article that tackles the issue of language variation from a broad vantage point, as well as a number of articles that address more specific topics. Moreover, as we will make clear in this introduction, a couple of papers in this volume build on topics and analyses that have featured in earlier LIVY-volumes. This is encouraging, as it suggests that current linguistic theorizing on language variation within the Minimalist Program may be converging on certain topics and methods.

In their paper "Node labels and features: stable and unstable dialects and variation in acquisition", Tom Roeper and Lisa Green start out from the apparent divide between the abstractness of grammatical principles in minimalism on the one hand and the subtle aspects of dialect variation on the other. They argue that if such an abstract theory can predict intricate aspects of variation, this can be viewed as providing strong support for the existence of UG. Key ingredient in their theoretical proposal is the distinction between nodes and features. The latter are stable when they are dominated by a matching node label, but unstable when they occur on a different, non-matching node or on a lexical item. Unstable features give rise to language variation. This flexible theoretical proposal is not only well equipped to deal with synchronic and diachronic variation, it also offers a new perspective on language acquisition: the child shifts from a(n unstable) feature representation to a (stable) node representation. Moreover, current grammars are assumed to simultaneously represent the undercurrent of several dialects, as long as they can all be mapped onto a single tree representation. This is reminiscent of much recent work on the possibility of multiple grammars, in particular that of Charles Yang (cf. in this respect Yang's contribution to LIVY 5).

Another recurrent theme can be found in the paper of Uli Sauerland, entitled "Copying vs. structure sharing: a semantic argument". Sauerland's paper is an

Linguistic Variation Yearbook 7 (2007), v–vii.
ISSN 1568–1483 / E-ISSN 1569–9900 © John Benjamins Publishing Company

extended argument in favor of a multidominance analysis of so-called focus dependency effects, whereby an elided phrase can function as a bound variable when
its antecedent is focused. As such, it fits in nicely with Peter Svenonius' contribution to LIVY 6 and Barbara Citko's paper in LIVY 5, as both these papers also defended that particular theoretical option, but for different empirical phenomena.
Sauerland discusses in detail how an analysis in terms of structure sharing not only
overcomes the problems facing traditional accounts of focus dependency (in terms
of binding or copying), but that it also makes a number of additional (and correct)
predictions. As far as language variation is concerned, his proposal predicts variation to be mainly situated on the PF-side, i.e. which copy or copies is/are spelled
out in a multidominance structure. A first glance at German wh-copying seems to
confirm this prediction, but a lot of work remains to be done.

In his contribution, Klaus Abels tries to move "Towards a restrictive theory of
(remnant) movement". He argues that the lack of a sufficiently restrictive theory of
movement prevents a proper explanation of the well-known linear asymmetries in
natural language within proposals that try to reduce the expressive power of phrase
structure (such as Kayne's (1994) anti-symmetry). He proposes to take the hardly
disputed ordering of theta-, case- and A'-related operations as a central theorem
(dubbed UCOOL). Abels then implements UCOOL in such a way that it includes
not only simple movement, but also subextraction from moved phrases (surfing
paths) and remnant movement (diving paths). This proposal receives strong support from a detailed investigation of the feeding and bleeding relations between A-
movement, scrambling, wh-movement and topicalisation. Moreover, it also provides a straightforward account for straight cross-serial dependencies in Germanic
and for the absence of inverse cross-serial dependencies. In both these respects, it
is shown to fare better than existing accounts in terms of remnant movement.

Marjo van Koppen focuses on "Agreement with coordinated subjects: a comparative perspective". She addresses the agreement relation between a complementizer Probe and a coordinated subject Goal. In such contexts, complementizers in
various Dutch dialects can agree either with the first conjunct (first conjunct agreement) or with the entire coordination (resolved agreement). The choice between
the two options is not free, but depends on the affix inventory of each dialect. That
is, the syntactic derivation of the various examples is identical, and the locus of
variation is situated exclusively in the post-syntactic lexicon. This analysis extends
straightforwardly to comparable agreement phenomena in Bavarian, Arabic and
Irish. The theoretical contribution of Van Koppen's paper is twofold. First of all, it
shows that when one Probe syntactically Agrees with multiple Goals, the ultimate
morpho-phonological spell-out of these syntactic relations is determined by the

post-syntactic morphological component. The second theoretical contribution of this paper resides in the claim that the internal structure of movement copies is invisible for Agree.

In "The Brythonic reconciliation", Mélanie Jouitteau argues that a long-standing and widely accepted typological difference between Welsh and Breton is in fact only apparent. While the former is traditionally characterized as VSO and the latter as V2, Jouitteau shows that both are V2-languages. The main difference between these two varieties of Celtic reduces to the fact that V2 in Breton is more 'conspicuous' than in Welsh. This difference derives from a different setting for two parameters: a lexical one determining which C-particles the various languages have at their disposal, and a syntactic one governing whether or not a language allows phonological features to be split off from lexical and semantic ones. If it does, it can move these phonological features to satisfy its V2-requirement. Jouitteau's account of this "expletive movement" is couched in Holmberg's (2000, 2005) implementation of the EPP.

The paper by Lisa Matthewson, Henry Davis and Hotze Rullman entitled "Evidentials as epistemic modals: evidence from St'át'imcets" examines evidential morphemes in St'át'imcets, a Northern Interior Salish language, and argues that they are epistemic modals. They run a large number of detailed tests in support of this conclusion and against a competing analysis, i.e. that the evidential morphemes are illocutionary operators. Their analysis raises serious doubts about the claim that a defining characteristic of epistemic modals is that they encode degree of speaker certainty. Matthewson, Davis & Rullman show that in St'át'imcets none of the modals encode quantificational strength and propose instead a parameter whereby modals encode either source of information or degree of speaker certainty, but never both at the same time.

Finally, we would like to thank the reviewers for this volume, for their much appreciated comments and critical remarks: Cecilia Poletto, Jason Merchant, Marcel den Dikken, Jairo Nunes, Dan Finer and one reviewer who preferred to remain anonymous.

Node labels and features
Stable and unstable dialects and variation in acquisition

Tom Roeper and Lisa Green
University of Massachusetts

We argue that the smallest shifts in grammar should give us the most precise insight into grammatical mechanisms. The often tiny differences captured by dialects become a natural focus for linguistic theory, precisely because of their variability and instability in the history of language and in the grammatical commitments of individual speakers. The notion of stability refers to where dialects differ, where registers add or drop features, where historical change moves, what proves difficult in the steps in acquisition, and where second language learners easily stumble. In a word, we argue that nodes are stable and features are unstable. In particular, node labels, which reflect head features in a feature bundle, are stable, while non-head features are unstable and subject to variation. We show that specific nodes in African American English, such as Negative Focus (CP) in negative inversion constructions, are stable (*Don't nobody play baseball.*). Also, particle positions (*he threw (up) the ball (up)*) and various features, like those associated with tense inflection (if it is under a V node not a T node) or presuppositionality (if it is under a CP node), are inherently unstable. Many other predictions for dialect, acquisition, and diachronic patterns follow as well.

Keywords: African American English, aspectual *be*, habitual *be*, interpretable features, minimalism, multiple grammars, negative focus, negative inversion, presuppositionality, stable nodes, tense, uninterpretable features, Universal Grammar, unstable features

Linguistic Variation Yearbook 7 (2007), 1–26.
ISSN 1568-1483/ E-ISSN 1569-9900 © John Benjamins Publishing Company

Introduction

Not all dialect variation is of the same stripe. Some features seem stable over generations and others seem to shift from speaker to speaker. Some dialect features are easily grasped by outsiders, and others will escape an outsider's control for a lifetime. Such large differences should tell us something about Universal Grammar (UG), or rather, should be predicted by a good theory.

We argue that, in general, the smallest shifts in grammar should give us the most precise insight into grammatical mechanisms. To utilize a metaphor: the second hand on a clock is more closely linked to a clock's spring mechanism than the hour hand. For this reason, the often tiny differences captured by dialects become a natural focus for linguistic theory, precisely because of their variability and instability in the history of language and in the grammatical commitments of individual speakers. The notion of stability refers to where dialects differ, where registers add or drop features, where historical change moves, what proves difficult in the steps in acquisition, and where second language learners easily stumble. By hypothesis, all variation must occur within the boundaries of UG. Modern minimalism appears to increase vastly the abstractness of principles of grammar. None of the formal anchors appear to have fixed connections to the surface of grammar: phases, features, node labels, and feature satisfaction are inherently open concepts which could allow tremendous dialect variation. If such an abstract theory provides room for and predicts the most subtle aspects of variation, then variation provides strong support for it if, in mechanical detail, the principles of UG are reflected.

On the other hand, taking an acquisition perspective, any increase in descriptive power, any failure to make a direct connection to instructive triggers in the input, will make the acquisition path more difficult to see. Therefore, any distinctions which create more possibilities complicate acquisition and create domains of probable discrepancy for those whose knowledge of grammar is passive. These claims are obviously broad enough to lead to many predictions beyond those we consider. Still we regard this reasoning as quite pedestrian, rather close to common sense and perhaps a clarification of what is already assumed by many people.

1. Technical background

Hierarchical phrase structure, often isolated by movement operations, is one of the best established features of modern grammar. However, the labels on nodes themselves have always been – and increasingly been – subject to reanalysis and remain uncertain theoretical objects.

Current syntactic theory in the minimalist framework has focused upon feature matching, movement, and the separable properties of interpretable/uninterpretable features. Chomsky (2005, 2006) has focused upon two notions: 1) that interpretable features have a semantic value and 2) that nodes have labels that reflect those interpretable features and motivate syntactic operations or drive all operations. This point is captured in the following way: "If an element Z (lexical or constructed) enters into further computations... The optimal assumption is that this information is provided by a designated minimal element of Z, a lexical item W (Z itself, if it is an LI), which is detectable by a simple algorithm; *the label of Z*, the head projected in X-bar theories" (Chomsky 2006). With respect to uninterpretable features, Chomsky argues: "Since the values of these features are determined by context, the simplest assumption is that they are unvalued in the lexicon, thus properly distinguished from interpretable features, and assigned their values in syntactic configurations."[1] We can represent the difference schematically:

(1)

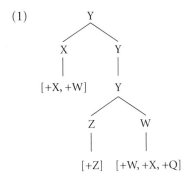

If [W] is present under the W node, then the feature bundle under [W] can move to [X] and delete the [X] feature. If [Q] is not linked to a node label, then it is inherently unstable and may be deleted or not recognized. If [X] is generated in a position where it does not match the higher node, then it is unstable as well, though it should be more stable since it is represented elsewhere in the tree and motivates movement. Therefore, the only completely stable nodes are those which are generated below an identical node and not moved (W). Our goal will be to argue for the feature/node contrast without fully carrying out implications for the technology of interpretable/uninterpretable features.

One major consequence for this perspective is that one cannot assume the Universal Base Hypothesis is more than a rough configurational assumption. For instance, UG will dictate that the Complementizer Phrase (CP) will dominate the Inflection Phrase (IP), but the present and/or exact content of these nodes cannot be assumed by the language learner (e.g. some Asian languages may have no IP).

This in turn means that an acquisition device must assemble evidence to decide exactly what the node label contains. If details of dialect variation and the acquisition path receive a natural explanation in terms of a feature/node contrast, then this non-intuitional evidence has a very significant role in the empirical work justifying formal distinctions. We will argue that tree structure allows a very straightforward method to represent multiple dialects, or multiple grammars as recent theoretical work labels them (Kroch 1997; Roeper 1999; Yang 2003). In fact, what is labeled Standard (Mainstream) English is really a representation of several grammars with some redundancies that are compatible with a single tree, which we illustrate in Section 3.

2. Stable and unstable features

We begin with examples of stable and unstable features that illustrate the feature/node contrast in (1) and then move to more complex examples. We show how the distinction can account for intra- and inter-dialectal variation. Our focus will be upon African American English (AAE).

2.1 Stable features

Stable features are either universal or dialect-specific features that define a node.

2.1.1 ASPECT *as a stable node*
African American English differs most from other varieties of English in exhibiting a rich tense-aspect component, and we argue that a stable node label for ASPECT exists in AAE. Tense-aspect markers *be*, *BIN*, and *dən*, which are similar to verbal forms in mainstream and other varieties of American English, are used in AAE. Aspectual (or habitual) *be* (be_{asp}) (2) indicates that an eventuality recurs, and *BIN* (3) indicates that an eventuality or some part of an eventuality is in the remote

past. Finally, the marker *dən* (4) indicates that the eventuality is in its resultant state, or according to Terry (2005), introduces stativity.[2]

(2) Bruce be running in the park.
 'Bruce is usually running in the park'

(3) a. Bruce BIN running in the park.
  'Bruce has been running in the park for a long time'
  b. Bruce BIN ran in the park.
  'Bruce ran in the park a long time ago'

(4) Bruce dən ran in the park.
 'Bruce has already run in the park'

On syntactic and structural grounds, these markers can be argued to be generated in ASPECT (ASP), head of the Aspect Phrase (ASPP). While these markers are compatible with certain adverbs, they do not simply redundantly specify the same information conveyed by the adverbs. For instance, be_{asp} is compatible with frequency adverbs that specify the time period during which an eventuality holds or occurs. Along these same lines, the marker *dən* is compatible with adverbs that further specify the time of the event or interacts with the topic time. (See Terry (in press) for a discussion of adverbs and topic time modification in *dən* constructions.) Adverbs that occur with *BIN* do not generally modify the long period indicated by *BIN*, probably because the marker already indicates that the period is long. For instance, in *Dee BIN running for thirty minutes.* 'For a long time, Dee has been running for thirty minute stretches', *for thirty minutes* modifies periods of short instantiations of running events (Green 2007).[3]

When we consider the aspectual markers in questions and negative contexts, in which they are supported by auxiliaries (e.g., *do* and *have*), it becomes clear that the node in which the supporting auxiliaries are generated is higher than ASPP, as in the following examples:

(5) a.   Bruce <u>don't be</u> running.[4]
  'Bruce isn't usually running'
  a'. <u>Do</u> Bruce <u>be</u> running?
  'Is Bruce usually running?'
  b. Bruce <u>ain't/haven't BIN</u> running.
  'Bruce hasn't been running for a long time'
  c. Bruce <u>ain't/haven't dən</u> ran.
  'Bruce hasn't already run'

The sentences in (5) can be generated in a structure in which the TENSE node is higher than ASPP, and the features of the ASP node determine the auxiliary that supports the aspectual marker.

(6)

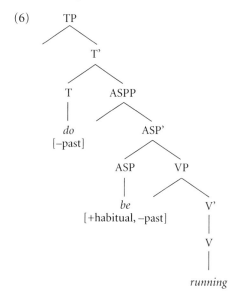

Be_{asp} carries the features [+HABITUAL, −PAST], and the auxiliary *do* is generated in the Tense node when be_{asp} needs to be supported in questions and negative constructions (5). Given the structure in (6), *do* is inserted to host [−PAST]; however, it is not clear whether the auxiliary also hosts some additional feature, such as [+HABITUAL], that is in agreement with the features associated with be_{asp}:

(7)

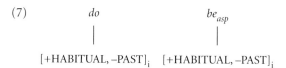

Because another auxiliary, *ain't*, is inserted to host the markers *BIN* and *dən*, it seems that these host auxiliaries are not simply pleonastic, as is the case of *do* in general *do*-support constructions. That is, these auxiliaries may also bear other features, in addition to [TENSE], that are associated with the aspectual markers they are inserted to host. Given that the higher node is a TP, we will only represent a [−PAST] feature in the head position of T in be_{asp} constructions although it is unclear whether auxiliaries also carry aspectual information. The option of realizing both tense and aspect features on a single head is discussed in terms of feature scattering in Giorgio and Pianesi (1997).

There should be no doubt that the distribution of features has to be highly constrained. If the representation of agreement between *do* and *be$_{asp}$* is correct, then the ASPP node carries an additional feature that is non-aspectual, just like the -*s* on the verb node in MAE, which is also unstable. The supporting auxiliary *do* in *be$_{asp}$* constructions can never host [+PAST]; therefore, the following sentence is ungrammatical:

(8) *He didn't be playing baseball. (cf. *He don't be playing baseball.*)

Here we predict that the Mainstream American English (MAE) speaker with passive knowledge of AAE will not acquire the additional [−PAST] feature because it is not a reflection of the ASP node label. Thus MAE speakers may know that habitual *be* is [+HABITUAL], without recognizing an extra Tense feature that would block a link to the Tense marker. Without such a feature, nothing would block the generation of a [+PAST] marker in Tense. We also predict that children will not be sensitive to this restriction when they first recognize habitual *be*. Thus, we predict that agreement, depending upon features, is unstable.

There is further clear evidence that *do*, not *be$_{asp}$*, is in Tense, or in some higher projection. The aspectual marker cannot occur in C(omplementizer) in questions (9a), nor can it host negation (9b):

(9) a. *Be Bruce running?
     b. *Bruce ben't running.

Examples such as those in (9) provide evidence that *be$_{asp}$* is stable for aspect; the marker is generated under ASP and does not move. The sentences with *do*-insertion are important forms of overt evidence that show that the child can use Tense separate from Aspect in AAE.

In MAE aspectual information is linked to the Tense node or is carried by a special affix, such as -*ing*. That is, in MAE auxiliary elements in Tense are automatically associated with Tense. The MAE speaker will naturally assimilate the higher Aspect node to a Tense node in cases like *He be running* and give the interpretation 'He is running.'[5] This result has been experimentally demonstrated in studies with child speakers (Jackson 1998; Green and Roeper 2007), in which it has been shown that developing AAE-speaking children associate *be$_{asp}$* with a habitual reading more often than non-AAE-speaking children. Here there is a node clash. The MAE speaker has no ASP node and, therefore, assimilates *be$_{asp}$* to the Tense node, giving it a [+PRESENT] interpretation, and misses the habitual property involved.

Resistance to the ASP node in AAE is predictable from the fact that AAE and MAE contrast at the node level. Suppose the MAE speaker hears *He don't be running* (4a), then he has the same information that the child has and can generate the ASP node, and mark it as a dialect node without changing any other nodes in his MAE tree.

In addition, a possible property of a node, not of a feature, is that it can be recursive, or in the sense of Rizzi's (2004) cartographic approach, a single node can be split into different nodes. In AAE, different types of ASP nodes can cooccur. The markers be_{asp} and *BIN* can occur with *dən* (10a, b), but be_{asp} and *BIN* do not cooccur (10c):

(10) a. Bruce be dən ran in the park.[6]
          'Bruce has usually already run in the park'
      b. Bruce BIN dən ran in the park.
          'Bruce ran in the park a long time ago'
      c. *Bruce be BIN/BIN be running in the park.
          'For a long time, Bruce has had the habit of running in the park'

Given the co-occurrence restrictions, the aspectual markers can be generated in the following structure, in which there are two instantiations of ASPP for the different markers:

(11)

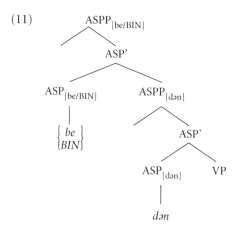

The aspectual markers in the sentences in (10a, b) can be generated in the structure in (11), because they contribute different kinds of aspectual information: habituality and stativity, respectively. The sentence in (10c) will be correctly ruled out because *be/BIN* are both forms of the habitual in that context, and only one can occur at a time. However, *be* and *dən* and *BIN* and *dən* can coocur in recursive ASPP nodes because each marker contributes a different type of tense-aspect information.[7]

2.1.2 *Negative inversion and the stable CP$_{NegFoc}$ node*

The Negative Focus (NegFoc) feature is instantiated in Negative Inversion (NI) constructions in AAE (Green 2007). NI, a type of negative concord, is characterized by an initial negated auxiliary followed by a negative indefinite DP, as shown below:

(12) a. <u>Don't nobody</u> want no tea this morning.
          'Not a single person wants any tea this morning'
      b. <u>Can't nothing</u> stop me from drinking tea.
          'Not a single thing can stop me from drinking tea'

The analysis here is that the negated auxiliary is attracted to Focus (=C) by a negative focus feature [NegFoc]. The two negative elements, the negated auxiliary and negative indefinite DP, are interpreted as a single negation. The negative declarative constructions in (12a, b) bear a superficial resemblance to interrogatives, but they are not questions. They can be accounted for in an analysis in which the negated auxiliary moves to a position in the CP periphery. Here the NI structures in AAE are generated in a Rizzi-type (2004) split CP construction, in which the CP-node is split into a separate ForceP and FocusP (Green 2007). The preposed negated auxiliary widens the domain of quantification of the negative indefinite DP (along the lines of widening in Kadmon and Landman (1993)). The constructions in (12) are distinguished from questions by a feature on a C node that attracts them. The negated auxiliary in NI constructions is attracted to Focus by a [NegFoc] feature that defines the FocusP node and that is linked to a widened domain reading, and the negative indefinite DP is in Spec, TP.

(13)   ForceP (=CP)

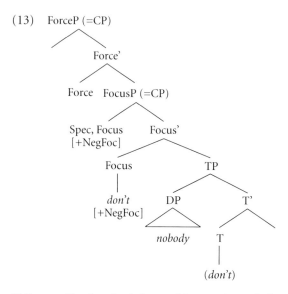

(14)   a.   Don't nobody be working on the 10th floor.
            'Not a single person is usually working on the 10th floor'
        b. $[_{CP}[_{C'}[NegFoc]DON'T_j]][[_{TP}nobody_i [_{T'}t_j]][_{NegP}[_{Neg'}t_j]][_{ASPP}[_{ASP'}be]]$
            $[_{VP}t_i[_{V'}working\ on\ the\ 10th\ floor]]$

As shown in (14b), the sentence in (14a) can be generated by raising the negative DP *nobody* to Spec, TP, and the negated auxiliary *don't* is attracted to Focus, where the [NegFoc] feature is checked. This explains the declarative reading, and it also predicts that these constructions have a focus reading, in which the negated auxiliary may be stressed. [NegFoc] is associated with a CP node, and it is stable in AAE.

The analysis of NI constructions in which the negated auxiliary raises to Focus accounts for the order of the negated auxiliary preceding the indefinite DP; however, the following constructions raise questions about an analysis in which the auxiliary is in a C position:

(15)   a.   That's the book [that didn't nobody read].
            'That's the book that not a single person read'
        b.   I don't care [if can't nobody see this page].
            'I don't care if not a single person can see this page'

In the sentences in (15a, b), the embedded clauses are introduced by *that* and *if*, respectively, which are both arguably in C. If they are in C, then the question is whether the negated auxiliary (e.g. *didn't*, *can't*) can also be in C. Sentences such as (15a, b) provide evidence that there are two C positions, as exhibited in the representation in (13), one occupied by the complementizer (*that, if*) (Force) and the lower C position (Focus) occupied by the negated auxiliary.

(16)   ForceP (=CP)

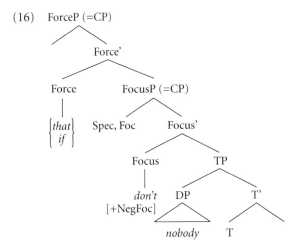

Given the analysis, it is not surprising that two C elements can occur, and, in fact, the results are even predicted. The FocusP (C) node is labeled for [NegFoc], so it is stable in AAE (as well as in other varieties of English in which NI occurs).

2.2 Unstable features

We now turn to unstable features, which give way to variation.

2.2.1 *Tense and aspect features*

A paradigm example of the distinction we pursue comes from the well-known analysis of morphological inflection in English advanced by Chomsky in the early 1990's. Chomsky (1995) argued that Tense features in English occurred under the VP and Verb nodes, not under a Tense node, where they moved via feature attraction to check off their features.

(17)

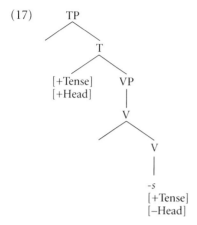

Our hypothesis then for English would be the following:

(18) a. Verb features will remain in English.
   b. Tense features may show unstable dialect variation.

This is in fact what happens in both MAE and other dialects of American English. We find that third singular (-*s*) and regular past inflection (-*ed*) are not obligatorily represented in AAE, and they are frequently dropped as a speech error (Deevey 2000). Speech errors and the grammar variation are not the same phenomenon, but they may both reflect where the grammar is unstable. Consider the examples from AAE:

(19) a. He run.
      'He runs'
   b. John bake the cake.
      'John baked the cake' (or 'John bakes the cake,' depending on the context)

It is also no accident that the verbal -*s* is linked to a generic interpretation and not to a real, anchored present tense. Its non-occurrence, therefore, has little impact upon interpretation. The past tense interpretation of (15b) can be derived from the context, so the non-occurrence of the -*ed* does not result in any loss of meaning either. In addressing the tense-aspect properties of AAE, DeBose and Faraclas (1993) argue that AAE is aspect prominent, and that tense values are based on aspect. Given the covert morphological tense marking in AAE, DeBose and Faraclas appeal to the Lexical Stativity Parameter (LSP) for tense-aspect interpretation. The LSP states that if there is no overt tense-aspect marking, a stative predicate is normally interpreted as non-past/noncompletive and a nonstative predicate is normally interpreted as past/completive (p. 371).[8]

Other grammars, like German, arguably generate inflection directly below the Tense node and, therefore, those inflections have greater stability. Clahsen, Eisenbeiss and Vainnikka (1994) have argued that V2 in German becomes invariable when the -st morpheme is fixed. This follows if the acquisition of -st constitutes a stable projection of the TP node which then requires V2 for feature satisfaction. Inflectional variation in Germanic languages is, of course, still present and calls for much more intricate explanations.

2.2.2 *Question inversion and the unstable* [+PRESUPPOSITION] *feature*
Data from matrix and embedded questions show that AAE allows inversion in both clause types. First, as shown in (20), matrix questions can be signaled by subject-auxiliary inversion (20a) or by question intonation (20b), in which the auxiliary stays in its base position. The auxiliary cannot be deleted in this context, of course, because it signals modality:[9] Auxiliaryless true yes-no questions can also occur: She be running to school? 'Is she usually running to school?'.

(20) a.   Can she leave?
      b.   She can leave?

While the sentence in (20b) can be used in rhetorical contexts, it also has a productive reading as a true yes-no question. The non-inverted true yes-no question is not a "special question." Obenauer (2004) refers to special questions in Pogotto as those non-standard wh-questions that have bare wh-phrases and are structurally different from regular wh-questions. He argues that these "surprise questions, rhetorical questions, and can't-find-the-value-of-x questions are derived by adding functional structure 'on top of' the structure derived in StQs [standard questions]" (p. 343).

We argue that in English there are two features, [+Q] and [+PRESUPPOSITIONALITY] ([+PRESUP]) on the higher Spec, CP (i.e. Force) label. The [+PRESUP] feature also moves to Force, where the [+Q] feature occurs. As we will explain in what follows, the [+PRESUP] feature is optional in questions and varies across dialects. The [+PRESUP] feature is a syntactic approximation to a link to the semantic (or pragmatic) system that can enforce or lift presupposition in the c-command domain. We present the notion of presuppositionality with the feature [+PRESUP], which no doubt calls for a more complicated analysis. The major point is that [+PRESUP], which refers to a presupposed proposition, is not a Force-type feature, so it is not a reflection of a node. The [+Q] feature is part of the CP Force label, and the [+PRESUP] feature is a Probe that looks for a Goal, but does not define a head. Thus, under our view, [+PRESUP] is predictably unstable. The variation in (20) is a result of the Probe feature being satisfied by movement (20a) or by c-command without movement (20b). In the latter case, [+PRESUP] is checked or licensed by a Q-intonation morpheme (20b), as in Cheng and Rooryck (2000).

Appealing to the [+PRESUP] feature may be a way to account for the question variation differences between MAE and AAE, in which we argue that there is a broader range of intonation in AAE that can invoke the [−PRESUP] feature. That is, even when inversion does not occur in AAE, the question may also be an open proposition, so the sentence *He be sleeping in that car?* may not presuppose that he usually sleeps in that car. When inversion does not occur in MAE, then a question intonation pattern keeps the presupposition, but allows a tag question: *He can sing, can't he?*. The inverted form which lifts the presupposition blocks the tag question that presupposes it:

> *Can he sing, can't he?*.

Embedded questions are similar to matrix questions in that they also allow inversion. The examples in (21) show that embedded questions can be formed by subject auxiliary inversion as well as by non-inversion, in which case the complementizer (*whether/if*), not an auxiliary, is in C.

In the case of questions, the auxiliary is attracted to Force (C) by a [+Q] feature:

(21) a.   It's gonna ask you [do you wanna make a transfer].
      a'. ...[if you wanna make a transfer].
      a". *...[if do you wanna make a transfer].
      b.   We on our way to Oklahoma. We trying to see [can we can work out March].
      b'. ... [if we can work out March].
      b". *...[if can we work out March]
      c.   I wonder [do it be like the water we drink].
      c'. ... [if it be like the water we drink]
      c". *... [if do it be like the water we drink] (from Green 2002)

As shown in the sentences in (21a, b, c) and (21a', b', c'), either an inverted auxiliary or a complementizer, respectively, can occur in the embedded C position. However, they cannot both occur at the same time (21a", b", c") because they are targeting the same C (=Force) position.

(22)

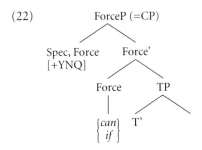

In comparing embedded yes-no question inversion to embedded NI (15), we are able to see the differences in positions that the question and negated auxiliaries in those constructions target. Auxiliaries (as well as complementizers) in questions target the Force node, while negated auxiliaries in NI target the Focus node. The conclusion is that complementizers and auxiliaries in questions cannot co-occur (21a", b", c") because they both target Force, but complementizers and negated auxiliaries (15) can because the former occur in Force and the latter in Focus.

The major difference between matrix and embedded yes-no questions in AAE is exemplified below:

(23) a. *It's gonna ask you [$_C$__ you wanna make a transfer]. (cf. 21a)
      b. *We on our way to Oklahoma. We trying to see [$_C$__ we can work out March]. (cf. 21b)
      c. *i) I wonder [$_C$__ it be like the water we drink]. (cf. 21c)

While inversion is optional in matrix questions, it is obligatory in embedded questions when the C position would be left empty. AAE and MAE overlap in the requirement that the complementizer position be filled in embedded clauses; however, they differ in that AAE allows C to be filled with either an auxiliary, resulting from inversion, or a regular complementizer, in which case inversion has not applied. It may be that in this case, because an unstable [+PRESUP] feature is involved, we get idiosyncrasy in that there is no optional inversion in embedded clauses as there is in matrix questions. In the case of embedded questions, the [+PRESUP] feature obligatorily moves to C if the position would be left empty. This movement is forced because there is no intonational Q feature that is compatible with subordination intonation.

This feature- and node-based analysis can also account for *wh*-questions:

(24) a. Why can she have that book?
      b. Why she can have that book?
      c. *Can she have that book why?
      d. *She can have that book why?

Wh-movement is obligatory (cf. (24a, b) and (24c, d)) because it is associated with the stable Spec, CP node, but auxiliary inversion in these questions is optional. Given that the [+PRESUP] feature is unstable, we predict the variation in auxiliary inversion that is shown in (24a, b).

In the remainder of the paper, we consider stable nodes/unstable features from the viewpoint of multiple grammars and patterns in acquisition.

3.   English and multiple grammars

We will now argue that the stable nodes/unstable features distinction provides a natural way to analyze those domains in which a number of authors have argued that a speaker and a child in the process of acquisition will maintain multiple grammars and allow one to dominate if it dominates either by virtue of frequency (Yang 2003) or by evidence of productivity as with recursion. We can now ask: How does a person manage the substantial overlap between grammars and what prevents them from swimming into each other and becoming impossible to discriminate? We cannot answer all of this question, but we may have an answer to an important part: whatever can be represented as an independent node on a tree will remain stable. A classic case is the particle construction, with seemingly redundant positions in English, which appears to be in transition from a separable connection to the verb (25) to an inseparable Anglo-Saxon variety (26):

(25)   pick the ball <u>up</u>

(26)   pick <u>up</u> the ball

What is notable is that if this change is occurring, it is occurring very slowly because each particle position occupies a separate position in a tree, and, therefore, remains stable and, to some degree, attracts slightly different semantics.

As an exercise, let us maximize the variety of grammars that are captured in a single tree. This is not the tree of any grammar, but a conglomerate representation that could illustrate why we can keep features from different grammars in a stable form. This tree as an abstraction expresses compatibility among grammars and suggests that such compatibility is a feature of our knowledge. Without it – where only features differentiate grammars – confusion is invited. Consider these parts of the trees as reflecting primarily one or another grammar family: German (GER), Anglo-Saxon (AS), African American English (AAE), and Latinate (Lat), with everything unmarked as Mainstream American English (MAE):

(27)

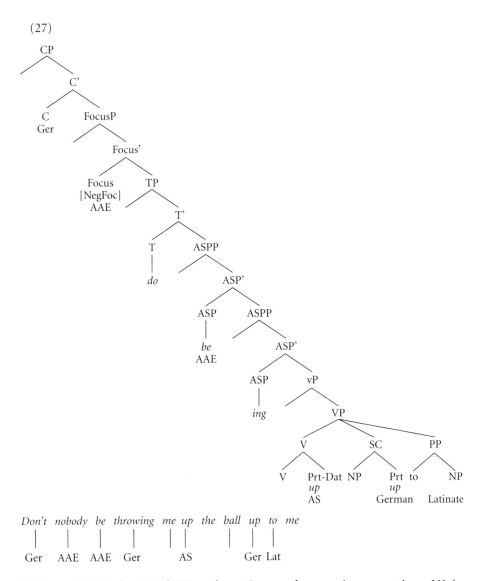

Don't nobody be throwing me up the ball up to me
| | | | | | | | |
Ger   AAE   AAE   Ger   AS   Ger Lat

We have labeled the initial CP node as German because it can motivate V2 in quotation structures like (28) and express Tense overtly:

(28)   "Nothing," said Bill.

One can argue that V2 for quotation involves a different landing site – a further split in CP; however, it is still part of the Germanic V2 system operating on main verbs. It is possible that there are further splits in the CP, as many suggest, and as we have suggested for AAE. It would be natural to see the cartographic approach altogether as leading to a conceptualization of this kind.

We have labeled the PP *to me* as Latinate because it is reliably used with Latinate verbs, and others as well. The double object appears to be a reflection of Anglo-Saxon since it occurs with AS verbs. This is an extreme characterization of what we feel to be largely parts of English in the broad sense, where most speakers can represent the dialectal variations they hear with surprising ease. The double object appears to be a reflection of Anglo-Saxon since it occurs with Anglo-Saxon verbs. Interestingly, the structure can carry further dialect variation.

At the feature level, once again, interestingly, we find further dialect variation: there is a non-reflexive personal dative in Appalachian English, as well as in other varieties of Southern American English (part of AAE as well):

(29)   I am going to cook me up eggs.

Here we have a non-reflexive benefactive dative, an unstable dialect feature. It has slightly different properties from (30) (Wolfram and Christian 1976, Christian 1991, Conroy 2007):

(30)   I am going to cook myself some eggs.

The reflexive indicates the recipient, but without the special benefactive flavor. Since the dative is a feature of AS already, its special role in Southern American English varieties is unstable and less clear to the MAE speaker who might waver in judging part of MAE. The semantics of why the coreference exists without the reflexive marking is, of course, an interesting independent topic.

This state of affairs follows directly from our hypothesis that there is only a feature difference [+benefactive, ±reflexive] and not a node difference. It follows that benefactive dative remains a shadowy dialect feature while two positions for the particle, despite its redundancy, are perceived as part of a single grammar, although we can see it as a dialect split of modern English from German.

4.   Case study: Acquisition of possessive

Our theory provides a lens through which one can examine many stages of acquisition. Consider this case drawn from Galasso (1999). The first generalization is that children first use a default accusative case instead of possessive:

(31)   a.   <u>Me</u>: I want me bottle. Where me Q-car? That me car. Have me show. Me turn. Me cat. Me pen. (2;6-2;8)

   b.   <u>You</u>: No you train. It's you pen. It's you kite. It you house? (3;2)

   c.   <u>Him</u>: I want to go in him house. Him bike is broken. It's him house.

   d.   <u>Mine</u>: Mine banana. Mine bottle. Mine car. Mine apple. Mine pasta. (2;4)

The same phenomenon can be found among specific language impaired children where several other modules (e.g., wh-movement, reflexive) can be advanced, but Case assignment remains deficient or delayed:

(32)   Me sister name Dawne. Her give me Dad a lobster, a two lobster, Me Mom put in here, cook them, forgot to take them eyes out.... (Roeper, Ramos, Seymour, and Abdul-Karim, 2001).

Default accusative, we assume, is in effect not to have any Case marking at all. However, note that this Case does not require a special node for reference. The determiner head is filled by the lexical information onto which, in some grammars, a further possessive Case is attached, a non-head feature. In English the node is filled, but no extra Case feature is demanded or present:

(33)

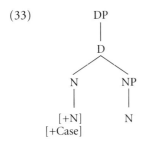

What happens when the shift to an adult grammar occurs? Here our argument demands that an independent node arise. In fact, it seems that one does. The notable fact about possessives is that they can apply to an entire phrase:

(34)   the man in the corner's hat

A form that is radically ungrammatical in other languages is perfectly acceptable in English and produced by six-year-olds. What this requires is that there is a separate POSS node that is a sister to an NP:

(35)

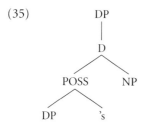

Now the stage is set for recursion, which is precisely what occurs:

(36)   my father's brother's dog's collar

Children do not realize the recursive properties of possessives immediately, as we would predict and as this dialogue reveals (from Roeper 2007):

MOTHER:	What's Daddy's Daddy's name?
SARAH:	uh.
MOTHER:	What's Daddy's Daddy's name?
SARAH:	uh.
MOTHER:	What is it?
	What'd I tell you?
	Arthur!
SARAH:	Arthur! Dat my cousin.
MOTHER:	Oh no, not your cousin Arthur.
	Grampy's name is Arthur.
	Daddy's Daddy's name is Arthur.
SARAH:	(very deliberately) No, dat my cousin.
MOTHER:	oh.
	What's your cousin's Mumma's name?
	What's Arthur's Mumma's name?
SARAH:	uh.
	oh.
MOTHER:	Thinking?
[Sarah nods]	

And in the example from the disordered child (32), we find no case as in *me sister hat*, which would exhibit recursion without the possessive node. This shows that the child initially is able to drop possessive '-s because it is first analyzed as an additional case feature, not reflecting a node. Then it must be reanalyzed as a node which permits recursion. The first stage is only possible because the crucial feature is not a head feature.

5.   Acquisition splitting

It is a common assumption that children seek to maximize falsifiabiliy. One manifestation is to define something in such a narrow way that it is immediately modified by new evidence. If an English and German child both hear:

(37)   the boy
       'den Jungen'

and both associate features for singular, accusative, masculine with the article, then the German child will be correct from the outset. The English child, however, will quickly hear examples such as the following:

(38)   the girl ⇒ drop gender feature
       the girls ⇒ drop number feature
       the girls are ⇒ drop accusative feature

They will be led to the correct grammar. Note, however, that no change in the tree occurs; the node is stable with shifting features associated with it. A natural alternative to the maximization of features and their systematic deletion would be the capacity to split features into two nodes. Here we have an important move which, following our theory, would be difficult to reverse but may occur a number of times. It follows in the footsteps of linguistic theory, which has advocated many "split-node" analyses.

    Hollebrandse and Roeper (1997) provide an analysis of splitting as a natural part of the acquisition process in which a child begins by considering Tense to be exclusively on a verb when -ed occurs and then, when they hear *did*, they reanalyze -ed as either occurring on or destined to be moved to the Tense node. The same occurs for the realization of *make* as a causative, which occurs later if it is first linked lexically to causative verbs like *break*. In other words, the child learns *John broke the bowl* before he generates *John made the bowl break*.

6.   L2 diagnostic

Now let us use the same kind of analysis to see if we can crack open an old observation about L2. It has frequently been noticed that L2 speakers (German speakers, in particular, and others) do not honor the constraint on progressives that limit them to action verbs, so they produce sentences such as the following, although they are rejected by native speakers as quite odd:

(39)   a.   I am believing what you say.
         b.   I am knowing the answer.

This small problem may occur so reliably and so persistently, immune to correction even by explanation because deep processes are at work. An observation by Wagner (2006) may be useful in addressing the issue. Wagner observed that children initially analyze the past tense *-ed* morpheme as being linked to telic verbs. Thus children will use *painted* while they still say *he walk* to mean *he walked*.

Following our model, if we argue that the child is 1) attaching *-ed* to the V node and 2) seeking agreement between the telic properties of the verb and the affix, which fits maximizing falsifiability, then the child will set the stage for splitting.

(40)

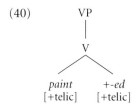

If the child hears *didn't paint*, then the Tense node is established as higher than the verb, and the verb will move to that node to satisfy the Tense feature.

(41)

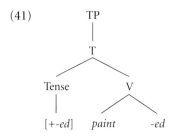

When the child hears *walked*, the telic feature is then dropped from the representation.

The case with progressive *-ing* is the same, but the restriction, we argue, holds. The child initially hears *-ing* on verbs and links them to the active feature and, therefore, statives are not allowed.

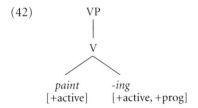

Then the child reanalyzes the *-ing* as a part of the *be+ing* aspect marker within the TP node (which will carry a [+progressive] feature):

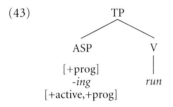

Lexical restriction [+active] on [-ing] is carried forward. Nothing causes a change in the feature.

The L2 speaker does not pass through this stage, but rather projects [-ing] as a progressive marker directly into an ASP node that is higher than the verb.

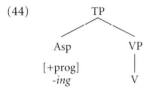

This would follow most naturally from the fact that an L2 speaker's L1 has a TP node already; therefore, the projection is immediate. The lexical restriction is never established under agreement because [-ing] is never in a configuration that would justify adding a [+active] feature via agreement. In addition the attracting feature is simply [+V]. There is nothing requiring [+V,+active], so *I am believing* can be generated. Thus we have found that our theory captures the microscopic detail of L2.

Conclusion

We have pursued a simple theoretical distinction – nodes versus features – made possible by the refinements of modern minimalism. It allowed us to address dialect variation in terms of stable nodes and unstable features. We made the strong claim that current grammars simultaneously represent the crosscurrents of several dialects if they can be mapped onto a single tree. The analysis led to a theory of how to capture certain developmental steps: a shift from a feature representation to a node representation.

Many other stages in acquisition and distinctions among dialects may submit to a splitting analysis. For instance, Blom and Wijnen (2005) provide evidence that the child gradually shifts to a modal interpretation for verbs. We can model that shift as first being in terms of a feature on a lexical item, then a feature on a verb node, and finally acquisition splitting, allowing an independent ModalP within the TP. Once the feature is part of a node label, the label is stable, but the evolution may not be immediate.

Chomsky has remarked on occasion that technical solutions should be reanalyzed into "leading ideas." Our proposal is, one hopes, a step toward extracting the leading ideas within the abstractions of minimalism.

Notes

1. See Collins (2002), for unlabelled structures which still derive information from lexical items. Hinzen (2006) seeks to have the node labels carry more information allowing thematic interpretation as well. Of each of these approaches, we would ask how they capture the dynamics of dialect variation.

2. *BIN* is written in capital letters to indicate that it is stressed, and the marker *dən* is written with a schwa to indicate that it is generally unstressed.

3. In some cases in which adverbs specifying the length of the long period occur in these *BIN* constructions, they are introduced with a pause: Bruce BIN left PAUSE an hour ago.

4. In general, overt 3rd singular marking in AAE is variable at best.

5. The higher ASPP that we refer to here is the node for grammaticalized aspect markers. Both AAE and MAE must also have other lower ASPP categories for aspectual elements such as the progressive (-ing) and perfect (-en).

6. In AAE, either the simple past or past participial form of the verb will occur. In general, the same verb form is used in simple past and past participial contexts, depending on the verb.

7. We predict similarly in MAE that doubling will not occur if an extra identical node is called for and that is precisely correct. Sentences like *John must will play baseball.* are never recorded in the acquisition literature as mistakes to which children are prone or that occur at all (unless in

the "might could" dialect region). However, where another node exists, precisely this overgeneralization can occur. It has long been recorded (going back to Menyuk 1969) that children may say: Must John will play baseball? This is possible because both positions, CP and ModalP, exist independently; therefore, the child feels that it should be possible to fill them both.

8. Something along the lines of the LSP has also been proposed for Kwa languages in factitive constructions.

9. Auxiliaryless true yes-no questions can also occur: She be running to school? 'Is she usually running to school?'.

References

Blom, E. and F. Wijnen (2005). Development need not be disappointing: The demise of the root infinitive and related changes in Dutch language acquisition. Ms. Utrecht University.

Cheng, L. L-S. and J. Rooryck (2000). Licensing wh-in-situ. *Syntax* 3, 1–19.

Chomsky, N. (1995). *The Minimalist Program*. MIT Press, Cambridge.

Chomsky, N. (2005). Three factors in language design. *Linguistics Inquiry* 36, 1–22.

Christian, D. (1991). The personal dative in Appalachian speech. In P. Trudgill and J. K. Chambers (eds.), *Dialects of English: Studies in Grammatical Variation*. Longman: New York.

Chomsky, N. (2006). Approaching UG from Below. In H-M Gärtner and U. Sauerland (eds.), *Infinity + Recursion = Language*. Berlin: Mouton De Gruyter.

Clahsen, H., S. Eisenbeiss, and A. Vainnikka (1994). The seeds of Structure: Analysis of the Acquisition of Case-Marking. In T. Hoekstra and B. Schwartz (eds.), *Language Acquisition Studies in Generative Grammar*. (pp. 85–116).

Collins, C. (2002). Eliminating labels. In S. D. Epstein & T. D. Seely (eds.), *Derivation and Explanation in the Minimalist Program* (pp. 42–64). Oxford: Blackwell.

Conroy, A. (2007). The personal dative in Appalachian English as a reflexive pronoun. In Orgeta-Santos, J. Sprouse, and M. Wagers, *UMWIPiL 16* (pp. 63–88). University of Maryland.

DeBose, C. and N. Faraclas (1993). An Africanist approach to the linguistic study of black English: Getting to the roots of tense-aspect-modality system and copula systems in Afro-American. In S. S. Mufwene (ed.), *Africanisms in Afro-American Language Varieties* (pp. 364–387). Athens, GA: University of Georgia Press.

Deevy, P. (2000). Agreement checking in comprehension: Evidence from relative Clauses. *Journal of Psycholinguistic Research* 29, 69–79.

Galasso, J. (1999). The acquisition of functional categories: A case study. Unpublished PhD dissertation, University of Essex.

Giorgio, A. and F. Pianesi (1997). *Tense and Aspect: From Semantics to Morphosyntax*. Oxford: Oxford University Press.

Green, L. (2002). *African American English: A Linguistic Introduction*. Cambridge: Cambridge University Press.

Green, L. (2007). Negative Inversion and Negative Focus in African American English. Ms. University of Massachusetts.

Green, L. and T. Roeper (2007). The Acquisition Path for Tense-Aspect: Remote Past and Habitual in Child African American English. *Language Acquisition* 14, 269–313.

Hinzen, W. (2006). Minimalist foundations of language evolution: On the questions of why language is the way it is. *Proceedings of the 6th International Conference on the Evolution of Language*. 115–122.

Hollebrandse, B., and T. Roeper (1997). The concept of *of*-insertion and the theory of INFL in acquisition. In C. Koster and F. Wijnen (eds.), *Proceedings of GALA*. Groningen: Centre for Language and Cognition.

Kadmon, N. and F. Landman (1993). Any. *Linguistics and Philosophy* 16, 353–422.

Jackson, J. (1998). Linguistic aspect in African American English speaking children: An investigation of aspectual be. PhD dissertation, University of Massachusetts, Amherst.

Menyuk. P. (1969). *Sentences Children Use*. Cambridge: MIT Press.

Obenauer, H-G. (2004). Non-standard wh-questions and alternative checkers in Pagotto. In H. Lohnstein and S. Trissler (eds.), *The Syntax and Semantics of the Left Periphery* (pp. 343–383). Berlin: Mouton De.

Rizzi, L. (ed.). (2004). *The fine structure of CP and IP: The Cartography of Syntactic Structures, Volume 2*. Oxford: Oxford University Press.

Roeper, T., E. Ramos, H. Seymour, and L. Abdul-Karim (2001). Language disorders as a Window on universal grammar: An abstract theory of agreement for IP, DP, and V-PP. *Brain and Language* 77, 378–397.

Roeper, T. (1999). Universal Bilingualism. *Bilingual Language Cognition* 2, 169–186.

Roeper, T. (2007). *The Prism of Grammar: How the Study of Child Language Illuminates Humanism*. Cambridge: MIT Press.

Terry, J. M. (2005). Past perfective and present perfect in African American English. In H. Verkuyl, H. de Swart, and A. van Hout (eds.), *Perspectives on Aspect* (pp. 217–232). Springer Publishing Co., Dordrecht.

Terry, J. M. (In press). Past-time denoting adverbs and the African American English preverbal done construction: A case of variable judgments. In *Proceedings of the 42nd Annual Meeting of the Chicago Linguistics Society* (Volume 1: The Main Session). Chicago: Chicago Linguistics Society.

Wagner, L. (2006). Aspectual bootstrapping in language acquisition: Transitivity and Telicity. *Language Learning and Development* 2, 51–77.

Wolfram, W. and D. Christian (1976). *Appalachian Speech*. Washington D.C.: Center for Applied Linguistics.

Yang, C. (2003). *Knowledge and Learning in Natural Language*. Oxford: Oxford University Press.

Author's address:

Department of Linguistics
226 South College
150 Hicks Way
University of Massachusetts
Amherst, MA 01003
USA

roeper@linguist.umass.edu

Copying vs. structure sharing
a semantic argument

Uli Sauerland

The term *Focus Dependency* describes an important phenomenon at the syntax-semantics interface: Elided material can exhibit bound-variable-like behavior when its antecedent is a focussed phrase in the same sentence. In the past, focus dependency has been analyzed as actual binding or by means of copying. This paper presents a new account of focus dependency that relies on the syntactic idea of structure-sharing. Structure-sharing allows sub-phrases to be syntactically linked to more than one position of a phrase marker. The proposal better explains focus dependency than existing accounts considering data from sentence-boundedness, insensitivity to c-command, extraction from the focus-dependent material, and the formal link to the antecedent. It also achieves a theoretical unification with other phenomena where structure sharing has been made use of, specifically movement.

Keywords: focus, binding, ellipsis, parallelism

1. Introduction

There is an important and, in my opinion, insufficiently studied phenomenon at the syntax-semantics interface:[1] An elided phrase or parts of it can depend on an earlier overt occurrence of the same phrase in way that resembles variable binding. One type of example showing this phenomenon is Kratzer (1991) well-known Tanglewood sentence (see (34) below). The phenomenon, however, is much more wide-spread. For the purposes of this paper, I use the term *Focus Dependency* for the phenomenon at issue. I understand focus dependency in the following way:

(1) *Focus Dependency:* An elided occurrence of a phrase XP can co-vary in interpretation with a focussed occurrence of the same phrase XP.

Linguistic Variation Yearbook 7 (2007), 27–51.
ISSN 1568–1483 / E-ISSN 1569–9900 © John Benjamins Publishing Company

Working independently of each other, Hardt (1999) and Schwarz (1999) first systematically investigated focus dependency: Schwartz's (1999) example (2) illustrates focus-dependency by a VP. The example allows a reading where it entails that you do not say I should not sing when I sing. This reading is based on a focus dependency of the elided VP $\triangle_1$ on *whistle* in the first conjunct and a parallel dependency in the second conjunct.

(2)   (Schwarz 1999:(33))
       When I whistle you say I shouldn't $\triangle_1$, but when I sing you don't $\triangle_2$.
       $\triangle_1$ = whistle, $\triangle_2$ = say I shouldn't sing

Example (2) also allows a second reading that entails that, when I sing, you do not say that I should not whistle. But, it is easy to show that a distinct focus dependency reading is available. The following scenario does the job: You hate my whistling, but like my singing. Furthermore I have a tendency to break into whistling when I sing. So, whenever I whistle or sing, you always tell me not to whistle. In this scenario, it is not true that, when I sing, you don't say I shouldn't whistle. Since (2) is true in the scenario, it can only be true because of the focus dependency reading. Focus dependency is puzzling because there is strong evidence that an elided phrase must be very similar in interpretation to another phrase in the same discourse (Hankamer and Sag 1976; Rooth 1992). But this is not the case with focus dependency: no other phrase has the same or even a very similar meaning to the elided phrase *say I shouldn't sing*.

In this paper, I argue that focus dependency should be analyzed in terms of structure-sharing, a syntactic configuration also know as multi-dominance. I first show some problems with existing analyses, before presenting my own proposal. I then review the predictions of my analysis in Section 3.

2.   The proposals

2.1 Binding based analyses

Both Schwarz (1999) and Hardt (1999) analyse examples like (2) as involving a special kind of binding relationship. In its crudest form, this type of analysis assumes that this binding relationship is created by a syntactic mechanism – covert movement to a c-commanding position. This creates the LF-representation in (3). In the first conjunct, the VP *whistle* is extracted from the *when*-clause and then binds a VP-pro-form in the elided VP. In the second conjunct, the VP *sing* undergoes parallel covert movement and then also binds a VP-pro-form in the elided VP in the second conjunct.

(3) [whistle]$_{VP}$ λ_i [When I t$_i$ you say I shouldn't [pro$_i$]$_{\triangle_1}$],
     but [sing]$_{VP}$ λ_j [when I t$_j$ you don't [say I shouldn't t$_j$]$_{\triangle_2}$]

Ellipsis is predicted to be licensed in (3) in the same way as with sloppy readings of VP-ellipsis. In particular, Rooth (1992) account of VP-ellipsis licensing carries over: The constituent consisting of λ_j and its complement as a focus domain is identical in interpretation to the constituent consisting of λ_i and its complement in the first conjunct.

However, Schwarz (1999) already points out two problems for the binding analysis: lack of c-command and that extraction is possible from the putative variable. Lack of c-command is illustrated by (2) where *whistle* and *sing* are embedded in a conditional clause and therefore do not c-command the elided VP. Generally, covert movement is assumed to be blocked in such a case because quantifiers cannot take scope outside of a *when*-clause. The scopal restriction still holds in examples with a focus dependency (specifically, an NP focus dependency), as (4) shows.

(4) When I want many books, you buy some $\triangle_1$, but when I want many toys, you
     don't $\triangle_2$.
     $\triangle_1$ = books, $\triangle_2$ = buy some toys.

Schwarz and Hardt each address the lack of a c-command restriction in their own way. Schwarz (1999) points out that there is also no c-command restriction for sloppy interpretations in VP-ellipsis as Tomioka (1999) discusses in detail. (5) is one example where a sloppy interpretation is available, though c-command does not obtain.

(5) (Tomioka 1999:219 who credits unpublished work by M. Wescoat)
     The police officer who arrested John insulted him, and the police officer who
     arrested Bill did $\triangle$, too.
     $\triangle$ = insult him

However, I do not think that Tomioka's proposal for (5) should be taken as the basis for the analysis of focus dependency because Tomioka's proposal itself has problems (Elbourne 2002). Tomioka (1999) proposes that *him* is analyzed as the definite description *the person he arrested* both in the overt clause and in the elided VP in (5). This is what Elbourne (2002) calls a D-type analysis of the pronoun *him*. However, the version Tomioka relies on suffers from the problem of the formal link: Tomioka's analysis would predict that (6) too should have an interpretation of the pronoun as *his wife*.[2]

(6) *The police officer who married Sue kissed her, and the married fireman did too $\triangle$.

$\triangle$ = kiss the fireman's wife

Elbourne (2002) argues that D-type pronouns generally cannot stand for any salient description, but are derived by NP-ellipsis. If Elbourne is correct (and (6) supports his analysis further), then Tomioka's analysis of (5) cannot be maintained. In conclude therefore that Schwarz's suggestion to reduce focus dependency to Tomioka's analysis cannot be correct.

At the same time, I still believe that there is a close relationship between Tomioka's data and focus dependency. In fact, I propose that Tomioka's examples are special cases of focus dependency. This analysis is illustrated for (5) in (7).[3]

(7) The police officer who arrested John insulted him $\triangle_1$, and the police officer who arrested Bill did $\triangle_2$, too.

$\triangle_1$ = John, $\triangle_2$ = insult Bill

Now consider Hardt's (2003) proposal to overcome the lack of c-command. He assumes that there is a second binding mechanism called center binding that operates without a c-command restriction. A series of starred pronouns, pro*, refers to the discourse center, and focus can set a new discourse center. For (5), Hardt would assume the representation in (8).

(8) The policeman who arrested John$_F$ hit him*, and the policeman who arrested Bill$_F$ did [hit him*]$_\triangle$, too.

But, Hardt's center binding, too, has at least two problems: the formal link (again) and examples with multiple antecedents.[4] Concerning the formal link, Hardt might say about (7) that the phrase *married fireman* is not sufficient to introduce the fireman wife as a new discourse center. However, in other examples the formal link is still a problem for Hardt. Consider the German examples in (9):

(9) a. Wer mit dem Auto   kommt, muß es/*ihn parken.
       who with the car.NEUT comes must it/*him park
    b. Wer mit dem Wagen   kommt, muß ihn/*es parken.
       who with the car.MASC comes must him/*it park

Both examples in (9) allow a focus dependency because both can be continued with *aber wer mit dem Rad kommt, nicht* ('but who comes bike, does not [have to park it]'). Hence the pronoun following *muß* in (9) should be able to be pro* in both (9a) and (9b). But the analysis does not predict that the pronoun must match the grammatical gender of the NP it is anaphoric to.

A further problem for center binding are examples with multiple focus dependencies such as (10). Here Hardt would have to say that two discourse centers are involved and that *she* and *it* each refer to one of them. However, a restriction to one backward looking discourse center is established in centering theory (Grosz et al. 1995). So, Hardt's proposal must be crucially different from centering theory, and therefore has no independent motivation.

(10)   When a woman buys a blouse we ask that she try it on, but when a man buys a shirt we don't △.
△ = ask that the man try on the shirt

I conclude therefore that the lack of a c-command restriction creates a problem for a binding analysis of focus dependency.

The second problem for the binding analysis in general are examples with sluicing like (11). (11) demonstrates the possibility of extraction from the putative variable:[5]

(11)   If you email someone you can look up later who $\triangle_1$, but if you call someone you can't $\triangle_2$.
$\triangle_1$ = you emailed t, $\triangle_2$ = look up who you called t

Building on Ross (1969), Merchant (2001) has argued that sluicing should be analyzed as IP-deletion with syntactic extraction out of the deleted IP. But if the sluiced phrase in both conjuncts in (11) is analyzed as an IP-variable, there is no site from which extraction of *who* could take place.

There is also a class of examples where extraction out of the focus dependent material is impossible, but for independent reasons as we shall see. Such examples were first pointed out by Merchant (2004) and have been further discussed by Tomioka (2007). I summarize Tomioka's discussion. One of Merchant's examples is (12), which cannot receive the indicated focus-dependent reading.

(12)   *Fred read the book that he was supposed to $\triangle_1$, and Eric also reviewed the one that he was $\triangle_2$
$\triangle_1$ = read, $\triangle_2$ = supposed to review

However, Tomioka shows that the availability of focus-dependency is not at issue in (12). Rather, it must be an independent constraint on ellipsis. The two arguments Tomioka gives for this conclusion are that (12) does not even allow a reading that does not depend on focus dependency and that furthermore example (13) does marginally allow a focus dependency. Since (12) is structurally almost identical to (13), it is plausible that the illformedness of (12) is due to a version of the MaxElide constraint discussed in Section 3.9, as Tomioka also concludes.

(13) A: Why are you so upset with Fred? He bought the books he was supposed to $\triangle_1$, right?

B: $^?$Yeah, but then, he read the books that he wasn't $\triangle_2$.

$\triangle_1$ = buy, $\triangle_2$ = supposed to read

I conclude therefore that, in principle, extraction from an focus dependent phrase is possible. This entails that neither version of the binding analysis provides a satisfactory account of focus dependencies.

2.2 The copy and focus based analysis

A second kind of analysis was proposed by Kratzer (1991) (building on a sketch of Rooth 1985). Kratzer's aim is to make the analysis of focus 'variable-like'. Her specific implementation is based on an LF-copying analysis of ellipsis, which also copies a focus marks into the elided VP. Focussed constituents are marked with additional indices as in (14). The copying process ensures that the focus marks in the overt constituent and in the elided constituent are coindexed.[6] Kratzer, herself, develops her analysis on for the Tanglewood example in (34), but it is easy to extend the account to other cases. In example (2), two steps of copy operations apply to the surface representation (14a): in (14b) the VP from the first conjunct is copied into the second conjunct, and then the smaller VP is copied in each conjunct resulting in (14c).

(14) a.   When I whistle$_{F_1}$, you say I shouldn't $\triangle$, but when I sing$_{F_2}$, you don't $\triangle$

b.   When I whistle$_{F_1}$, you say I shouldn't $\triangle$,
but when I sing$_{F_2}$, you don't [say I shouldn't $\triangle$]$_\triangle$

c.   When I whistle$_{F_1}$, you say I shouldn't [whistle$_{F_1}$]$_\triangle$,
but when I sing$_{F_2}$, you don't [say I shouldn't [sing$_{F_2}$]$_\triangle$]$_\triangle$

The focus alternatives of a phrase, Kratzer defines as the set of values $[\![XP]\!]_f^G$ for any focus assignment G for which this is defined. A focus assignment is a typed Tarskian variable assignment: It maps a pair of an index i and a type τ to an individual of type τ. A focussed constituent is interpreted as follows:

(15) a.   normal semantic value: $[X_{F_x}]^g = [X]^g$

b.   focus semantic value: $[\![X_{F_x}]\!]_f^{g,G} = G(n,\tau)$ where τ is the semantic type of $[X]^g$.

Note that Kratzer's proposal for focus dependency also accounts for sloppy interpretations without c-command by way of an NP-ellipsis analysis of pronouns. For example (5), this analysis is shown in (16): Recall that proper names are analyzed as NP-complements of a null determiner. In each conjunct, the focussed proper name NP is copied to the NP-position following the pronoun.

(16) The police officer who arrested John$_{F_1}$ insulted him [John$_{F_1}$]$_\triangle$, and the police officer who arrested Bill$_{F_2}$ did [insult [Bill$_{F_2}$]$_\triangle$]$_\triangle$

However, Kratzer's proposal has two kinds of problem: problems with clause-boundedness and problems for LF-copying analyses of VP-ellipsis. Consider first clause-boundedness of focus-dependency. This was originally described by Safir (2005). He observes that a sloppy interpretation is not available in (17):

(17) *John is a dealer and criminal. Luckily, the police arrested him. Bill is an even worse dealer and criminal. Unfortunately, the police didn't $\triangle$.
       $\triangle$ = arrest Bill

Kratzer's analysis, however, predicts a sloppy interpretation to be available in (17). The derivation of (17) involves two steps of copying as in (18): first the VP is copied into the last clause, then the two empty NPs following the pronouns are filled.

(18) a. John$_{F_1}$ is a dealer and criminal. Luckily, the police arrested him $\triangle$ Bill$_{F_2}$ is an even worse dealer and criminal. Unfortunately, the police didn't [arrest him $\triangle$]$_\triangle$

      b. John$_{F_1}$ is a dealer and criminal. Luckily, the police arrested him [John$_{F_1}$]$_\triangle$ Bill$_{F_2}$ is an even worse dealer and criminal. Unfortunately, the police didn't [arrest him [Bill$_{F_2}$]$_\triangle$]$_\triangle$.

Syntactic copying for ellipsis resolution cannot be sensitive to clause-boundaries because the antecedent of an elided VP can be in a different clause. One possibility to rule out the sloppy interpretation in (18), would be to force copying in an earlier clause to take place before a later clause is processed. However, this would incorrectly rule out a sloppy interpretation in (19), as well.

(19) Because John is a dealer and criminal, the police arrested him. But, though Bill is an even worse dealer and criminal, the police didn't $\triangle$.
       $\triangle$ = arrest Bill

Hence, I conclude that focus dependencies are sensitive to clause boundaries, but not to c-command. Kratzer's analysis incorrectly predict no clause boundary effects. I should add that while I argue for the clause-boundedness restriction using

Safir's NP-ellipsis example, the point can also be made with VP-ellipsis examples: (20) is a case in point.

(20) *Last week, John was about to sing. Fortunately, you convinced him not to $\triangle_1$. Yesterday, John was about to whistle. This time, I did $\triangle_2$.
($\triangle_1$ = sing, $\triangle_2$ = convince him not to whistle)

Furthermore, arguments against the LF-copying analysis of VP-ellipsis argue against Kratzer's analysis. Such arguments have been given first by Rooth (1992) and Fox (1999) for VP-ellipsis, and later also by Merchant (2001) for sluicing (IP-ellipsis).

2.3 The structure sharing analysis

I assume like Kratzer that focus dependency involves a syntactic relationship. However, this is not established by copying, but by structure sharing. Structure sharing is possible in syntactic theories that allow multi-dominance like those of Gärtner (2002) and Svenonius (2005). Such theories assume that one phrase can occupy two positions of a syntactic tree. I represent structure sharing as in (21). Here, the VP *whistle* occupies both the VP position in the *when*-clause and the complement position of *whistle*, and the VP *sing* occupies the same two positions in the second clause.

(21)   when I [—]_F you say I shouldn't [—]_△
                    whistle
        when I [—]_F you don't [say I shouldn't —]_△
                    sing

I assume that material that is structure-shared in this way must not be pronounced more than once – at least, this restriction makes correct predictions for English, while languages that have productive copying constructions may differ (cf. Kobele 2006). Then the analysis predicts for English that focus dependencies depend on ellipsis (see below). I furthermore assume that, the semantic value of the structure shared material is determined independently each time it is linked to a position in a structure. This assumption allows a sloppy interpretation of structure-shared material of the kind illustrated by (22):[7]

(22)   When I phone my mother, I assume you do as well $\triangle_1$, but when I email my father, I don't $\triangle_2$.
        $\triangle_1$ = phone your mother, $\triangle_2$ = assume that you email your father

My proposal furthermore relies on a particular analysis of focus: I assume that the focus alternatives are generally defined by reference to LF-structures.

(23)   XP is a focus alternative to YP if and only if there is a sequence of replacements applying to YP that result in XP, where each step replaces a phrase dominated by the focus feature F with a phrase of the same syntactic category.

Such a syntactic definition of focus alternatives has been argued for by Fox (2000). New support for it comes from observations of Krifka (2001) for a ban on complex foci and Artstein (2004) on focus on meaningless word parts. Artstein argues that *stalagmite* should be the only non-trivial focus alternative of *stalacTITE* with focus on the final syllable. While Artstein argues for a proposal where meaningless word-parts can be assigned a kind of compositional meaning, the facts can also captured by the replacement in (24) within the syntactic analysis of focus alternatives.

(24)   YP = John saw a stala$[$cTITE$]_F$ → XP = John saw a stalagmite.

Krifka (2001) points out the question-answer paradigm in (25): While VP focus in (25a) is possible, it is not possible to have the two phrases VP consists of each separately in focus. Since any possible action of John's might be described as him doing something somewhere, a purely semantic condition of focus licensing such as Schwarzschild (1999) does not predict (25b) to be odd.

(25)   What did John do?
    a. $[$Drive to BERLin$]_F$
    b.   #$[$DRIVE$]_F$ $[$to BERLIN$]_F$

While Krifka proposes an account of (25) using structured meanings, the current purely structural account also predicts (25): While in (25a) replacing the entire VP with *do something* yield a focus alternative the question provides, (25b) requires a preceding question consisting of a verb and a directional or locative adverbial.

Structure sharing is predicted to interact with focus in a specific way. Namely, structure shared material will be focused in all positions it is linked to if and only if one of the positions it is linked to is dominated by an F-mark. Consider the account of (2): *whistle* and *sing* are focussed as shown in (24). Since I assume that elided material cannot be focussed, the focus marks of the two verbs must only be associated with the first position they are linked to. To license VP-ellipsis, I assume following Rooth (1992) that some constituent YP containing the elided VP must be such that a focus alternative of YP occurs in the previous discourse. In structure (24), this condition is fulfilled if we consider the YP indicated in (26): Within YP, *sing* is dominated by an F-feature and therefore replacing *sing* with *whistle* is a focus alternative of YP.

(26)

$$
\underbrace{\text{when I } [\text{—}]_F \text{ you don't } [\text{say I shouldn't } [\underbrace{\text{—}}_{\text{sing}}]_\triangle}_{\text{YP}}
$$

Note however, that YP must include the *when*-clause for ellipsis to be licensed. In (27), a smaller domain for ellipsis licensing is indicated. But, in this domain no F-mark dominates *sing*, and therefore replacing *sing* with *whistle* does not result in a focus alternative.

(27)

$$
\text{when I } [\text{—}]_F \underbrace{\text{you don't } [\text{say I shouldn't } [\underbrace{\text{—}}_{\text{sing}}]_\triangle}_{\text{YP}}
$$

This interaction between the parallelism domain and focus dependency will become important below.

3.   Predictions of the analysis

In this section, I first show that the structure sharing analysis predicts those properties of focus dependency already discussed above. I then show how additional facts about focus dependency corroborate the structure sharing analysis.

3.1 Category indifference

The examples of focus dependency discussed up to now, have already shown that focus dependencies are available for any category: VP in (2), NP in (4), IP in (11). This state of affairs is exactly predicted by the structure sharing analysis because there is no motivation to restrict structure sharing to a particular syntactic category.

3.2 Basic configurational requirements

The basic configurational requirements of a focus dependency were also already introduced. Example (2) shows that focus dependency is not constrained by c-command. Example (17) shows that a sentence boundary blocks a focus dependency. Clause boundedness is a natural restrictions for structure sharing because syntactic structures are build clause by clause, and therefore no interclausal syntactic relationships exist. Whether c-command constraints syntactic operations is rather debated. For example, Bobaljik and Brown (1997) argue that copying should not be constrained in this way. I adopt this assumption for structure sharing rather than copying. Then it is predicted that structure sharing is available in examples like (2).

3.3 Extraction

The analysis predicts no restriction on extraction from elided phrases that receive a focus-dependent interpretation. This follows in some way, however, from the category indifference of structure sharing. Consider again the sluicing example (11) (repeated in (28)).

(28)   If you email someone you can look up later who $\triangle_1$, but if you call someone you can't $\triangle_2$.
       $\triangle_1$ = you emailed t, $\triangle_2$ = look up who you called t

In this case, I assume that VP structure sharing as shown in (29a) is not possible since presumably *someone* and the trace of extraction of *who* are not formally identical. However, the representation shown in (29b) remains available if structure sharing is truly category indifferent.

(29)   a.   a.   *If —— you look up later who$_j$ [—]$_\triangle$
                      └———————————┘
                        you email someone

       b.   b.   email
                                           ┌———————————————┐
                   If —— —— someone you look up later who$_j$ [—— —— t$_j$]$_\triangle$
                       └————————————————————————————┘
                            you

Further support for the availability of multiple structure sharing comes from (30), which allows a partially focus dependent interpretation.

(30)   When I play the violin, you say I shouldn't $\triangle_1$, but when I sit at the piano, you don't $\triangle_2$.
       $\triangle_1$ = play the violin, $\triangle_2$ = say I shouldn't play the piano

This interpretation is captured by the representation in (31):

(31)   when I sit at [—]$_F$, you don't [say I shouldn't play —]$_\triangle$

the piano

However, it remains to be investigated to what extent such mixed readings are available. For example, the indicated mixed interpretation seems to be hard to obtain in (32).

(32)   When I kill a fish, you say I shouldn't $\triangle_1$, but when I catch a squid, you don't $\triangle_2$.
$\triangle_1$ = kill the fish, $\triangle$ = say I shouldn't kill the squid

3.4 Formal link

Examples (6) and (9) above provide evidence for a formal link between the two elements of a focus dependency. On the structure sharing analysis, the formal link is forced because the two elements of a focus dependency are the same syntactic material. Consider for example the structure-sharing analysis for (9b) in (33). Because the noun *car* with grammatical gender MASC is linked to two positions in the syntactic structure, both must have the same grammatical gender.[8]

(33)   who with — comes must him it.MASC — park

the.MASC car.MASC

The four properties of focus dependency discussed in this and the previous subsections are all the properties already mentioned in the discussion of the binding and focus based approaches. I showed that these properties are straightforwardly captured by the structure sharing analysis, while they created difficulties for the other two proposals. In the following subsections, I discuss properties of focus dependency not mentioned yet in this paper.

3.5 Bound-variable like behavior

The bound-variable like behavior is clearly displayed by Kratzer's (1991) Tanglewood example in (34).[9]

(34)   I only went to [Tanglewood]$_F$ because you did $\triangle$.
$\triangle$ = go to Tanglewood

Kratzer notes that (34) is different from (35) with double-focus. Namely, the focus alternative to the overt and elided occurrence of *Tanglewood* in (34) must covary, while only (35) allows the continuation *I didn't go to Lubbock because you went to Williamstown*, which requires a non-covarying focus alternative.

(35)   I only went to [Tanglewood]$_F$ because you went to [Tanglewood]$_F$.

The difference between (34) and (35) follows from the fact that only (34) allows the structure sharing analysis in (36). For (35), such a representation is not available since I assume that structure shared material must not be pronounced more than once.

(36)   I only went to [—]$_F$ because you did [go to —]$_\triangle$

                              Tanglewood

3.6 Ellipsis requirement on dependents

The contrast between examples (34) and (35) already shows that a focus dependency requires ellipsis of the dependent. This also holds for examples like (2) where the focus dependency is required for ellipsis licensing as Schwarz (1999) discusses. Example (37) shows that when *sing* in (2) is not elided, but spelled out, it must be focused.

(37)   (Schwarz 1999:(8b))
       When I [WHISTLE]$_F$ you say I shouldn't $\triangle$, but when I SING you don't say I
       shouldn't [SING]$_F$/# sing
       $\triangle$ = whistle

The difference between (2) and (37) follows on the structure sharing analysis from the condition that structure shared material must be pronounced only in one position. While in (37) structure sharing is possible in the *when*-clause, this is not sufficient to license destressing of the second occurrence of *sing*.

    Schwarz also considers already the case in (38) with ellipsis in the second conjunct, but not in the first. Schwarz claims that (38) allows the focus dependent reading, but reports in a footnote that it is not as easily available as in other cases. For my informants, (38) did not allow the focus dependent interpretation easily, hence I mark it here as being only very marginally available.

(38) (Schwarz 1999:(12) with different judgment)
*[?]When I whistle you say I shouldn't whistle, but when I sing you don't $\triangle$.
$\triangle$ = say I shouldn't sing

A similar intermediate status is obtained for the sloppy interpretation of (39).

(39) *[?]The policeman who arrested John hit John, and the policeman who arrested Bill did too $\triangle$.
$\triangle$ = hit Bill

The intermediate status of (38) and (39) is predicted by the structure sharing analysis. While the second conjunct of (38) can have the structure sharing analysis in (40), the focus alternative obtained by replacing *sing* with *whistle* is not available in the discourse as an antecedent because the first conjunct does not allow a structure sharing analysis.

(40)   when I [—]$_F$ you don't [say I shouldn't [—]$_\triangle$
        sing

However, this focus alternative is entailed by the first conjunct. There is evidence that VP-ellipsis can be licensed via an entailment (Rooth 1992; Fox 1999) in some cases. The marginality of VP-ellipsis in (38), I propose, follows from the fact that there is an alternative completion of the ellipsis site, namely *say I shouldn't whistle*, which is licensed without drawing an entailment from the antecedent first.

3.7 Antecedent focus requirement

The three analysis of focus dependency differ with respect to the role of focus on the antecedent:[10] For the binding based analysis, focus plays no role; for the focus based analysis, focus must be on the antecedent; and for the structure sharing analysis, the antecedent must be part of a focus. (41) is a test for the distinction between the latter two analyses. The German translation of (41) is acceptable in the context of a discussion of whether I have problems talking with Mary and her family.

(41)   When I met Mary's father, I talked to him and when I met [her]$_F$, I did $\triangle$, too.
        $\triangle$ = talk to Mary

The acceptability of (41) is predicted by the structure sharing analysis, but not by the focus based analysis. (42) shows the structure sharing analysis of the second conjunct of (41): *her* contains an elided definite description *Mary* that is structure shared, but *her* itself is in focus. Therefore, the replacing *Mary* with *Mary's father* is a focus alternative of (42).

(42)   when I met [her [——]△ I did [talk to ——]△
                        Mary

On the focus based analysis, however, the antecedent *Mary* itself must bear a focus mark, which would then be copied into the ellipsis site. But the antecedent *Mary* in (41) is itself elided, and the prior occurrence of *Mary* is not necessarily focussed.[11] I conclude therefore that (41) provides an additional argument against the focus based analysis.

On the binding based analysis, it is easy to account for (41) because binding does not depend on focus. To distinguish between the predictions of the binding based analysis and the structure sharing analysis, examples where the antecedent in a focus dependency is not part of a larger focus are necessary. Unfortunately it is difficult to find relevant facts, and I leave this matter for future research.[12]

3.8 Dependency parallelism

Dependency parallelism is a condition Fiengo and May (1994) observe for the sloppy interpretation of a bound pronoun. It requires the antecedents of the two pronouns to be in structurally parallel positions. In Sauerland (1998), I point that a sloppy interpretation is unavailable in (43) in contrast with (5).[13]

(43)   *The policeman who John talked to read him his rights and the policeman who
        arrested Bill did △, too.
        △ = read Bill Bill's rights

Dependency parallelism follows from the structure sharing analysis because ellipsis can only be licensed in a domain that includes the antecedent: For (43), this would be the domain YP indicated in (44). But, no focus alternative of (44) occurs in the discourse.

(44)   YP
        the policeman who [arrested]F [——]F did [read him —— his rights]△
                                    Bill

The focus based analysis does not predict the dependency parallelism condition because it does not assume any condition other than LF-copying for ellipsis licensing. Of the binding based analyses, only those predict dependency parallelism that require a wide domain like (44) for ellipsis licensing. This is the case for the extraction analysis described first in Section 2.1, but not for the center index based analysis of Hardt (2003).

3.9 Structure sharing and MaxElide

MaxElide is a new condition on ellipsis licensing requiring the deletion of as much of a parallelism domain as possible. The existence of such a condition was to my knowledge first observed by (Fiengo and May 1994:244) and Merchant (in print). I follow here the discussion of Takahashi and Fox (2005). As stated above, I assume that a parallelism domain (or ellipsis licensing domain) is a phrase such that a focus alternative of it occurs in the discourse. For ellipsis licensing, I assume the two conditions in (45):

(45) a. Ellipsis of XP must be licensed by a parallelism domain YP that dominates XP. (Rooth 1992)
      b. MaxElide: There must be no XP′ dominated by YP and dominating XP such that XP′ can be elided.

As Takahashi and Fox (2005) argue, MaxElide has no effect in many examples because the position of parallelism domains is flexible. For example, ellipsis can target either the higher or lower phrase in (46) depending on the choice of parallelism domain.

(46) (Takahashi and Fox 2005:(12))
      a. John said Mary likes Peter. BILL also did [say she likes Peter]$_\triangle$
                                                    parallelism domain
      b. John said Mary likes Peter. BILL also said she does [like Peter]$_\triangle$
                                                              parallelism domain

MaxElide only has an effect when small parallelism domains are blocked. Following Rooth (1992), Takahashi and Fox (2005) assume that binding blocks small parallelism domains. Therefore, a sloppy interpretation is blocked when ellipsis is not maximal as in (47b) and (48b).

(47) ((Takahashi and Fox 2005:(5)) after (Sag 1976:131))
      a. John said Mary hit him, and BILL λ_x also did [x say Mary hit x]$_\triangle$
                                                              parallelism domain

b.   *John said Mary hit him, and BILL λ_y also y said $\underbrace{\text{she did [hit } y]_\triangle}_{\text{parallelism domain}}$

(48) (Williams 1977:122)

  a.   John is proud that thereare pictures of him there, and
       $\underbrace{\text{BILL } \lambda_x \text{ is } [x \text{ proud that there are pictures of } x \text{ there}]_\triangle}_{\text{parallelism domain}}$, too.

  b.   *John is proud that there are pictures of him there, and
       BILL λ_x is x proud that there are $\underbrace{\text{[pictures of } x \text{ there}]_\triangle}_{\text{parallelism domain}}$, too.

The different accounts of focus dependency make different predictions for the interaction with MaxElide. The deciding factor is whether ellipsis licensing requires a focus domain that includes the antecedent. Since binding based analyses other than Hardt's and the structure sharing based analysis require such a wide parallelism domain, they predict that MaxElide effects should be observed with focus dependencies. The center binding and the focus based analysis make the opposite prediction. The facts in (49) and (50) bear out the prediction of the former set of analyses.

(49) a.   The policeman who arrested John threatened to hit him $\triangle_1$, and the policeman who arrested Bill did $\triangle_2$, as well.
           $\triangle_1$ = John, $\triangle_2$ = threaten to hit Bill
      b.   *?The policeman who arrested John threatened to hit him $\triangle_1$, and the policeman who arrested Bill threatened to $\triangle_2$, as well.
           $\triangle_1$ = John, $\triangle_2$ = hit Bill

(50) a.   When I sing you say it is nice that I do $\triangle_1$, but when I whistle you don't $\triangle_2$
           $\triangle_1$ = sing, $\triangle_2$ = say it is nice that I whistle
      b.   *When I sing you say it is nice that I do $\triangle_1$, but when I whistle you don't say it is $\triangle_2$
           $\triangle_1$ = sing, $\triangle_2$ = nice that I whistle

Specifically the structure sharing analysis predicts the contrast in (50) in the following way: Consider the structure of the second conjunct in (51). The only parallelism for which the first conjunct is a possible antecedent is the entire second conjunct because any domain that does not include the *when*-clause does not contain an F-feature dominating *whistle*. Therefore MaxElide dictates the the biggest subconstituent of this domain that can be elided must be: ellipsis of the VP headed by *say* is forced.

(51)   when I [——]_F you don't [say it is nice that I do ——]_△
                                                                whistle

I conclude that the interaction of MaxElide and focus dependencies provides another argument against the center binding and the focus based analysis of focus dependencies.

3.10 Cross-over constraint

Focus-dependency is subject to a kind of cross-over constraint. (Tomioka 1999:220) observes that a sloppy interpretations is unavailable in (52) (see also (Safir 2005:51)).

(52)   *The guy who likes him gave John a present, and the guy who doesn't
        △ gave Bill nothing.
        △ = likes Bill

On the structure sharing analysis, (53) requires an additional constraint. One possibility is a requirement that there is a condition that structure shared material must always pronounced in the left-most position it is linked to. This condition is violated in the structure (53).

(53)   the guy who likes him —— gave [——]_F a present
                                                    John

However, this purely linear constraint faces a problem with psych-verbs. Fiengo and May (1994) point out that (54) does not allow the sloppy reading that is indicative of a focus dependency, even though the linearity constraint is satisfied.[14]

(54)   *A rumor about John annoyed him, but a rumor about Bill didn't △
        △ = annoy Bill

Another difficult case is brought up by Tomioka (2007). He points out the example in (55), which does allow a focus dependency though the linearity constraint is violated.

(55)   If you tell me to $\triangle_1$, I will gladly quit drinking, but even if the Queen did $\triangle_2$,
       I would never quit smoking!
       $\triangle_1$ = drink, $\triangle_2$ = tell me to quit smoking

Tomioka claims that what I call structure-sharing is generally not subject to weak
crossover. While I agree with the conclusion, that it is not exactly weak crossover
that is at issue, it seems likely to me that something additional is going on in (55).
Note that with NP-deletion in (56), a focus dependency is blocked.

(56)   *If I want to talk to him, I call my father, but if you do $\triangle$, you don't call your
       mother
       $\triangle$ = want to talk to your mother

I therefore propose that both (54) and (56) fulfill the linearity constraint on the
pronunciation of structure-shared material that I proposed at the relevant level of
representation, but that there can be subsequent purely phonological movement
as Sauerland and Elbourne (2002) have argued. Specifically, the positions prior to
this movement would be the following: A position somewhere below and to the
right of the experiencer in the psych-verb case (54), and a position below the subject immediately adjacent to VP for the condition in (55). For the condition, I
assume furthermore that the linearity is such that if two occurrences of structure
shared material are adjacent either one can be pronounced.

   This proposal predicts an interaction between focus dependency and Condition C similar to the interaction between variable binding and Condition C with
preposed conditionals observed by Chierchia (1995). Specifically, my account predicts that (57a) should not allow a focus dependency, while (57b) should. This
prediction needs to be tested more thoroughly, than I have been able to up to now,
but there seems to be a slight contrast in the predicted direction.

(57)   a.   [??]If a lady asks me to $\triangle_1$, she can always take flowers from my garden, but
             even if my wife does $\triangle_2$, she must never deposit garbage there.
             $\triangle_1$ = take flowers from my garden, $\triangle_2$ = ask me to deposit garbage there
       b.   [?]If she asks me to $\triangle_1$, a lady can always take flowers from my garden, but
             even if my wife does $\triangle_2$, she must never deposit garbage there.

I conclude therefore that, while the crossover constraints on focus dependencies
are complex and still insufficiently explored, an account in terms of order and
adjacency at PF is presently a possible analysis of the facts as they are know. This
kind of explanation is, of course, consistent with the structure sharing analysis I
have proposed.

4.   Conclusion

This paper argues for an analysis of focus dependency on the basis of structure sharing. A structure shared phrase is connected to at least two positions of a phrase marker as shown in (58). This material must remain unpronounced in one position it is linked to, but can even be part of a focussed phrase in the other. (58) is then pronounced with *whistle* in the left position and with pitch accent on *whistle*.

(58)   when I [—]-F you don't say I shouldn't —
                                                  whistle

Interestingly, structure sharing is predicted to interact with focus in a specific fashion and this provides the argument for structure sharing I developed in this paper. In a configuration like (58), the unpronounced material following *shouldn't* is in a very specific way related to focus: It is not focussed when we consider a constituent that does not include the F-feature dominating the first position *whistle* is linked to. But, it is focussed when we consider a constituent that includes the first position. Furthermore, the focus alternatives of *whistle* covary in the two positions *whistle* is linked to. As I have shown all these properties are desirable for the account of focus dependencies.

Focus dependency has so far been usually given purely semantic accounts. In many cases, these accounts have in one way or another expanded the inventory of semantic mechanisms; for example, by focus indices (Kratzer 1991), unrestricted QR (Schwarz 1999), center binding (Hardt 2003), or step-by-step ellipsis resolution (Tomioka 2007). One of the main points of this paper is that, from a semantic point of view, focus dependency looks like other cases where structure sharing has been invoked in syntactic theory. Therefore, I propose that the right strategy is to use the same syntactic mechanism for all such cases, and let the syntacticians handle the consequences of this conclusion. My move does entail that the locality restrictions on movement cannot be explained by restrictions on structure sharing since focus dependency is not subject to locality conditions. This view seems compatible with the view of Merchant (2001) that locality conditions on movement are due to interface properties, rather than core syntax, but as far as I know this view is still regarded with scepticism in syntax.

My proposal also entails that structure sharing rather than just copying must be a permissible syntactic operation since it is not straightforward to achieve the same results with only copying. If just the lexical material without the focus feature is copied as in (59), the copy is not focussed at all, which predicts no focus dependencies. If the copy may also include the focus feature as in (59b), still covariance in the focus alternatives is not achieved. Kratzer (1991) therefore proposed to index foci as in (59c). But as I have shown above, (59c) still is insufficient because a) the focus is visible even within a constituent not including the overt focus mark, and b) the focus is only transferred by copying if it is on or within the phrase that is copied.

(59) a.   when I [whistle]$_F$ you don't say I shouldn't *whistle*
      b.   when I [whistle]$_F$ you don't say I shouldn't [*whistle*]$_F$
      c.   when I [whistle]$_{F_1}$ you don't say I shouldn't [*whistle*]$_{F_1}$

Therefore, I conclude that structure sharing is needed in syntax, and that it is furthermore far less constrained than previously thought. I reach this conclusion based on data from English in this paper. I should note that the structure-sharing account predict cross-linguistic variation to be quite limited with respect to the relevant conditions, as the basic structure-building operations should not vary among languages. The one area where I would expect variation is the pronunciation of structure-shared material: English, as I argued above, is subject to a constraint that permits structure sharing only if all but one occurrence of the structure shared material are part of an elided structure. It seems quite plausible that this constraint does not apply in the same way in languages with overt copying constructions, and then we expect these languages to exhibit focus-dependencies with two overt occurrences. One example of this seems to be German: German *wh*-copying has been analyzed as pronunciation of multiple copies (Barbiers et al. 2007), but could also be analyzed as structure sharing with multiple pronunciation of the same material. The fact that sluicing can be combined with *wh*-copying as in (60) shows that a focus dependency is possible, arguing in favor of the structure sharing analysis.

(60)   Wer   hat   Maria gesagt wer   kommen wird,   und   wann △.
       Who   has   Mary   said   who   come   will   and   when

       △ = hat   Maria gesagt wann kommen wird
            has   Mary   said   when   come   will

       'Who did Mary say is coming and when?'

This indicates that there is indeed the cross-linguistic variation regarding the pronunciation of structure shared material that I expect. Unfortunately, I have not seen any relevant data from other languages that allow overt copying such as Yoruba in the relativized predicate construction (Kobele 2006:212–245).

Notes

* I would like to thank Hans-Martin Gärtner, Bernhard Schwarz, Michal Starke, one anonymous reviewer, and audiences in Barcelona, Berlin, and Gargnano for their comments on this work. I also thank many native speakers for responding to my judgment queries, especially Philippa Cook. I am also grateful for the financial support of the DFG through grant SA 925/1-2. Of course, I alone am responsible for all the shortcomings. An earlier, shorter version of this paper appeared in the proceedings of Sinn und Bedeutung 11.

1. As I revise this paper for publication, I have become aware of interesting new work by Merchant (2004) and Tomioka (2007) which discuss the phenomenon at hand in some detail.

2. Elbourne (2001) makes a similar point with example (61). Tomioka's analysis incorrectly predicts an interpretation where R is interpreted as *person he arrested* to be available.

(i)   Scenario: Officer Jones arrested a pimp.
       Every police officer who arrested a murderer insulted him [the R], and Officer Jones insulted him [the R] too.

3. I follow Geurts (1997) in assuming that proper names are NPs with an empty definite determiner.

4. Furthermore, Hardt's proposal does not predict clause-boundedness as Safir (2005) points out. I discuss the relevant fact in 17 below.

5. Schwarz's own example does not make this point as forcefully as (11) since it involves sluicing with *why*, which might be base-generated in a VP-external position (Tsai 1994). Tomioka (2007) independently constructed examples similar to (11) and also concludes that syntactic extraction from the focus dependent material is possible.

6. See Sauerland (1998) for an analysis similar to Kratzer's that does not rely on LF-copying.

7. I assume here following Heim (to appear) that the bound pronouns *my* and *your* in (22) have no semantically interpreted features.

8. Note that the predicted entailment is also unidirectional: If there is structure sharing of NPs, then there must be agreement in grammatical gender. Agreement in grammatical gender can independently arise from NP-ellipsis without structure sharing as discussed in Sauerland (2007).

9. Similar examples are of course possible with a VP focus dependency and probably with other categories too:

(i)   I only SING because you told me to.

10. Bernhard Schwarz (p.c.) alerted me to this fact.

11. One could, of course, assume that when copying to fill ellipsis sites, the source is always the first occurrence of a phrase in a discourse, which usually would bear focus. But, this seems implausible to me.

12. (61) is my best current attempt, but it's not presently clear whether intonational marking *do* can create a VP-focus.

(i) $^{??}$When I sing you say I shouldn't. I started to whistle, because when I do, you don't.

13. (Tomioka 1999:222) argues for a different conclusion. However, his examples allow implicational bridging (cf. Rooth 1992): For example, the first conjunct of (61) – one of Tomioka's examples – entails that people in New York hate its subway system. (43) controls for implicational bridging.

(i) Those who live in New York hate its subway system, and people in Tokyo do △, too.

14. This point requires further investigation, though. It seems that for VP focus dependencies there is no contrast between transitive verbs and psych-verbs in (61).

(i) Usually people who snore hate/bother other people who do △$_1$, but people who sleepwalk don't △$_2$.
     △$_1$ = snore, △ = hate/bother other people who sleepwalk

References

Artstein, Ron, 2004. 'Focus below the word level', *Natural Language Semantics* 12, 1–22.

Barbiers, Sjef, Olaf Koeneman, and Marika Lekakou, 2007. 'Syntactic doubling and the structure of chains'. Talk at GLOW 2007, University of Tromsø, Norway.

Bobaljik, Jonathan D. and Sam Brown, 1997. 'Inter-arboreal operations: Head-movement and the Extension Requirement', *Linguistic Inquiry* 28, 345–356.

Chierchia, Gennaro, 1995. *Dynamics of Meaning*. University of Chicago Press.

Elbourne, Paul, 2001. 'E-type anaphora as NP-deletion', *Natural Language Semantics* 9, 241–288.

Elbourne, Paul, 2002. *Situations and Individuals*, Doctoral Dissertation, Massachusetts Institute of Technology.

Fiengo, Robert and Robert May, 1994. *Indices and Identity*. MIT Press, Cambridge, Mass.

Fox, Danny, 1999. 'Focus, parallelism, and accommodation'. In T. Matthews and D. Strolovitch (eds.), *Proceedings of SALT 9*, 70–90. Cornell University, CLC Publications, Ithaca, N.Y.

Fox, Danny, 2000. *Economy and Semantic Interpretation*. MIT Press, Cambridge, Mass.

Gärtner, Hans-Martin, 2002. *Generalized Transformations and Beyond: Reflections on Minimalist Syntax*. Akademie Verlag, Berlin, Germany.

Geurts, Bart, 1997. 'Good news about the description theory of names', *Journal of Semantics* 14, 319–348.

Grosz, Barbara J., Scott Weinstein, and Aravind K. Joshi, 1995. 'Centering: A framework for modeling the local coherence of discourse', *Computational Linguistics* 2, 203–225.

Hankamer, Jorge and Ivan Sag, 1976. 'Deep and surface anaphora', *Linguistic Inquiry* 7, 391–428.

Hardt, Daniel, 1999. 'Dynamic interpretation of verb phrase ellipsis', *Linguistics and Philosophy* 22, 185–219.

Hardt, Daniel, 2003. 'Sloppy identity, binding, and centering'. In *Proceedings of SALT 13*. CLC Publications, Cornell University.

Heim, Irene, to appear. 'Features on bound pronouns'. In D. Adger et al. (eds.), *Φ-features*, Oxford University Press, Oxford, UK.

Johnson, Kyle (ed.), in print. *Topics in Ellipsis*. Oxford University Press, Oxford, UK.

Kobele, Gregory M., 2006. *Generating copies: An investigation into structural identity in language and grammar*, Doctoral Dissertation, UCLA.

Kratzer, Angelika, 1991. 'The representation of focus'. In A. von Stechow and D. Wunderlich (eds.), *Semantik: Ein internationales Handuch der zeitgenössischen Forschung (Semantics: An International Handbook of Contemporary Research)*, 825–834. de Gruyter, Berlin.

Krifka, Manfred, 2001. 'For a structured meaning account of questions and answers'. In W. Sternefeld and C. Féry (eds.), *Audiatur Vox Sapientiae. A Festschrift for Arnim von Stechow*, 287–319. Akademie Verlag, Berlin, Germany.

Merchant, Jason, 2001. *The Syntax of Silence: Sluicing, Islands, and the Theory of Ellipsis*. Oxford University Press, Oxford, UK.

Merchant, Jason, 2004. 'A deletion solution to the sloppy ellipsis puzzle'. Handout from a talk delivered at the 75th Meeting of the LSA.

Merchant, Jason, in print. 'Variable island repair under ellipsis', In Johnson (in print), 132–153.

Rooth, Mats, 1985. *Association with focus*, Doctoral Dissertation, University of Massachusetts, Amherst.

Rooth, Mats, 1992. 'Ellipsis redundancy and reduction redundancy'. In S. Berman and A. Hestvik (eds.), *Proceedings of the Stuttgart Ellipsis Workshop*. Arbeitspapiere des Sonderforschungsbereichs 340, Bericht Nr. 29, IBM Germany, Heidelberg.

Ross, John Robert, 1969. 'Guess who?' In R. I. Binnick, A. Davison, G. M. Green, and J. L. Morgan (eds.), *CLS 5*, 252–278. Chicago.

Safir, Kenneth, 2005. *The Syntax of (In)dependence*. MIT Press, Cambridge, Mass.

Sag, Ivan, 1976. *Deletion and logical form*, Doctoral Dissertation, Massachusetts Institute of Technology, Cambridge, Mass.

Sauerland, Uli, 1998. *The meaning of chains*, Doctoral Dissertation, Massachusetts Institute of Technology, Cambridge, Mass.

Sauerland, Uli, 2007. 'Flat binding: Binding without sequences'. In U. Sauerland and H.-M. Gärtner (eds.), *Interfaces + Recursion = Grammar? Chomsky's Minimalism and the View from Syntax-Semantics*, 197–254. Mouton de Gruyter, Berlin, Germany.

Sauerland, Uli and Paul Elbourne, 2002. 'Total reconstruction, PF movement, and derivational order', *Linguistic Inquiry* 33, 283–319.

Schwarz, Bernhard, 1999. 'Silent verb phrases as bound variables'. Manuscript, University of Massachusetts, Amherst.

Schwarzschild, Roger, 1999. 'GIVENNESS, AVOIDF and other constraints on the placement of accents', *Natural Language Semantics* 7, 141–177.

Svenonius, Peter, 2005. 'Extending the extension condition to discontinuous idioms', *Linguistic Variation Yearbook* 5, 227–263.

Takahashi, Shoichi and Danny Fox, 2005. 'MaxElide and the re-binding problem'. In E. Georgala and J. Howell (eds.), *Proceedings of SALT 15*. Ithaca, N.Y.

Tomioka, Satoshi, 1999. 'A sloppy identity puzzle', *Natural Language Semantics* 7, 217–248.

Tomioka, Satoshi, 2007. 'A step-by-step guide to VP ellipsis resolution'. In Johnson (in print).

Tsai, Wei-Tien Dylan, 1994. *On economizing the theory of A-Bar dependencies*, Doctoral Dissertation, Massachusetts Institute of Technology, Cambridge, Mass.

Williams, Edwin, 1977. 'Discourse and logical form', *Linguistic Inquiry* 8, 101–139.

Author's address:

Zentrum für Allgemeine Sprachwissenschaft
Schützenstr. 18
10117 Berlin
Germany

uli@alum.mit.edu

Towards a restrictive theory of (remnant) movement*

Klaus Abels
Universitetet i Tromsø (CASTL) and University College London

A restrictive theory of syntax needs both a restrictive theory of structures and a restrictive theory of operations. Much recent effort has gone into narrowing the class of allowable structures and a lot has been learned. This paper proposes that operations are linearly ordered on an essentially constituent by constituent basis. A universal constraint on the ordering of operations in language is proposed whose function is to fix the order in which operations apply. This constraint is deployed using a generalized prohibition against improper movement. The proposal captures some but not all effects of what has traditionally been called the freezing principle. It is argued that empirically exactly the right cut is made. It is further argued that the proposal rules out an entire class of remnant movement derivations, including the analysis of cross-serial dependencies in Nilsen (2003) and the analysis of order-preservation in Koopman and Szabolcsi (2000).

Keywords: remnant movement, cross serial dependency, improper movement, linear correspondence axiom, LCA, linear order, cycle, freezing principle, syntax

1. Introduction: A plea for a restrictive theory of operations

Syntactic theory should explain linear asymmetries in language. Why is rightward movement so much more restricted than leftward movement (Ross (1967), Perlmutter and Postal (1983/1972), Bach (1971))? Why aren't OV-languages simply the mirror image of VO-langues (see Kayne (1994, 2005) for some illustrations)? Why are there verb-second languages but no verb-second-last languages? Why are noun phrases asymmetric in a typological perspective (Greenberg (1963), Cinque (1996, 2005); Abels and Neeleman (2006))? Questions like these are in the background throughout this paper.

Linguistic Variation Yearbook 7 (2007), **53–120**.
ISSN 1568–1483/ E-ISSN 1569–9900 © John Benjamins Publishing Company

Over 10 years ago now, Kayne (1994) suggested that part of the answer to such questions could be the Linear Correspondence Axiom (LCA). The LCA claims that all phrases in natural language follow the template in (1). I will refer to this as the rigid specifier-head-complement (S-H-C) hypothesis. The LCA also claims that all movement operations are leftward.

(1)
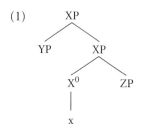

Obviously, the rigid S-H-C hypothesis, if true, can be no more than a partial answer to the questions raised in the first paragraph. No matter how restricted the theory of phrase structure is and no matter how serious the restriction to leftward movement may seem, an unduly permissive theory of movement can still undermine the explanatory effort expressed in the rigid S-H-C hypothesis. All of the structures that cannot be directly generated under the rigid S-H-C hypothesis can be brought back through movement operations, (2). The symbol ⤳ can be read as follows: Any analysis which is incompatible with the rigid S-H-C hypothesis because it contains the structure on the left can be made compatible by replacing all occurrences of the structures on the left hand side of the arrow by the structures on the right hand side. Head-final structures can be emulated through short movement operations, (2a), right specifiers and adjuncts can be simulated through the introduction of silent functional elements, f and g in (2b). Finally, any rightward movement operation can be emulated by a two-movement sequence, where the second step involves remnant movement, as in (2c). The structural and movement types indicated in (2) are not just hypothetical figments of my imagination; Kayne (1994: 50–54) chooses (2a) to analyze right headedness–although the analysis was later revised in Kayne (1999, 2004); Cinque (2005) uses structures like (2b) to treat right adjuncts, and Kayne (1998) employs structures abstractly like (2c) to treat certain cases of quantifier scope.

(2)   a.   Right Heads:

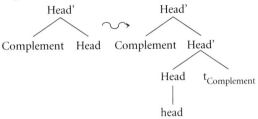

  b.   Right Specifiers and Adjuncts:

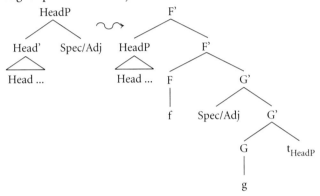

  c.   Rightward Movement:

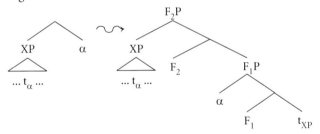

Excessive transformational power allows reformulating any analysis not conforming to the rigid S-H-C hypothesis in terms of it. Therefore, the LCA is more restrictive and predictive than the older, symmetric theory of structure and movement only in conjunction with a restrictive theory of movement.[1]

   I concentrate on remnant movement in this paper. Some of the other issues, those raised by the movements in (2a) and (2b), are discussed in some detail in Abels and Neeleman (2006). The conclusion drawn there is that the massive use of roll-up movement in the current literature removes the empirical content of the claim that complements follow heads and that specifiers precede heads (Richards

(2004: Chapter 2) comes to a similar assessment). Moreover, Abels and Neeleman argue that such roll-up movement violates otherwise valid generalizations concerning pied-piping, stranding, and anti-locality. They conclude that generating complements to the left or to the right of a head and allowing left and right specifiers and adjuncts allows a more restrictive theory of movement that can dispense with entire classes of movement. Their claim is that a theory that dispenses with the rigid S-H-C hypothesis can reduce the amount of movement that needs to be assumed not only quantitatively but qualitatively. This helps in the ultimate explanation of linear asymmetries. I assume this reasoning here and make use of trees with left and right complements and left and right specifiers. However, nothing in this paper hinges on this choice and adherents of the rigid S-H-C hypothesis may mechanically transform all structures which are incompatible with it into compatible ones by assuming the required functional and agreement heads as indicated in (2a) and (2b). In other words, this paper does not bear directly on the question of base structures but is about the shape of a restrictive theory of movement.[2] I will assume throughout that rightward movement is banned (for an attempt at deriving this independently of the LCA see Abels and Neeleman (2006)). This ban might still have empirical and explanatory content. All depends on the theory of movement it is embedded in.

As we just saw, too permissive a theory of movement makes the strict S-H-C hypothesis empirically contentless. A theory of movement that was restrictive in certain ways was in the background when Kayne's book was first published, hence, the rigid S-H-C hypothesis was viewed as a great explanatory success.

In the early and mid nineties the proper-binding condition was still widely assumed, remnant movement (as in (2c)) was considered exotic or impossible, and Müller (1998) felt compelled to spend an entire chapter on reconciling proper-binding-condition effects with the existence of remnant movement. The proper-binding-condition – in the formulation argued for in Lasnik and Saito (1992: 90) – says: "Traces must be bound throughout a derivation" (see Fiengo (1977: 45) for the original formulation). Under Lasnik and Saito's formulation, the proper-binding condition rules out any derivation along the lines in (2c), because the trace of alpha within the fronted XP is not bound at the stage of the derivation depicted. With the proper-binding condition as background, the ban against rightward movement predicts that derivations like (2c) are unavailable, that is, there should be a complete absence of rightward movement even superficially.

A second restriction on movement that was widely assumed was the freezing principle. The freezing principle (Ross (1967); Wexler and Culicover (1980)) prohibits movement from a moved constituent. Given the VP internal subject hypothesis, the freezing principle predicts that subjects moved to [Spec,TP] should be islands for extraction – some counterexamples are discussed below in Section 2. Together with the LCA the freezing principle also appears to rule out all extraction from preverbal obejcts in OV languages, (3), because all such extraction involves extraction from a moved constituent.

(3) a.   X ... [$_{DP}$ ... t$_X$ ...] ... V Aux [t$_V$ t$_{DP}$]
      b.   X ... [$_{VP}$ ... [$_{DP}$ ... t$_X$ ...] ... V] Aux ... t$_{VP}$

This view is clearly too restrictive, as (4) shows – this example is discussed below in (23).

(4) ... weil   darüber   niemand { ein |* das} Buch   lesen
      ... because there-about nobody   [a   the   book t$_{darüber}$] read
      wollte
      wanted
      ... because nobody wanted to read {a|*the} book about that

The discussion above is slightly oversimplified. Every violation of the freezing principle can be circumvented if remnant movement is freely available, as (5) shows (see Collins (1994, 1997); Müller (1998) for pertinent discussion of chain interleaving).

(5)   Freezing Principle:

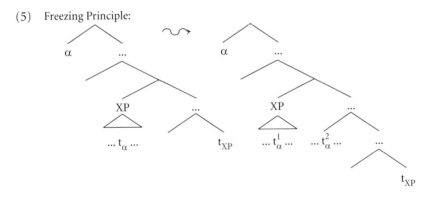

In a theory with the proper-binding condition and without other restrictions on remnant movement, the freezing principle has no content. This underscores yet again that the power of remnant movement needs to be sharply restricted.

    While the proper-binding condition and the freezing principle used to be accepted by many, it has become clear since the publication of Kayne (1994) that the proper-binding condition cannot be entirely correct; the arguments for the existence of remnant-movement are just too strong (for an overview of the arguments from German VP-, PP-, and NP-topicalization see Müller (1998: Chapter 1), see also Hiraiwa (2002), Abels (2002)). Likewise, the existence of what appears to be rightward movement cannot be completely denied; there is, for example, a consensus now that the structure for Heavy NP Shift under Kayne's (1994: 71–78) analysis is incorrect. Under that analysis the "heavy-shifted NP" simply remained in its low VP internal position. It seems now that the "heavy-shifted NP" moves out of VP. There are two implementations for this: the traditional rightward movement analysis and a remnant-movement analysis (den Dikken (1995); Rochemont and Culicover (1997); Kayne (1998) among others). Both of them give rise to gross constituent structures along the lines of those generated by the traditional rightward movement analysis. Of course, the long-standing observation still stands that what observationally looks like rightward movement has properties very different from those of leftward movement. Finally, I review examples below that suggest that the freezing principle cannot generally be correct.

These remarks show that, if the explanatory project which motivated the LCA, to account for linear asymmetries in languages, is to succeed, a restrictive theory of operations, movement in particular, is required. The proper-binding condition and the freezing principle need to be replaced by more empirically adequate constraints. This is the focal question of this paper. To investigate it, I look at improper movement and related phenomena that bear on the sequencing of movement operations and claim that there are non-trivial constraints on such sequencing. These constraints severely limit remnant movement (see Grewendorf (2003) for a related proposal) and extraction from moved constituents.

The suggestion I develop in this paper is to treat the ban against improper movement – at the very least for heuristic purposes – as a phenomenon rather than an epiphenomenon. Stated in the abstract, the phenomenon seems to be that movement operations must apply in a strictly ordered sequence to any given phrase. I hypothesize that there is a Universal Constraint on Operational Ordering in Language, UCOOL for short, operative in all languages. As a first and very coarse approximation this constraint takes the form in (6). Here and throughout A-movement and movement for Case designate the same operation.

(6) $\theta \ll$ A-mvt $\ll Op$

While (6) is just a restatement of the ban against improper movement, I suggest below that the phenomenon of improper movement is much more general than usually assumed. It is more general in two ways. First, more types of movement need to be taken into account. Second, while the ban against improper movement is usually construed as a ban against consecutive movements of the same phrase, I suggest below that it also regulates extraction out of moved phrases and remnant movement, that is, it will carry a lot of the empirical burden of the freezing principle and the proper-binding condition. I give a unifying formulation for these three cases below, which is a Generalized Prohibition against Improper Movement (GenPIM).

The similarity to Williams' (2002) Generalized Ban On Improper Movement (GBOIM) is not accidental. This paper is the attempt of capturing important parts of Williams' Level Embedding Conjecture in a framework with bottom-up tree generation and to develop certain consequences not considered by Williams.

Drawing mostly on German with occasional glances at English, I give empirical justification for generalizing improper movement in just this way in Section 2. The claim to universality for the fine-grained hierarchy of operations proposed below remains programmatic. Preliminary investigations of Czech, Serbo-Croatian, and Spanish reveal patterns of data in line with the expectations generated by UCOOL, but I cannot discuss them in this paper for reasons of space. I take the German and English facts discussed to be strong empirical evidence for the claims made here.

Some of the assumptions argued for in Section 2 are then brought to bear on the issue of cross-serial dependencies. First I observe that of the two logically possible types of cross-serial dependencies only one is actually attested. This asymmetry is directly predicted by the conjunction of assumptions defended in the first part of the paper.

I also show that the remnant-movement derivation of unbounded cross-serial dependencies proposed in Nilsen (2003) necessarily violates the conjunction of the Generalized Prohibition against Improper Movement with the assumption that operations are linearly ordered. The same is true of a number of analyses in Koopman and Szabolcsi (2000), of which their analysis of order preservation is discussed as an example. The results from the first part of the paper thus form an argument against these remnant-movement analyses. The argument is further buttressed by the fact that both of the remnant-movement analyses discussed overgenerate in that they willy-nilly give rise to the unattested type of cross-serial dependencies.

2. UCOOL and GenPIM

In this section I show that an accurate description of a wide range of facts can be given if we assume that there is a constraint on the order in which operations, specifically movement operations, apply to a given constituent. I call this constraint the Universal Constraint on Operational Ordering in Language or UCOOL, (7). UCOOL demands that θ-related operations have to apply first, followed by Case related operations, followed by operator movement. This is, of course, the received wisdom.[3]

> (7)   The Universal Constraint on Operational Ordering in Language (UCOOL) –
> *to be refined*
> θ ≪ A-mvt ≪ *Op*
> I will say that θ-operations are a *lower* type of operations than A-movement (Case), and that Case-operations are a *higher* type of operations than θ-operations.

The discovery of the ban on improper movement was an automatic side-effect of the move from construction specific transformations to general operations and conditions on them (Chomsky (1973: 243 fn. 24, p. 253 # 110c); May (1979); Chomsky (1981: 195–204)). Move α run amok would make improper movement possible. The Government and Binding framework managed to keep the derivational part of the theory maximally general, maintaining Move α, by appealing to representational conditions and devices. Thus, in Lectures on Government and Binding Chomsky appeals to the projection principle and the theta criterion to rule out certain instances of improper movement and, following May (1979), to binding theoretic properties of traces to rule out others. However, the notions on which Chomsky's derivation of the ban on improper movement rested are no longer available. Deep structure has been abolished in minimalist theorizing and the projection principle with it. Trace theory has been given up in favor of the copy theory of movement; the binding theoretic assumptions concerning different types of traces are therefore no longer available. Under Chomsky's inclusiveness condition, the explicit manipulation of indices required to make the binding theoretic account work is no longer available either. At present there is no minimalist account of the ban against improper movement.

UCOOL allows us to approach the relevant facts. It establishes three pairwise orders, none of which seem controversial: θ ≪ A-mvt, θ ≪ Op, and A-mvt ≪ Op.

In the framework of Government and Binding theory θ-roles were assigned at deep structure, ensuring that θ-role assignment could not be fed by movement operations. This assumption is carried over into minimalism by Chomsky (1995: 312–313), who explicitly rules out movement into theta positions. He relies on a configurational approach to θ-theory (rather than a feature based one) and the curious additional claim (p. 313) that "[i]f α raises to a θ-position TH, forming the chain CH = (α, t), the argument that must bear a θ-role is CH, not α. But CH is not in any configuration, and α is not an argument that can receive a θ-role."

Others have argued that movement into θ-positions should be allowed (see Bošković (1994); Bošković and Takahashi (1998); Hornstein (1999, 2001); Landau (2003); Culicover and Jackendoff (2001); Boeckx and Hornstein (2003); Polinsky and Potsdam (2002); Ramchand (to appear) for discussion). A look at the derivations proposed by the proponents of movement into θ-positions shows that θ-roles are always assigned in the lowest positions an argument finds itself in, never in positions that are only reached via case or operator positions.

Simple factual considerations suggest that the consensual position is true, as (8) is intended to indicate.

(8) a. *I asked who [$_{CP}$ t$_{who}$ [John should meet Mary]]
     b. *I (was) expected t$_I$ to be discovered a proof.

Thus, although there is no consensus on whether movement from θ-position to θ-position exists, there is a consensus that movement from a case to a θ-position or from an operator to a θ-position does not exist. Thus we get θ ≪ A-mvt and θ ≪ Op.

The remaining case, the ordering between movement to a case position and movement to an operator position is usually simply stipulated. A typical example is Chomsky and Lasnik's (1995: 91) assumption that apart from uniform chains, "[t]he only other legitimate LF objects are operator-variable constructions (α, β), where α is in an $\overline{A}$ position and β heads a legitimate (uniform) chain." As a description this seems consensual. Simple examples suggesting the factual correctness of the consensus are given in (9). All of this motivates A-mvt ≪ Op.

(9) a. [$_{CP}$ What [$_{IP}$ t$^3_{what}$ seems [$_{IP}$ t$^2_{what}$ to have been said t$^1_{what}$?]]]]
     b. *[$_{CP}$ What [$_{IP}$ t$^3_{what}$ seems [$_{CP}$ t$^2_{what}$ that [$_{IP}$ it was said t$^1_{what}$?]]]]
     c. John asked whose book to read.
     d. (i) *Whose book was asked [t$_{whose\ book}$ [{t$_{whose\ book}$ | PRO | there} to be read t$_{whose\ book}$]].
         (ii) *Whose book was asked [t$_{whose\ book}$ {whether | that | Ø} [{ it | there} was read t$_{whose\ book}$]].

UCOOL makes the consensual point regarding operational sequencing explicit.

I hasten to add that it would be desirable to derive the hierarchy or its effects from deeper principles, but for the moment it is unclear how to do this. Anyway, the fact that an explanation at a deeper level is currently missing should not deter us from investigating and using the hierarchy. The situation is exactly parallel for structural hierarchies: although currently there is no explanation for the CP-IP-VP hierarchy and its cartographic avatars, such hierarchies are used to explain language internal and cross-linguistic facts as well as facts from language acquisition. This mode of reasoning is an explanation at one level, the level called explanatory adequacy in Chomsky (1965), but of course not at a deeper level. I assume that UCOOL can be an explanatory device just as much (or little) as the Cinque hierarchy can and relegate the search for a deeper explanation to further inquiry.

Setting aside the eternal troublemakers for the ban against improper movement (*tough*-movement and relative clauses) for some other occasion, the hierarchy may be taken to restate what appears to be a fact across languages, namely, that an argument begins its derivational life in a θ-position. It may (or may not) then go on to receive case and move in connection to this. And it may (or may not) then move on to an operator position.

This classic trichotomy into θ-related, case-related, and operator-related operations was well suited to a trichotomous (CP-IP-VP) clause structure. The explosion of clause structure demands a more fine-grained approach to operational types as well. In other words, just like phrase-structure hierarchies have expanded from the simple $[_{CP}[_{IP}[_{VP}...]]]$ to encompass ever more fine-grained structures (see Larson (1988); Pollock (1989); Alexiadou (1997); Rizzi (1997); Cinque (1999, 2002); Belletti (2004); Rizzi (2004b); Cinque (2006) among many others), so our inventory of operations presumably needs to be refined (Sternefeld (1992); Müller and Sternefeld (1993); Starke (2001); Williams (2002); Grewendorf (2003)) and UCOOL be adjusted accordingly.

The dichotomy of A- vs. Ā-movement, going back to Postal (1971), is insufficient quite independently. It is often assumed that A-movement allows the moved element to act as the binder for anaphors and reciprocals from the landing site of movement, (10a), while Ā-movement does not, (10c). From this perspective (10b) is incomprehensible; whatever operation is responsible for inverting the order of the *to-* and the *about*-PP cannot be A-movement, because of the contrast between (10a–ii) and (10b–ii), but it cannot be Ā-movement either, because of the contrast between (10b–iii) and (10c–iii). The binding pattern seen in (10b) is not particularly rare and it is found with mittelfeldscrambling in German and so-called A-scrambling in Japanese.[4]

(10) a. (i)   *It seems to each other ('s best friends) that the twins are smart.
         (ii)   The twins seem to each other to be smart.
         (iii) the twins seem to each other's best friends to be smart.
     b. (i)   *John talked to each other ('s best friends) about the twins.
         (ii) *John talked about the twins to each other. (see Postal (1971))
         (iii) John talked about the twins to each other's best friends.
     c. (i)   *John believes each other ('s best friends) to be fond of the twins.
         (ii) *Which twins does John believe each other to be fond of.
         (iii) *Which twins does John believe each other's best friends to be fond
              of.

A more comprehensive and fine-grained hierarchy of operations seems to be called
for.

UCOOL allows us to approach and state the relevant facts. UCOOL com-
presses a number of logically independent hypotheses into a single statement.

(11) a. Movement operations are ordered asymmetrically or antisymmetrically;[5]
         on both construals (asymmetry and antisymmetry) the claim is that if a
         movement operation σ feeds a different movement operation τ, then τ
         does not feed σ; the difference is that an antisymmetric ordering allows
         movement of some type to feed movement of the same type, while this
         is ruled out under an asymmetric ordering;
     b. the ordering of operations is total, i.e., for every pair, σ, τ, of movement
         operations σ feeds τ or τ feeds σ;
     c. the ordering of operations is universally fixed.

The three claims are logically independent. The conjunction of the three is the
empirically strongest position, and it is the position I will adopt. As mentioned,
for the three types of operations in (6), the claims in (11), including universality
of the ordering, are uncontroversial.[6]

I will now investigate some properties of the deployment of UCOOL. Many
questions arise immediately. A first set of questions concerns the hierarchy itself:
Is it a linear order? Or is it a partial order? What counts as a type of operation? How
many such types are there? For the purposes of this paper, I will remain somewhat
vague concerning the exact boundaries of my notion of operation. However, any
movement will count as an operation. Finally, I assume that, as a first approximation, the feature-types that enter into the computation of relativized minimal-
ity/attract closest define the operational types. The appeal to relativized minimality, to make sense, presupposes recent work on relativized minimality substantially
refining the classes involved as compared to Rizzi's (1990) original three classes

(see Starke (2001); Rizzi (2004a, 2006) and related work). To extend to θ-roles, it also presupposes the essential correctness of Hornstein's (1999) approach to the locality of control in terms of closest attract.

A second set of questions is of a far reaching but somewhat technical nature: How exactly is this hierarchy deployed? Should it regulate the application of operations per derivation? Per cycle? Per phase? Or should it regulate the application of operations per feature? Per syntactic terminal? Per lexical item? Per word? Per constituent? I attempt to provide answers to these questions below.

A third set of question is less directly technical but even more far reaching: What is the relation between UCOOL and the Cinque hierarchy? Is one parasitic upon the other? If so, which one derives from the other? Can a (partial) shift of the explanation away from the Cinque hierarchy and onto UCOOL solve some of the paradoxes and anomalies that arise under the current understanding of the Cinque hierarchy? While it is important to keep the third set of questions in mind as the exploration of UCOOL unfolds, trying to answer them strikes me as premature at the moment. We first need to establish a much firmer understanding of UCOOL itself.

2.1 How UCOOL is deployed: GenPIM

Under a theory that generates syntactic structures bottom up, we can safely discard the option of deploying UCOOL at the level of the entire derivation, that is, it doesn't make much sense empirically to demand that all θ-role assignment happens before all A-movement before all $\overline{A}$-movement; θ-role assignment, A-movement, and $\overline{A}$-movement will happen in embedded clauses before they can happen in higher clauses.[7] This suggests that UCOOL must apply to smaller domains than entire derivations. An obvious candidate would be the derivational cycle (the phase). However, construing of UCOOL as a constraint on operations per cycle gives rise exactly to the problems we are trying to solve. Consider example (9b). In the lower phase, in the domain of the embedded clause, UCOOL is not violated. Though *what* fails to get Case, it receives a θ-role first and later undergoes $\overline{A}$-movement, which would conform to UCOOL if it were deployed at the phase level. In the upper phase, *what* does not receive a θ-role but it is moved to an A-position followed by movement to an $\overline{A}$-position, again, in conformity with UCOOL applied per phase. Cyclicity in this sense, then, cannot be the answer.[8]

Looking at the problem from the other end of the size scale, relativizing UCOOL to features will certainly not do. A single feature under standard assumptions is responsible for a single type of operation. There is no point in imposing an ordering on a single operation, it will vacuously comply with the order. For an ordering statement to have consequences, it has to apply at least to bundles of features. A moment's reflection reveals that head-sized, morpheme-sized, or word-sized bundles of features are not large enough to deal with improper movement – despite the fact that at this level features are assumed to be ordered (Chomsky (1993); Brody (2000); Stabler (1997)). Consider again (9d). Everything goes fine for *whose*. It may or may not receive a θ-role from *book*, it receives genitive Case internally to the DP *whose book* and then triggers $\overline{A}$-movement. UCOOL is satisfied. Likewise, *book* receives a θ-role and later Case in the matrix [Spec, TP]. Again, UCOOL is satisfied. So what went wrong?

What went wrong is that the entire phrase (qua pied-piping) was involved in high type $\overline{A}$-operation first and later in a lower type of operation, an A-operation. UCOOL must be deployed so as to ban this. This entails that ordering features within a head or a word is at best irrelevant. The constraint has to apply to all parts of the moving constituent. I suggest below that it applies even beyond the moving constituent to all ancestor nodes of the moving constituent which are part of the phrase marker at the moment when movement takes place. In other words, I suggest to extend the ban against improper movement from the identity case, (12a), to cases that do not regularly come under its purview: subextraction out of a moved constituent, (12b), and remnant movement, (12c). Notice that under classical GB assumptions no ordering problems arose, because (12b) and (12c) were simply ruled out: (12b) – by the freezing principle, (12c) – by the proper-binding condition.

Sauerland (1996) innovates aquatic metaphors for the configurations in (12b) and (12c). He calls the configuration in (12b) a *surfing* path, because constituent Y uses constituent X as its surfboard to ride up the tree. He calls (12c) a *diving* path, because constituent Y jumps ship and lets X pass without it. I will use these metaphors for their expressive value.

(12) a.   The standard case (identity):

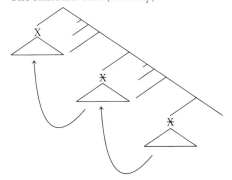

b.   Surfing path (subextraction, descendant moves second):

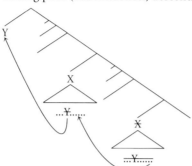

c.   Diving path (remnant movement, ancestor moves second):

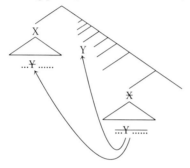

I suggest to deploy UCOOL as stated in the Generalized Prohibition against Improper Movement, GenPIM, (13). GenPIM, together with the definition of affectedness in (14), generalizes the ban against improper movement from the trigger of movement to the moving constituent itself and beyond it to all constituents affected by the movement. The notion of affectedness captures all and only the three cases mentioned above in (12): identity, subextraction, remnant movement.[9]

(13)   Generalized Prohibition against Improper Movement (GenPIM)
       No constituent may undergo movement of type τ if it has been affected by movement of type σ, where $\tau \ll \sigma$ under UCOOL.

(14)   A constituent α is *affected* by a movement operation iff
       i. α is reflexively contained in the constituent created by movement, and
       ii. α is in a (reflexive) domination relation with the moved constituent.

What (14) says is that when a constituent X is moved, this movement affects not only the moving constituent itself (it is in a reflexive domination relation with itself) but also the constituents that make up X (the elements that X dominates), and the nodes along the path of movement (understood in terms of domination) since those dominate X in the pre-movement configuration. Every node which is not affected is unaffected. Therefore, specifiers and heads along the path of movement are unaffected and so are all constituents "higher up" in the tree. This is illustrated in (15), where the nodes affected by movement of X are circled and the unaffected nodes are not.

(15)

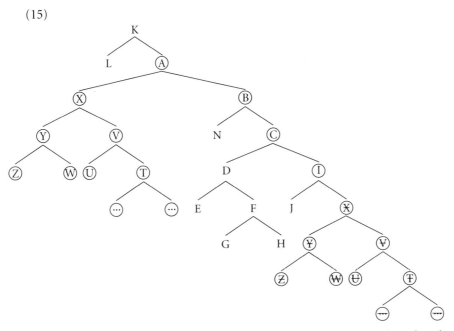

The notion of affectedness seems a bit complicated at first. However, it makes the conceptually desirable claim that when a constituent moves, this has an effect not only on the moving constituent alone but on the rest of the structure as well. Compare GenPIM with a standard formulation of the ban against improper movement in (16). They differ in the boldfaced part.

(16)   No constituent may undergo movement of type σ if it has **undergone** movement of type τ, where σ ≪ τ under UCOOL.

The standard understanding makes sure that movements undergone by a particular constituent do not violate UCOOL, but the effect of movement is sharply localized: the moved constituent is affected, the attracting head presumably is affected, but nothing else is. The standard understanding isolates the effect of movement and localizes it in the moved constituent and the attractor. This isolating view of movement opens the door to accounts where arbitrary formal features on abstract heads drive movements of arbitrarily picked constituents. Under the isolating view of movement, movement never does any harm, since nothing else in the theory or the structure is affected by such movements. The notion of affectedness denies this isolating view of movement – as did the all too rigid old theory with the proper-binding condition and the freezing principle. The denial of the isolating view of movement gives rise to a theory which is more strongly integrated, because every movement has an effect on a well-defined, potentially very big, part of the structure. Together with the idea that operations are ordered a(nti)symmetrically and drawn from a universal ordered set, GenPIM puts immediate constraints on what is possible. This seems clearly desirable to me, if only because the resulting theory will be much stronger in the sense of being more easily falsifiable than a theory without these assumptions. The sections of this paper that deal with cross-serial dependencies illustrate precisely this property: certain analyses become impossible in principle under the view advocated here.

But even if it is granted that a non-isolating approach to movement is conceptually desirable, I need to address the apparent complexity in the definition of affectedness. Assume in the background a theory of syntax which countenances only tree extending merge and move, that is, a theory which obeys Chomsky's (1993) extension condition. On a derivational view of syntactic relations (Epstein (1999); Epstein et al. (1998)) an operation can only ever have an effect on syntactic items which are already part of the representation when the operation is performed. In (15), the nodes K and L are not yet part of the representation when X moves, hence, they cannot be affected by that movement. Thus, bottom up tree generation together with a derivational view of syntactic relations derives the first part of (14), which need not be stipulated. With this said consider again (15) excluding K and L from consideration now. The predominant view of movement in the minimalist program is one of remerge: the constituent X is (externally) merged in the lower position and then remerged (internally merged) in the higher position. With this understanding of movement the nodes circled are simply all nodes that enter into a domination relation with X. This restatement alone is a considerable simplification of the notion of affectedness: Movement of X affects all nodes in a domination relation with X. Affectedness, in a derivational perspective, is simply the symmetric version of domination.

There still remains the flavor of a disjunctive definition in (14): "α is in a domination relation with β iff α dominates β **or** β dominates α." Disjunctive definitions are suspect because they merely list cases instead of bringing about a unification. However, the particular disjunction given here does not disjoin arbitrary terms without an obvious relation to each other. It rather creates symmetry from the asymmetric domination relation. Brody (2000: 29) reminds us that "[i]n the better developed sciences it is the departures from symmetry rather than the symmetries that are typically taken to be in need of explanation." If, as I argue below, affect-edness is an important notion, the priority of symmetry over asymmetry would cast doubt on the assumption that the asymmetric domination relation is truly fundamental. What would need to be explained is not the symmetric notion of affectedness, but the asymmetric notion of dominance.

Developing this speculation just one step further, we might assume that there is an underlying symmetric relation "affect" and the asymmetry of the dominance comes from derivational subsequence: α dominates β iff α and β stand in the (symmetric) affect relation and α was derived after β was derived. Affectedness might then – possibly together with the equally symmetrical relation of sisterhood – be *the* fundamental syntactic relation. To appreciate this, consider the c-command relation. Chomsky (2000) defines it as the composition of sisterhood with dominance. If affectedness is indeed a syntactic relation, then c-command need not be defined at all. It falls out: X c-commands Y iff at the time when X is (externally or internally) merged into the tree, X is not in the "affect" relation with Y (see Abels (2003: Chapter 2 Section 3) for further discussion).

I now turn to GenPIM. Although GenPIM is not a derivational constraint as given, a derivational metaphor might make it more tangible. A constituent, X in (15), has a number of things it needs to do in its derivational lifespan, that is, a given constituent might contain a number of unchecked or active features. These are ordered in terms of urgency by UCOOL. X may not undergo a less urgent (higher) operation unless all the more urgent (lower) ones have been completed. Similarly, and this is the contribution of GenPIM over (16), X may not undergo a less urgent (higher) operation if any of its parts still have more urgent business to do, this will yield restrictions on (12b). Conversely, if one of the constituents that contain X in the pre-movement structure still has urgent business to do, then X will have to wait with its less urgent business, which will yield (12c).

The generalization from (16) to GenPIM will be justified in the next sub-section. Before we look at the empirical justification, a few final comments and clarifications are in order.

First, the way it is presently formulated, GenPIM has to be understood as being about final landing sites of movement. Despite the derivational metaphor above, it cannot be understood directly as a constraint on derivations (unless the standard assumption is given up that successive cyclic movement is launched before the target of movement is merged into the tree). I make no attempt to reformulate

GenPIM in derivational terms here. The primary goal of the present paper is to investigate the correctness of the proposal and to demonstrate a specific prediction of UCOOL together with GenPIM.

Second, there is an asymmetry in GenPIM which is absent in (16). (16) makes reference to moving constituents both in the protasis and in the apodosis. Gen-PIM on the other hand makes reference to moving constituents in the apodosis but to affected constituents in the protasis. I leave this asymmetry unmitigated here. Whether the stronger symmetrical formulation where both protasis and apo-dosis make reference to affected constituents is tenable will have to be investigated independently.

2.2 A case study

Clearly, the scope of GenPIM goes well beyond the realm usually considered to fall under improper movement. Consider the following simple table, which represents a presumed subpart of the Universal Constraint on Operational Ordering in Language. I have left out θ-operations here, but I added the operation of scrambling (by which I specifically refer to movement into a pre-subject position in the German mittelfeld) and split the entry for $\overline{A}$-movement into *wh*-movement and topicalization – topicalization again of the German vorfeld variety.[10] The left-to-right and top-to-bottom ordering of operations corresponds to a (part) of the hierarchy of movement operations one would postulate for German (see Grewendorf (2003) for a similar proposal regarding the hierarchy of operational types and Sternefeld (1992) for a structural formulation of the hierarchy).

(17)

	A-mvt	Scrambling	*wh*-mvt	Topicalization
A-mvt		✓	✓	✓
Scrambling	*		✓	✓
wh-mvt	*	*		✓
Topicalization	*	*	*	

The table is to be read as follows: Rows are taken as the first step of movement, columns – as the second. The first row claims that A-movement feeds the other three types of movement, the second – that scrambling feeds *wh*-movement and topicalization but not A-movement, the third – that *wh*-movement feeds topicalization but not the other two types of movement, and the forth – that topicalization feeds none of the other three types of movement.

The diagonal of the table is left blank. The reason is that I left open the question whether the ordering of operations is asymmetric or antisymmetric, (11a). If it is antisymmetric, the diagonal should be populated by checkmarks. If it is asymmetric, the diagonal should be filled in with asterisks. Some considerations that bear on this involve the question whether the individual steps of successive cyclic movement should count, that is, whether a step in successive cyclic A-movement should count as A-movement, whether a step in successive cyclic *wh*-movement should itself count as *wh*-movement, and so on. If so, then we conclude that the ordering is antisymmetric. Similarly, if the movement analysis of control is correct, then the fact that subject control predicates can stack indicates that the ordering is antisymmetric and the cells along the diagonal of the table should get a checkmark. If, on the other hand, we interpret the fact that DPs do not move from structural case to structural case position and that *wh*-phrases do not leave their scope positions for further *wh*-movement once they have reached them as evidence that movement of the same type may not iterate (see Rizzi's (2006) Criterial Freezing), then we are led to conclude that the ordering is asymmetric. In this case the diagonal of the table is to be populated by asterisks.

Similar considerations apply to surfing paths. We might interpret the fact that *wh*-extraction out of a *wh*-moved constituents is possible (see Rizzi (2006: 13 ex. (36b)), Chomsky (1986: 26); Starke (2001: 54)), as an indication that the ordering of operations is antisymmetric. It seems equally plausible to claim, however, that in these cases the two movements have different properties (see Starke (2001) for discussion), in which case the ordering would be asymmetric.

Finally, there is a well known restriction on remnant movement: remnant creating movement and remnant movement may not be of the same type (Müller (1998: Chapter 5); Kitahara (1997); Hiraiwa (2002); Grewendorf (2003)): remnant creating *wh*-movement never feeds remnant *wh*-movement; remnant creating topicalization never feeds remnant topicaliztion; etc. This restriction is often referred to as Müller's generalization. Taken at face value, Müller's generalization suggests that the ordering of operations is asymmetric, hence the diagonal should be filled with asterisks. However, some of the literature just mentioned argues that Müller's generalization follows from the minimal link or the A-over-A condition; in a structure like (18), the interrogative complementizer, $^2C^0$, cannot attract the lower *wh*-element, pied-piping ZP, and leave the higher *wh*-element to be attracted by $^1C^0$ with concomitant (remnant) pied-piping of YP, because the first step violates closest attract or the A-over-A condition. If this reasoning is correct, then it is unnecessary to derive Müller's generalization from an asymmetric ordering of operations and an antisymmetric ordering will do the job. I make crucial use of Müller's generalization later on in the paper, but either way of deriving it will serve the purposes of the argumentation at that point.

(18) $[\,{}^1C^0_{[+wh]} \ldots [\,{}^2C^0_{[+wh]} \ldots [_{YP}\, wh \ldots [_{ZP} \ldots wh \ldots]\,]\,]\,]$

I therefore leave the decision whether the ordering of operations is asymmetric or antisymmetric open and the diagonal of the table blank.

Identity

Suppose we interpret the table as a table of the combinability of operations applying to one and the same constituent, the identity case in (12a). The first row of the table now says that a constituent that has undergone A-movement may subsequently undergo scrambling, *wh*-movement, or Topicalization. The second row says that a constituent that has undergone scrambling may not subsequently undergo A-movement, but may undergo subsequent *wh*-movement or topicalization. The third row says that *wh*-moved constituents may – according to the hierarchy – undergo topicalization bot not A-movement or scrambling. Finally topicalization does not feed any other operation.

The actual distribution of the data corresponds very closely to that given in the table. In particular there is no reason to believe that the operational sequences marked with an asterisk ever occur. It follows that no pair of operations σ, τ can be in a symmetric feeding relation. This observation strongly supports the assumption that all operations are a(nti)symmetrically ordered with respect to each other, (11a). The totality of the ordering is supported to the extent that all the cells with a checkmark in the table can be shown to correspond to grammatical sentences.

I take it to be clear that A-movement, that is case marking, may precede scrambling, *wh*-movement, and topicalization and that topicalization cannot feed any of the other operations (see Sternefeld (1992) for the relevant data). In other words, the first and the fourth row of the table are not disputed. It is less clear whether the second and third row are entirely correct. *Wh*-movement does not seem to feed topicalization in German.[11] Thinking along fairly standard lines, one may imagine that topicalization of an argument requires the existence of an identifiable discourse referent as topic, whereas a *wh*-question would be used to establish or identify such a referent. It would then follow that the same argument cannot be both questioned and topicalized and the fact that *wh*-movement does not feed topicalization would not bear on the ordering of operations.[12]

Whether scrambling feeds *wh*-movement is a disputed issue. The observation (von Stechow and Sternefeld (1988: 466), Fanselow (1990), Müller and Sternefeld (1993, 1996), Müller (1998: 39–40), Pesetsky (2000: 70–83), Grewendorf (2001: 110

fn. 37)) that *wh*-phrases in German are not usually allowed to scramble in multiple *wh*-questions suggests that scrambling does not feed *wh*-movement. On the other hand, the ban against scrambling *wh*-phrases is not rigidly observed (Beck (1996: 6–7), Sauerland (1996), Fanselow (2001, 2004)). In particular it is possible to scramble *wh*-words in front of quantified and other operator-like subjects, (20) (from Fanselow (2001: 414)).

(19) a. ?*Wann hat wem   der   Mann geholfen?
          when has who$_{DAT}$ the$_{NOM}$ man helped
          When did the man help whom?
      b. Wann würde wem   nur ein Held helfen?
          when would who$_{DAT}$ only a   hero help
          When would only a hero help whom?

A strong argument for the assumption that scrambling feeds *wh*-movment is given by Wiltschko (1997, 1998) (see Fanselow (2004); Pesetsky (2000); Grewendorf (2001) for discussion). As is well known scrambling does not give rise to weak cross-over effects, (20a) vs. (20b), and it is clause-bound, (21).

(20) a. *Früher haben seine$_k$ Eltern jeden   Studenten$_k$ unterstützt.
          earlier have his   parents every.ACC student.ACC supported
          In the past his$_k$ parents supported every student$_k$.
      b. Früher haben jeden   Studenten$_k$ seine$_k$ Eltern   unterstützt.
          earlier have every.ACC student.ACC his   parents supported
          In the past his$_k$ parents supported every student$_k$.

(21) *Gestern   hat jeden   Studenten Hans gesagt, dass seine
      Yesterday has every.ACC student.ACC Hans said   that his

      Eltern   unterstützen
      parents t$_{every\ student}$ support

Short *wh*-movement does not give rise to weak crossover effects, (22a), but long *wh*-movement does, (22b), but only in the higher clause, not in the clause where the *wh*-word originates, (22c).

(22) a. Welchen   Studenten$_k$ unterstützen seine$_k$ Eltern?
          which.ACC student.ACC support   his$_k$ parents?
          Which student$_k$ do his$_k$ parents support?
      b. *Welchen   Studenten$_k$ glauben seine$_k$ Eltern, dass Maria
          which.ACC student.ACC believe his   parents that Maria
          unterstützt?
          supports
          Which student$_k$ believe his$_k$ parents that Maria supports?

    c.   Welchen   Studenten$_k$ glaubt   Maria, dass seine$_k$ Eltern
        which.ACC   student.ACC believes Maria that his$_k$ parents
        unterstützen?
        support?
        Which student$_k$ does Maria believe that his$_k$ parents support?

This schizophrenic behavior of *wh*-movement in German, Wiltschko argues, can be straightforwardly explained if *wh*-movement gives rise to weak crossover effects but can be fed by scrambling. In (22a) and (22c) the *wh*-phrase would undergo cross-over obviating scrambling before undergoing *wh*-movement, but this possibility is barred in (22b): (i) scrambling is clause-bounded, (21), and (ii) an improper movement derivation where the initial step of *wh*-movement feeds a scrambling step into the higher clause which again feeds the final step of *wh*-movement is blocked by UCOOL.[13]

The paradigm in (22) can be replicated for topicalization by simply replacing the word *welchen* – 'which' by *jeden* – 'every'. The judgments remain as given above. Topicalization is as schizophrenic when it comes to weak crossover as *wh*-movement. By parody of reasoning I conclude that scrambling also feeds topicalization in German. These conclusions are not shared by all researchers; thus, the discussion here remains necessarily somewhat inconclusive.

The facts seem to pattern overall as presented in the table. But even if scrambling fed neither *wh*-movement nor topicalization, this would not disconfirm the hypotheses formulated in UCOOL and GenPIM, since the relevant constructions might be ruled out by factors that are orthogonal to operational ordering, as in the case of *wh*-movement and topicalization above. The hypothesis would be disconfirmed only if feeding relations between operations were discovered that correspond to the part of the table below the diagonal or if mutual feeding-relations, that is, symmetry, was discovered. No such cases exist.

Surfing paths
In the discussion above I assumed that the rows and columns of table (17) are to be interpreted as subsequent movements of the *same* constituent, (12a). Suppose that instead we were to interpret the rows as movement of some constituent and the columns as movement of a subconstituent out of the moved one (Sauerland's *surfing*-paths). In other words, the rows label the prior movement of X while the columns label the subsequent movement of Y in (12b).

Traditionally these structures were ruled out categorically by the freezing prinicple. I will now review some evidence showing that the freezing principle is too strong and that UCOOL together with GenPIM offer a much more accurate description of the situation.

The first row of (17) now claims that A-movement should feed scrambling, *wh*-movement, and topicalization. An example of the first is furnished by (23b) on the assumption that objects in German move to Case positions. We can demonstrate that the prepositional adverbial *darüber* has moved out of the NP by observing the specificity effect in (23b) (for detailed discussion of this point see e.g. Müller (1998: 10–15)).

(23) a. ...weil   niemand { ein | das} Buch darüber   lesen wollte
          ...because nobody [a   the   book there-about] read wanted
          ...because nobody wanted to read {a|*the} book about that

      b. ...weil   darüber   niemand { ein |* das} Buch
          ...because there-about nobody [a   the   book t$_{darüber}$]
          lesen wollte
          read   wanted
          ...because nobody wanted to read {a|*the} book about that

Examples bolstering the second claim, that A-movement may feed *wh*-movement of a constituent contained in the moving item, are easy to come by. (24) furnishes a simple example of extraction from an A-moved argument.[14] The point made by this example stands independently of whether the ECM subject remains in the embedded infinitival or moves into the matrix. The fact that A-movement can feed *wh*-movement can also be made on the basis of the existence of exceptions to the subject-island condition like (25b) (Starke 2001: 36), which, according to Starke, is at worst slightly worse than the corresponding object extraction case, (25a). The same appears to be true in the English – and, to my ear, German – translations. (Notice that although the NPs from which extraction happens here are formally definite, they are semantically unspecific because of the inherently relational nature of the nouns.)

(24) a. Which football team do you want/expect [the manager of t$_{which\ football\ team}$] to pay a large fine?

      b. Which football team do you believe [the manager of t$_{which\ football\ team}$] to have paid a large fine?

      c. Which politician do you believe the rumors about to be false?

(25) a. De quel   film as   tu   raté   la   première partie
         of which film have you missed [the first   part   t]
         Which film did you miss the first part of?

     b. De quel   film est-ce que tu   crois que la   première partie
         of which film is-it   that you think that [the first   part   t]
         va   créer un scandale?
         goes create a   scandale
         Which movie do you think that the first part of would create a scandal?

Similar examples with topicalization from a subject are easy to construct, (26). The discourse particle *doch* and the temporal adverbial are introduced to make sure that the subject cannot remain VP-internally (for discussion of VP-internal subjects and discourse particles see Haider (1993); Diesing (1992) among many others).

(26) Von diesem Film hat der erste Teil doch letztes Jahr einen großen
      of this   film has the first part PRT last   year a   big
      Skandal ausgelöst.
      scandal caused
      The first part of this film caused a big scandal last year.

This shows that the claims made in the table based on UCOOL and GenPIM, that A-movement should feed scrambling, *wh*-movement, and topicalization is correct. The many cases where this is impossible will have to be ruled out on independent grounds.

The opposite, that is, examples where scrambling, *wh*-movement, or topicalization feed A-movement are strikingly bad. I discuss just a single case here as an example, (27) (from Sakai (1994: 300), discussed as a problem in Collins (2005)). The example shows that A-movement from a *wh*-moved constituent is impossible. The other types of example are equally bad. On the intended but ungrammatical construal where *Oscar* A-moves out of the *wh*-moved clause, (27b) ought to mean something like *It was asked how likely it was that Oscar would win*. What goes wrong from the present perspective is that A-movement of *Oscar* and $\overline{A}$-movement *how likely to win* occur in the wrong order since A-movement out of an $\overline{A}$-moved constituent is ruled out under GenPIM. Example (27c) is a control, suggested by the anonymous reviewer, to check whether the infinitive can be pied-piped at all if there is no prior raising out of it.

(27) a. Max asked how likely to win Oscar was
         [IP1 Max asked [CP2 [AP how likely t_j to win]i [IP2 Oscar$_j$ was t_i]]]

    b. *Oscar was asked how likely to win it was.[15]

        [IP1 Oscar$_j$ was asked [CP2 [AP how likely t$_j$ to win]i [IP2 it was t$_i$]]]

    c. Max asked how likely for Oscar to win it would be if he bought better equipment. (Gillian Ramchand, p.c.)

The second row of the table claims that scrambling should feed both *wh*-movement and topicalization. That this is correct is shown in (28a–b) and (29a) respectively.[16] There is a clear contrast between (28a–b), with *wh*-movement from a scrambled constituent, and (28c), with scrambling from a *wh*-moved constituent. Likewise, there is a sharp contrast between (29a), with topicalization from a scrambled constituent, and (29b), with scrambling from a topicalized one.

(28) a. Worüber   kann einen Südkurier-Artikel   selbst Peter

        what-about can   [a   Südkurier-article t$_{worüber}$] even Peter

        nicht am   Strand verfassen?

        not   at.the beach write

        For which topic is it the case that even Peter cannot write an article about it for the Südkurier when he is at the beach. (from (Kuthy and Meurers 1999: 27) attributed to Fanselow (1991))

    b. Über welchen deutschen Kaiser   hatte ein fertiges

        about which German   emperor had   [a done

        Manuskript   leider   keiner der anwesenden

        manuscript t$_{PP}$]$_{NP}$ unfortunately none   the present

        Historiker   anzubieten.

        historians t$_{NP}$ to.offer

        About which German emperor could none of the historians present offer a completed manuscript?

    c. *Gestern hat über   Karl den Großen keiner   gefragt, was   für

        yesterday has [about Charlemagne]$_{PP}$ nobody asked   what for

        eine Arbeit   er schreiben soll

        a   work t$_{PP}$ he write   should

        Nobody asked yesterday what kind of paper about Charlemagne he should write.

(29) a. Über   Karl den Großen hatte ein fertiges Manuskript

        [About Charlemagne]$_{PP}$ had [a   done   manuscript t$_{PP}$]$_{NP}$

        leider   keiner der anwesenden Historiker   anzubieten.

        unfortunately none the present   historians t$_{NP}$ to.offer

        About Charlemagne, none of the historians present could offer a done manuscript.

b. *Auf dem Kongress hat über   Karl den Großen keiner   gesagt
   at   the congress has [about Charlemagne]$_{PP}$ nobody said
   ein fertiges Manuskript   habe er anzubieten.
   a   done   manuscript t$_{PP}$ have he to.offer
   At the congress nobody said that he had a completed manuscript about
   Charlemagne to offer.

The final case, topicalization out of a *wh*-moved constituent is degraded, (30a).
However, there is still a contrast between (30a) and (30b) on the construal with
wh-movement out of a topicalized constituent.

(30) a. [??]Über   Karl den Großen weiß ich nicht, was   für ein
         [about Charlemagne]$_{PP}$ know I   not   [what for a
         Buch   er   schreiben will.
         book t$_{PP}$]$_{NP}$ he t$_{NP}$ write   wants.
         About Charlemagne I don't know what kind of book he wants to write.
     b. *Über   welchen deutschen Kaiser   sagt er ein fertiges
         [about which   German   emperor]$_{PP}$ says he [a   done
         Manuskript   hat keiner   anzubieten.
         manuscript t$_{PP}$]$_{NP}$ has nobody t$_{NP}$ to.offer
         About which German emperor does he say that, a completed manuscript,
         nobody can offer?

The generalized version of the ban against improper movement suggested above
conforms with the facts quite nicely. Empirically it is clearly superior to a theory that bans all extraction from moved constituents by appeal to the freezing
principle.

Diving paths
Finally, let us turn to the third interpretation we can give to the table in (17). Consider (12c) again. We can now interpret the rows as indicating a first movement
step of Y and the columns as the following remnant movement step of X.

   The first row of the table in (17) now claims that A-movement may be followed by remnant scrambling, remnant *wh*-movement, and remnant topicalization. All three cases exist. For *wh*-movement and remnant topicalization this can
be demonstrated even for English, (31).

(31) a. [How likely t$_{John}$ to win the race]$_{AP}$ is John t$_{AP}$?
     b. [Criticized t$_{John}$ by his boss]$_{VP}$ John has never been t$_{VP}$.

Scrambling of predicates in front of the subject in German is always somewhat degraded, (32a), based on Müller (1998: 226). It may be debatable whether the scrambled category α in (32a) contains the trace of the subject, since it may be that a smaller constituent than the full VP is fronted. The same is not true in (32b), where the subject is almost certainly extracted from α. To my ear, these examples have a similar, slightly degraded status.[17]

(32) a. $^{?}$...dass   ein Buch gelesen wohl   keiner   haben wird
          ...that [t$_{keiner}$ a   book read]$_α$ probably nobody t$_α$ have   will
          ...that in all likelyhood nobody has read a book

      b. $^{?}$...dass von einem Studenten   angefasst   kein einziges
          ...that [by a   student   t$_{NP}$ touched]$_α$ [no single
          Reagenzglas   werden durfte
          test tube]$_{NP}$ t$_α$ become may.PAST
          ...that no student was allowed to tough a test tube

The rest of the table under this interpretation is unproblematic. Müller (1998) has argued in great detail that scrambling may feed both remnant *wh*-movement, (33) (based on Müller (1998: 221–222)), and remnant topicalization, (34) (Müller 1998: 10).

(33) Was   für ein Buch   hat über   die Liebe   niemand
      [what for a   book t$_{PP}$]$_{DP}$ has [about the love]$_{PP}$ nobody   t$_{DP}$
      gelesen.
      read
      What type of book about love has nobody read?

(34) Ein Buch   gelesen hat darüber   keiner.
      [[a book t$_{PP}$] read]$_α$ has there-about no-one
      A book about that, nobody has read.

Finally, remnant topicalization can be fed by *wh*-movement. Such examples involve extraction from a *wh*-island, which always involves a certain amount of degradation. However, the example in (35a) is no more or less degraded than that in (35b) (based on (Müller 1998: 301)).

(35) a. $^{??}$Hans das Buch zu geben weiß ich nicht warum Fritz
          [Hans the book to give]$_α$ know I   not   why   Fritz t$_α$
          abgelehnt hat.
          refused   has
          I don't know why Fritz refused to give Hans the book.

b. ??Hans   zu geben weiß ich nicht was   Fritz   abgelehnt
[Hans t_was to give]_α know I   not   what Fritz t_α refused
hat.
has
I don't know what Hans refused to give Fritz.

The opposite feeding relations are never possible.[18]

2.3 Conclusion

The following table summarizes the facts reviewed above. As can be seen, they fit the expectations generated by the conjunction of UCOOLand GenPIM very well. In particular, all of the feeding relations which are ruled out by the conjunction of the two principles fail to occur and all of the feeding relation which are predicted to exist by the conjunction of the two principles do indeed occur. The only data point that might remain a bit dubious is the feeding relation between *wh*-movement and topicalization, where the deviance of the examples seems to have different sources, though: a pragmatic incompatibility and the *wh*-island effect.

(36)

		A-mvt	Scrambling	*wh*-mvt	Topicalization
A-mvt	identity		✓	✓	✓
	surfing path		✓	✓	✓
	diving path		?	✓	✓
Scrambling	identity	*		✓	✓
	surfing path	*		%	%
	diving path	*		✓	✓
wh-mvt	identity	*	*		*
	surfing path	*	*		??
	diving path	*	*		??
Topicalization	identity	*	*	*	
	surfing path	*	*	*	
	diving path	*	*	*	

The facts strongly support the idea that operations are asymmetrically ordered, that the ordering is total, that it is as hypothesized for German, (37), and that the same ordering applies for the identity case, the case of surfing paths, and that of diving paths. As mentioned at the beginning, the claim to universality remains a promise at this stage.

(37) $\theta \ll$ scrambling $\ll$ A-mvt $\ll$ *wh* $\ll$ topicalization

Except for Williams' theory, to which I turn immediately below, none of the existing theories of improper movement extend from the identity case to the cases of surfing and diving paths. These approaches thereby miss the generalization illustrated in (36) and formulated in UCOOL and GenPIM. These are strong grounds for adopting a system which incorporates or derives UCOOL and GenPIM. The method used here makes immediate predictions. Once two distinct operations are identified, they will have to find their place on the hierarchy since the order is, by assumption, total. The prediction is then that the feeding and bleeding relations to all other operations in the hierarchy are automatically fixed and fixed in identical ways for the identity case, the case of diving paths, and the case of surfing paths.

I now turn to a brief discussion of Williams (2002). Williams' theory has a fairly different architecture from Chomskyan minimalism and a summary of it would lead too far afield here (see Nevins and Hornstein (2005) for a brief synopsis). I will therefore concentrate on a particular prediction that emerges from Williams' theory. In Williams' theory (as in an earlier proposal by Sternefeld (1992)) the ordering and scope of operations is directly tied to the structural hierarchy in the clause. Williams derives a number of particularly strong claims: (i) Movements that happen later in the overall derivation target position higher in the functional hierarchy than movements that happen earlier; (ii) movements that happen later may be longer than all movements that happened earlier; (iii) the launching site of movement is systematically lower (not only in terms of c-command but also on the functional hierarchy) than the landing site of movement; and (iv) no movement may cross positions on the functional hierarchy that are higher on that hierarchy than the landing site. These claims all follow under Williams' architecture.

I limit the discussion to (iii) and (iv) here since only they are directly relevant to the topic of this paper. We can formulate them slightly more formally by construing the hierarchy of functional projections as a numbered series of heads, where the lowest head is numbered 1 and numbers go up steadily to the highest head (presumably situated in the complementizer domain). Property (iii) now says that if a constituent occupies a specifier or complement position of a head indexed i and undergoes movement which targets the specifier (or head-adjoined) position of a head indexed j, then $i \leqslant j$. Property (iv) says that if a constituent X has landed in the specifier position of a head indexed j, then the movement path may not have crossed the projections of any heads indexed k, where $k > j$. In a minimalist syntax with a Cinque hierarchy, these results follow for clause internal movement but not for cross-clausal movement. Under Williams' theory, the claim is completely general.

The ban against improper movement follows from (iii) and (iv) directly. Consider (38). (iii) rules out the derivation in (38a); the movement step from [Spec, CP] to [Spec, TP] is illicit under (iii) because C^0 is higher in the functional hierarchy than T^0. (iv) rules out the derivation in (38b); the movement step from the embedded object position directly to the matrix [Spec, TP] crosses along its way a head, C^0, which is higher in the hierarchy than the head which provides the landing site of that movement step, T^0.

(38) *What seems that it was said?
    a. [CP What [IP t^3_{what} seems [CP t^2_{what} that [IP it was said t^1_{what} ?]]]]
    b. [CP What [IP t^2_{what} seems [CP that [IP it was said t^1_{what} ?]]]]

Claims (iii) and (iv) are sufficiently general so that their conjunction rules out all of the cases of improper movement discussed above including the diving and surfing paths.

Nevertheless, I will not adopt Williams' proposal because it seems overly restrictive. Consider exceptional case marking in English, (39). Under the now standard analysis of exceptional case marking as involving raising to a non-thematic object position in the higher clause (see Postal (1974); Lasnik and Saito (1991); Davies and Dubinsky (2004) for discussion and references), the subject of the embedded infinitival clause moves to a low position in the matrix clause. Movement from the original subject position in the lower clause violates (iii) or (iv) (or both). Suppose for concreteness that the embedded infinitival is a TP. The position of negation in the matrix clause, to the left of the ECM subject, indicates that the ECM subject has not moved up to TP in the matrix. But in the embedded clause, the ECM subject must either move past TP without landing there, move through TP and land there, or originate in TP. In the first case, movement of the ECM subject would violate condition (iv). In the second two cases, movement of the ECM subject would violate condition (iii).[19]

(39)   John doesn't believe Mary not to have been telling the truth.

Similar problems arise with quantifier movement in French across complementizers, (40) (which is mentioned as a problem in Williams (2002); the Icelandic situation seems to be similar (Kayne 1998: 142 #55–6)). The quantifier originates in object position in the embedded clause and ends up in a position preceding the non-finite main verb and following the finite auxiliary in the main clause, (40b). If the quantifier crosses the complementizer *que* in one step, then that movement violates condition (iv). If there is an intermediate movement step to [Spec, CP], then the movement step from [Spec, CP] to the final landing site violates (iii).

(40)   French ((Kayne 1998: 141–142 # 52–3))

    a.   Il n'   a   rien   fallu   que je fasse.
       it neg has nothing been-necessary that i do
       It hasn't been necessary for me to do anything.

    b.   Il a   tout   fallu   que je leur   enlève.
       it has everything been-necessary that I them$_{dat}$ remove
       I had to take everything off them.

Examples of this type are not too hard to come by. Thus, long scrambling in Russian crosses complementizers (the complementizer *kak* introducing direct perception reports) but does not seem to necessarily end up in [Spec, CP] in the higher clause (Glushan (2006)). Hyperraising (Ura 1994) poses similar problems given that it apparently crosses complementizers but lands within TP (see Nevins (2004); Williams (to appear) for directly relevant discussion). Likewise cyclic movement across complementizers contained in lower clauses but ending up in a position to the right of the same type of complementizer in the higher clause are predicted to be impossible by the conjunction of (iii) and (iv). However, such cases do exist, (41).[20] The examples in (41) are from Kîîtharaka, a Bantu language spoken in Kenya. Kîîtharaka allows *wh*-in situ, partial *wh*-movement, and full *wh*-movement (see Muriungi (2005) for extensive discussion). The examples in (41) illustrate this pattern. They are synonymous, the only difference relevant to the discussion is the position of the *wh*-phrase *ûû* – 'what'.[21]

    The declarative complementizer in Kîîtharaka is *atî* – 'that'. In (41b–d) the *wh*-word has undergone partial *wh*-movement. Notice that partial *wh*-movement is compatible with the occurrence of a declarative complementizer in the clause hosting the partially moved *wh*-phrase, (41c–d). In both (41c) and (41d) the *wh*-phrase appears to the right of the complementizer *atî* – presumably because the landing site of partial *wh*-movement is below the complementizer position. The crucial example is (41d). Here the *wh*-phrase has crossed one instance of the complementizer *atî*, underlined in the example, but ends up to the right, that is, below, the other instance of the complementizer, circled in the example. Assuming a fixed position in the Cinque hierarchy for the complementizer in Kîîtharaka, we end up with a violation of (iii) or (iv).

(41)   Kîîtharaka (Peter Muriungi, p.c.)

    a.   U-   ri-   thugania atî John a- ug- ir- e atî Pat a-
       2nd.SG- pres- think   that John sm- say- perf- FV that Pat sm

       ug- ir- e   Lucy a- ring- ir- e   ûû
       say pres FV Lucy sm- beat- perf- FV who
       Who do you think that John said that Pat said that Lucy beat?

b. U-   ri-   thugania atî   John a-   ug- ir-   e   atî   Pat a-
   2nd.SG- pres- think   that John sm- say- perf- FV that Pat sm
   ug- ir-   e   n- û̂û̂ Lucy a-   ring- ir-   e   t_{wh}
   say pres FV F- who Lucy sm- beat- perf- FV
   Who do you think that John said that Pat said that Lucy beat?

c. U-   ri-   thugania atî   John a-   ug- ir-   e   atî   n- û̂û̂
   2nd.SG- pres- think   that John sm- say- perf- FV that F   who
   Pat a-   ug- ir-   e   Lucy n- a-   ring- ir-   e   t_{wh}
   Pat sm say pres FV Lucy F- sm- beat- perf- FV
   Who do you think that John said that Pat said that Lucy beat?

d. U-   ri-   thugania ⟨atî⟩ n- û̂û̂ John a-   ug- ir-   e
   2nd.SG- pres- think   that F- who John sm- say- perf- FV
   atî   Pat n- a-   ug- ir-   e   Lucy n- a-   ring- ir-   e   t_{wh}
   that Pat F   sm say pres FV Lucy F- sm- beat- perf- FV
   Who do you think that John said that Pat said that Lucy beat?

e. N- û̂û̂ u-   ku-   thugania atî   John n- a-   ug- ir-   e
   F   who 2nd.SG- pres- think   that John F   sm- say- perf- FV
   atî   Pat n- a-   ug- ir-   e   Lucy n- a-   ring- ir-   e   t_{wh}
   that Pat F   sm say pres FV Lucy F- sm- beat- perf- FV
   Who do you think that John said that Pat said that Lucy beat?

I take such cases to be sufficient grounds for rejecting Williams' proposal as too restrictive and will stick with UCOOL and GenPIM, which do not make the problematic predictions.

In the next section I turn to cross-serial dependencies. The assumptions strongly supported by the facts so far (a(nti)symmetry, totality, extension to surfing and diving paths) predict a particular linear asymmetry in the area of cross-serial dependencies. The prediction appears to be borne out. These assumptions also rule out a family of remnant movement accounts of cross-serial dependencies found in the literature. These accounts, ruled out under present assumption, also necessarily fail to predict the observed asymmetry. We can therefore reject the accounts in question.

3. Cross-serial dependencies

In the debates concerning the weak and strong generative capacity of human languages (Pullum and Gazdar (1982); Bresnan et al. (1982); Huybregts (1984); Shieber (1985); Higginbotham (1984); Culy (1985); Savitch et al. (1987)) the issue of unbounded cross-serial dependencies between non-identical elements played an important role. The other main issue were cross-serial dependencies between identical elements, that is, reduplicative processes in the broadest sense (see Stabler (2004) for important discussion and references). I ignore the case of reduplication here, since it does not bear directly on the issue of improper movement as far as I can see. Although unbounded cross-serial dependencies have remained important in the literature on mathematical linguistics (see Kracht (2003) and references given there), more descriptively oriented work (outside of West Germanic) has largely ignored them (though Tagalog is claimed to exhibit them in Maclachlan and Rambow (2002)).

In the so-called verb-raising construction Dutch famously exhibits crossing dependencies between verbs and their notional subjects, as in (42) from Bresnan et al. (1982). The standard German versions of such sentences show nesting dependencies, (43). The corresponding English construction is shown in (44). The same crossing pattern emerges for the dependencies between the verbs and their notional objects in Dutch. In addition there is, of course, a dependency between the verbs. The selectional dependency between the verbs goes from left to right in Swiss German, Dutch, and English and from right to left in German.

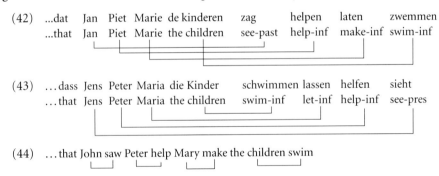

(42) ...dat   Jan   Piet Marie de kinderen   zag   helpen   laten   zwemmen
     ...that   Jan   Piet Marie the children   see-past help-inf make-inf   swim-inf

(43) ...dass Jens Peter Maria die Kinder   schwimmen lassen helfen   sieht
     ...that Jens Peter Maria the children   swim-inf let-inf help-inf   see-pres

(44) ...that John saw Peter help Mary make the children swim

Huybregts (1976) argues that the verb-raising construction is unbounded.[22] Speakers usually have difficulties with sentences containing cross-serial dependencies of length four or more. To defend the claim that the grammar of Dutch allows unbounded cross-serial dependencies, Huybregts gives the following arguments: First, a number of verbs can come in either order under verb raising, (45). Second, for the triple *let–help–teach* Huybregts shows that the verbs can come in any of the six mathematically possible orders, (46). Finally, the construction is recursive, since one and the same verb can occur more than once, (47). The apparent upper bound on the verb-raising construction is therefore usually attributed to processing complexity.

(45) All examples from Huybregts (1976: 43–44 ex. (15)–(19))

  a. let/see
      (i) …dat ik Cecilia een dokter zag laten komen
           …that I Cecilia a   doctor saw let   come
           …that I saw Cecilia let a doctor come
      (ii) …dat Cora ons twee nijlpaarden liet zien paren
           …that Cora us   two hippos   let see mate
           …that Cora let us see two hippos mate

  b. let/try
      (i) …dat ik Cecilia wodka liet proberen te drinken
           …that I Cecilia vodka let try   to drink
           …that I let Cecilia try to drink vodka
      (ii) …dat Cora ons Arabisch probeerde te laten spreken
           …that Cora us Arabic   tried   to let   speak
           …that Cora tried to let us speak Arabic

  c. try/help
      (i) …dat ik hem Cecilia probeerde te helpen verleiden
           …that I him Cecilia tried   to help   seduce
           …that I tried to help him seduce Cecilia
      (ii) …dat Cora ons de Petit Dru hielp proberen te
           …that Cora us the Petit Dru helped try   to
           beklimmen
           climb
           …that Cora helped us try to climb the Petit Dru

  d. help/teach
      (i) …dat ik Cecilia stijgijzers   hielp leren aantrekken
           …that I Cecilia climbing-irons helped learn on-put
           …that I helped Cecilia learn to put on climbing-irons
      (ii) …dat Cora ons kinderen leerde helpen oversteken
           …that Cora us children taught help   cross
           …that Cora taught us help children cross the street

  e. teach/see
      (i) …dat ik Cecilia een microbe leerde zien bewegen
           …that I Cecilia a   microbe taught see move
           …that I taught Cecilia to see a microbe move
      (ii) …dat hij ons Cora zag leren zwemmen
           …that he us Cora saw teach swim
           …that he saw us teach Cora to swim

(46) Huybregts (1976: 44 ex. (20)–(25))

a. …dat we hem 'n druide nijlpaarden laten helpen leren paren
…that we him a druide hippos   let   help   teach mate
…that we let him help a druid teach hippos mate

b. …dat we hem 'n druide nijlpaarden leren helpen laten paren
…that we him a druid hippos   teach help   let   mate
…that we taught him help a druide let hippos mate

c. …dat we hem 'n druide nijlpaarden laten leren helpen paren
…that we him a druid hippos   let   teach help   mate
…that we let him teach a druid help hippos mate

d. …dat we hem 'n druide nijlpaarden helpen leren laten paren
…that we him a druide hippos   help   teach let   mate
…that we help him teach a druid let hippos mate

e. …dat we hem 'n druide nijlpaarden leren laten helpen paren
…that we him a druid hippos   teach let   help   mate
…that we teach him let a druide help hippos mate

f. …dat we hem 'n druide nijlpaarden helpen laten leren paren
…that we him a druide hippos   help   let   teach mate
…that we help him let a druid teach hippos mate

(47) Examples (a–bi) from Huybregts (1976: 45–46 ex. (26)–(28)), (b.ii) from
Bresnan et al. (1982: ex. 4), (c) provided by Hans van de Koot, p.c.

a. (i) Ik heb hem Cecilia helpen helpen verhuizen
I have him Cecilia help   help   move
I have helped him help Cecilia move.

(ii) Hij heeft me een leeuw leren leren blaten
he has   me a   lion teach teach bleat
He has taught me teach a lion how to bleat

(iii) Ik heb hem Cecilia det schaap een leeuw laten helpen
I have him Cecilia that sheep a   lion let   help

leren helpen blaten
teach help   bleat
I have let him help Cecilia teaching that sheep how to help a lion
bleat

b. (i) Ik heb hem Cecilia iemand   det   shaap een leeuw laten
I have him Cecilia someone that sheeep a   lion let

helpen leren helpen leren blaten
help   teach help   let   bleat

I have let him help Cecilia teaching someone how to help that sheep teaching a lion how to bleat.

(ii) ...dat de leraar   Jan Marie de kinderen leerde laten

...that the teacher Jan Marie the children   taught let

leren   zwemmen

teache swim

...that the teacher taught Jan to make Marie teach the children to swim

c. (i) ...dat Jan de leraar   Marie de kinderen ziet helpen zien

...that Jan the teacher Marie the children sees help   see

zwemmen

swim

...that Jan sees the teacher help Marie see the children swim

With the previous literature I conclude that the grammar of Dutch allows unbounded cross-serial dependencies. The importance of the lack of a syntactic bound on the phenomenon can hardly be overestimated. As is well-known, verb raising gives rise to clause-union effects. (See Evers (1975); Haegeman and van Riemsdijk (1986) among many others and Wurmbrand (2006) for a recent overview.) Despite the clause-union effects, Huybregts' observations rule out an analysis along the lines of the functional restructuring approach that Cinque (2006) advocates for other cases of clause union. A Cinquean solution is incompatible with free ordering and recursion, that is, unboundedness.

Another example of cross-serial dependencies comes from standard Norwegian (Nilsen (2003:S. 72); Bentzen (2005)). The relevant construction is exemplified in (48) where all the adverbs must precede all the verbs. The scope relations between verbs and adverbs cannot be read off this string directly. Scope relations rather follow the linear left-to-right order in the ungrammatical (48b).

(48) a. ...at det ikke lenger   alltid helt   kunne ha   blitt
          ...that it   not any.longer always completely could   have been
          ordnet
          fixed

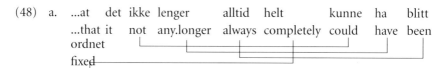

      b. *...at det ikke kunne lenger   ha alltid blitt helt   ordnet
          ...that it   not could any.longer have always been completely fixed

The cases of cross-serial dependencies exemplified here have one property in common: the left-to-right order of elements within each of the sub-sequences corresponds to the scope and/or selection within that sub-sequence. The verbs in the Dutch verb clusters come in their left-to-right order of selection. The same is true in the Norwegian example: both the auxiliaries and the adverbs take scope with respect to each other from left to right. I will call cross-serial dependencies where the left-to-right order corresponds to scope and selection within each sub-sequence *straight* cross-serial dependencies. Dutch and Norwegian exhibit straight cross-serial dependencies and so do Swiss German (Huybregts (1984); Shieber (1985)) and, according to the description in Maclachlan and Rambow (2002), Tagalog.

The opposite case would be an *inverse* cross-serial dependency, where the selectional and scope relations go from right to left. This hypothetical case is illustrated in (49), an inverted version of Shieber's famous Swiss German example, (50). To the best of my knowledge (see also Dehdari (2006) for a brief review of the literature) no case of an unbounded inverse cross-serial dependency has been discovered in human language.[23] This lack cannot be attributed to the lack of inverse orderings of arguments per se, since inverse orders of arguments are attested (e.g., postverbally in Kiowa (Adger et al. 2007) and in Malagasy (Pearson 2000)).

(49)   Inverse cross-serial dependency:
       ...that the barn the man the children we paint help let

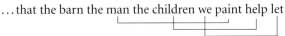

       ...that we let the children help the man paint the barn

(50)   ...das   mer   d'   chind   em   Hans es   huus   lönde
       ...that we.NOM   the children.ACC the.DAT Hans the.ACC house let
       hälfe aastriiche
       help   paint
       ...that we let the children help Hans paint the house

I claim that the absence of inverse cross-serial dependencies is not an accidental gap in the database, but reflects a deep property of language. I show below that the assumption that operations are a(nti)symmetrically, totally ordered and that that order applies in the identity, the surfing, and the diving cases alike (together with a number of independently motivated assumptions) predicts the absence of unbounded inverse cross-serial dependencies. Universal (51) is then another testable consequence of the assumptions argued for here.

(51)   Universal:
       UG does not allow unbounded inverse cross-serial depencies.

4. Deriving straight cross-serial dependencies

In this section I consider two types of derivation for straight cross-serial dependencies. Both of them rely strictly on leftward movement, but one relies heavily on
remnant movement while the other one does not. I compare the two approaches
with respect to their ability to predict the ban against inverse cross-serial dependencies, (51), and with respect to their compliance with the a(nti)symmetric, total, ordering of operations and GenPIM. The remnant movement account, it turns
out, does not predict the asymmetry nor is it compatible with the assumptions regarding ordering of operations in conjunction with GenPIM. Before continuing,
I need to justify the decision not to take into account any rightward-movement
analyses of verb raising. This is crucial, because the prediction regarding inverse
cross-serial dependencies follows only if rightward movement does not exist.

Traditional generative analyses of verb-raising in Dutch and Swiss German assume an underlying head-final structure and then transport the selected verb rightward around its selecting verb in some way (Evers (1975);
Haegeman and van Riemsdijk (1986)). The considerations of Section 1 suggest
that such analyses are wrong. An explanatory model of UG should countenance
only leftward-movement, which is clearly independently justified, and remnant
movement, which is also independently justified, but no rightward movement.[24]

The two analyses of cross-serial dependencies considered below therefore do
not invoke rightward movement.

4.1 Straight cross-serial dependencies without rightward movement and without remnant movement

In line with the argumentation so far, I will assume that there is a derivational
point where the structure of (50) is roughly as in (52a). The details of the structure do not matter; there might be additional VP-shells present; there might be
unpronounced controlled PROs; the c-command relations between the verbs and
their respective arguments might be locally reversed... What is important is that
the arguments are interspersed with – and locally related to – the verbs and that
the c-command relations among the arguments and among the verbs are as given
here. From an underlying structure with these characteristics, the cross-serial order can be derived by merging a licensing head with the property of attracting all
DPs into its specifier positions, as shown in (52b–c).[25]

(52)   a.

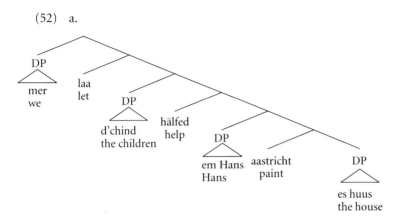

b.

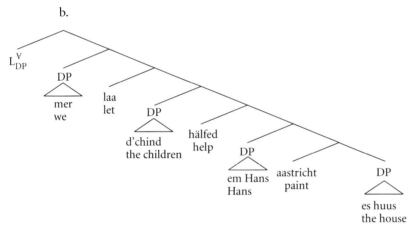

c.

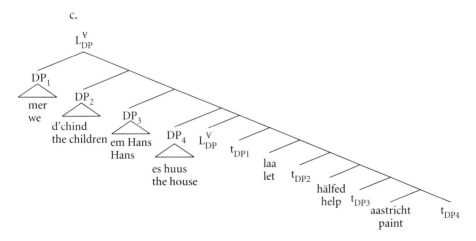

In order to derive the cross-serial order in (52c), I invoked two crucial assumptions. First, I assumed that there are heads that attract all (active) members of a given class, here DP: $L_{DP}^{\vee}$. The account draws on Bošković's (1999) theory of multiple *wh*-fronting in Slavic, where the existence of heads with the property "Attract all!" are postulated. Again the details are not particularly important here. An account that recursively stacks up as many DP-licensors as there are active DPs (constrained by convergence) would achieve the same result. Based on evidence like that reviewed in Section 3 it was conjectured that cross-serial dependencies can be unbounded. If this is correct, then some assumption along these lines (recursion of the same head, recursion of a sequence of heads, or attract all) is necessary to account for these constructions. A grammar where each of the arguments is moved into a dedicated position, that is, where each argument's landing site has different properties and a different label, cannot describe the facts adequately. Put yet another way, a linearly ordered, finite sequence of dedicated heads each attracting a single DP is insufficient.

Second, I assumed that movement processes, though they disturb the order between elements of different classes, are generally order preserving when it comes to elements of the same class. This intuition lies behind the various formulations of Relativized Minimality (Rizzi (1990); Chomsky (1995) for two prominent formulations). Relativized Minimality demands that pre- and post-movement structures – when relativized to a particular property, feature, or class of positions – be homomorphic: what was higher in the pre-movement structure is higher in the post-movement structure as well, (53a–b). Example (53) is intended to capture in the abstract the spirit of all formulations of relativized minimality. (53a) claims that if α and β are in the same class targeted by operation Δ and α c-commands β before the application of Δ, then α c-commands β also after the operations applies. The class of items relevant to the operation have identical c-command relations before and after the operation applies – though of course, α might move past other elements that are not in the class targeted by Δ. (53b) makes the same claim for β: applying Δ may not change the c-command relations between α and β. Note that derivations of the type in (53b) might be impossible because of the extension condition. This does not affect the point that Relativized Minimality per se allows such derivations.

(53)   For α, β $\in \Delta$, where Δ stands for some property, featurally defined class, or class of positions, $\prec$ the asymmetric c-command relation, and $\vDash_{\Delta}$ the relation of possible derivational subsequence through an operation targeting an element in class Δ:

a. $\alpha \prec \beta \vDash_\Delta \alpha \prec t\alpha \prec \beta$
b. $\alpha \prec \beta \vDash_\Delta \alpha \prec \beta \prec t_\beta$
c. $\alpha \prec \beta \nvDash_\Delta \beta \prec \alpha \prec t_\beta$
d. $\alpha \prec \beta \vDash_\Delta \alpha \prec \beta \prec t\alpha \prec t_\beta$

By contrast (53c) is disallowed by Relativized Minimality, because the pre- and post-movement orders are reversed. There is no homomorphism between the structures before and after Δ applies.

By the logic of order preservation derivations such as those in (53d) should also be allowed since the pre-movement c-command relations between α and β and the post-movement c-command relations are the same. This generalization of Relativized Minimality to chains is due to Starke (2001: Chapter 8), a concrete formulation is given in (54a).[26]

The empirical expectation this gives rise to is that order preservation should be common and that nesting dependencies should be rare. This expectation seems to be borne out (see Fanselow (1993); Richards (1997); Müller (2001); Starke (2001); Koopman and Szabolcsi (2000); Williams (2002); Fox and Pesetsky (2005) and the other contributions in that issue of Theoretical Linguistics among others). This view also makes concepts like equidistance Chomsky (1993) superfluous, which was designed specifically to allow an order preserving map between θ- and case-positions for subject and object. The cases (e.g., Kuno and Robinson (1972)) that were assumed to fall under the generalization that nesting paths are preferred to crossing paths (see Pesetsky's Path Containment Condition (1982)) will have to be reanalyzed.[27]

Again, any account of unbounded cross-serial dependencies must provide a general solution to the order-preservation problem. The unbounded nature of the phenomenon rules out a solution in terms of a linear sequence of dedicated projections. Relativized Minimality builds on the idea that movement is a homomorphic mapping (see above) and is therefore the most plausible candidate.

The crucial assumptions are summarized again below.

(54) Assumptions:
   a. If two or more items undergo the same type of movement, movement is order preserving
      (i) Relativized Minimality
            If X and Y are members of the same class, then an operation targeting that class may not cross X and Y.

(ii) *Crossing* – generalized version to accommodate (54d) (see Starke (2001))

X *crosses* Y iff all occurrences of Y asymmetrically c-command at least one occurrence of X; and at least one occurrence of X asymmetrically c-commands all occurrences of Y.

b. There are processes that correspond to the "attract-all" model in Bošković (1999).

c. Movement is to the left.

The Norwegian case, (48), can be dealt with along the same lines if we assume that there is a head which attracts all adverbs, $L^{\vee}_{Adv}$.

Derivations like these are fully consistent with the assumption that operations are ordered a(nti)symmetrically. The obvious question to ask at this point is whether the ban against inverse cross-serial dependencies, (51), can be derived. I postpone discussion of this question until Section 5 and turn to a second approach to straight cross-serial dependencies first.

4.2 Straight cross-serial dependencies with remnant movement

Nilsen (2003) and Bentzen (2005) generate straight crossing dependencies through a series of remnant movements. The crucial assumptions driving the accounts are given in (55).

(55) a. Above every verbal head there is an adverb lifter, that is, a head which attracts the maximal projection of the closest head with an adverbial in its specifier, $^{Adv}L^0$.

b. Above every functional head with an adverb in its specifier there is a verb lifter, $^{V}L^0$, that is, a head which attracts the maximal projection of the closest verbal head (V, auxiliary, modal).

On these assumptions, the Norwegian cross-serial dependency, (48), is derived as follows. First, the VP with the main verb is formed, (56). Subsequently the adverb is merged in the specifier position of a dedicated functional head, F^0_{Adv}, the associated verb lifter, $^{V}L^0_3$, is merged, and the original VP moves to its specifier position, (57).

(56)

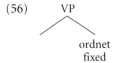

(57)

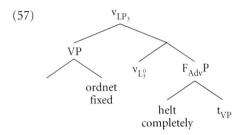

The next steps consist in merging the auxiliary *blitt* – 'become' and its associated adverb lifter, $^{Adv}L_3^0$. Then $F_{Adv}P$, containing only the adverb *helt* – 'completely', moves to the specifier of $^{Adv}LP_3$, (58).

(58)

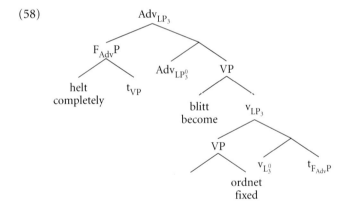

At this point the derivation appears to become an uneventful repetition of sequences of the same steps: A new adverb is merged in the specifier of a designated functional head, a verb lifter is merged on top of it, and the highest verb phrase, containing *blitt ordnet* – 'become fixed' moves, (59). Then another verb merges, an adverb lifter merges on top of it, and the closest $F_{Adv}P$, containing *alltid helt* – 'always completely' moves, (60).

(59)   V-lifter

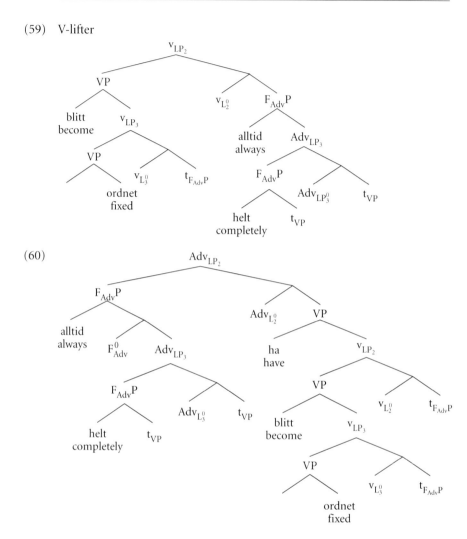

(60)

After another cycle through the "adverb, verb lifter, verb, adverb lifter" sequence, the structure is as in (61): The adverbs are collected in one constituent in an order-preserving fashion, the verbs are collected in another constituent, also in an order preserving fashion.[28]

(61)

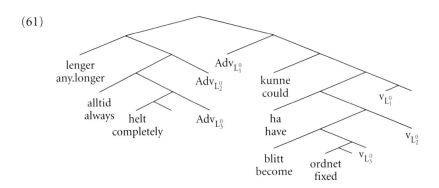

This is how the Nilsen-Bentzen system derives the cross-serial dependency between the adverbs and the verbs. The same type of analysis can be given for the Swiss German and Dutch cases, (62). All that is required for these languages are DP-lifters and XP-lifters, (62) below. The latter of which bring about the clustering of the verbs. The unbounded nature of the phenomenon is captured here by recursion through fixed sequences of identical lifters.

I will now show that the Nilsen-Bentzen approach to cross-serial dependencies is at odds with the assumptions argued for in Section 2. We saw that all movement operations are ordered with respect to each other. If the Nilsen-Bentzen account of cross-serial dependencies were correct, then all postulated movement operations would have to find their place in the linear sequence of operations. This would have to be true, in particular, of the VP-movement operation in (57), (59), and (61), and the movement of the F_{Adv}Ps in (58), (60), and (61). In other words, assumption (11b) demands that VP-movement and F_{Adv}P-movement be ordered with respect to each other: VP-movement $\ll F_{Adv}$P-movement or F_{Adv}P-movement $\ll$ VP-movement. Continuing the hypothetical argument, the step from (57) to (58) shows that VP-movement feeds F_{Adv}P-movement; hence, VP-movement $\ll F_{Adv}$P-movement. On the other hand, the step form (58) to (59) shows that F_{Adv}P-movement feeds VP-movement; hence, F_{Adv}P-movement $\ll$ VP-movement. We end up with a violation of the asymmetric ordering of operations.[29] The contradiction is unavoidable. It is in principle impossible to harmonize the Nilsen-Bentzen account of cross-serial dependencies with the conjunction of (11a), (11b), and GenPIM. Given the evidence reviewed in Section 2, this is a strong argument against the Nilsen-Bentzen approach to cross-serial dependencies. As we will see in a momement, the same problem plagues the analyses in Koopman and Szabolcsi (2000).

The problems that arose under (11a), (11b), and GenPIM for the analysis of Norwegian, arise again under the remnant movement analysis of Dutch and Swiss German (62). Movement of DP and of XP cannot be of the same type because of Müller's generalization. But they cannot be of different types either since then one of the remnant movements would sooner or later violate GenPIM. If anything, the problems for this analysis of the Dutch and Swiss German cross-serial dependencies is more severe than they were for the case of Norwegian. In Norwegian there is no reason to believe that the phenomenon is truly unbounded. This opens up a loophole. The analysis of Norwegian can be saved by assuming that the hierarchy of movements includes movement of VP_{ordnet}, F_{Adv_1}, VP_{blitt}, F_{Adv_2}, VP_{ha}, F_{Adv_3},... as separate types. They can then be hierarchically ordered as follows: $VP_{ordnet} \ll F_{Adv_1} \ll VP_{blitt} \ll F_{Adv_2} \ll VP_{ha} \ll Fs_{Adv_3}$... This is an unappealing but possible fix. The same solution is not available in the case of Dutch and Swiss German cross-serial dependencies because of the recursive nature of the phenomenon.

(62)

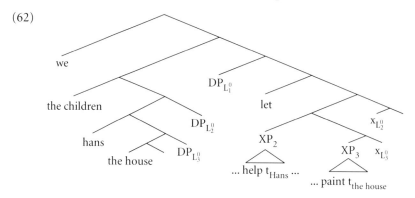

Let's consider the structures derived by the remnant-movement account of cross-serial dependencies. A careful look at them reveals two cross-serial dependencies each. In (61) the adverbs *lenger alltid helt* – 'any.longer always completely' and the verbs *kunne ha blitt* – 'could have become' form a straight cross-serial dependency; the abstract heads $^{Adv}L_n^0$ and $^{V}L_n^0$ – an inverse one. This inverse cross-serial dependency is formed as a by-product in the derivation. Similarly, in (62) the DPs *d'chind em Hans es huus* – 'the children Hans the house' are in a straight cross-serial dependency with the verbs *laa hälfe aastriiche*, while the abstract lifters $^{DP}L_n^0$ and $^{XP}L_n^0$ enter into an inverse cross-serial dependency. From the point of view of the Nilsen-Bentzen theory it is a coincidence that all heads involved in the inverse cross-serial dependency are abstract. In fact, I give a trivial adaptation below in Section 5.2 that derives an overt inverse cross-serial dependency. The fact that the

Nilsen-Bentzen approach cannot predict the linear asymmetry in (51) is a second argument against this approach.

I now turn to Koopman and Szabolcsi's (2000) theory of order preservation. It suffers from the same two problems as the Nilsen-Bentzen account of cross-serial dependencies: first it is incompatible with the conjunction of (11a), (11b), and GenPIM and second it generates inverse cross-serial dependencies as a derivational by-product.

Koopman and Szabolcsi (2000) assume that while movement of specifiers can be order-changing, the movement of complements is not because it is subject to the "move-one-category-at-a-time" constraint, (63a). Though the formulation is slightly cryptic, it is clear from context that Koopman and Szabolcsi intend (63a) to ensure that in a situation where XP contains YP as its complement, XP cannot move without previously evacuating YP. Since this is a general condition, if YP itself contains a complement ZP, then ZP will have to move prior to YP movement, etc. We need not concern ourselves with the exceptions in (63b) here.

(63) Movement (Koopman and Szabolcsi 2000: 43):

    a. by default, move only one category at a time.

    b. Exemption: Sequences of categories that may move together are (i) <YP+, YP>, where YP+ is a projection motivated by the modified LCA, (ii) sequences involving operator projections like RefP, DistP, F[oc]P, and the projection hosting the verb.

The move-one-category-at-a-time constraint entails, for example, that X and Y in (64) will not usually move by themselves but as part of their containing categories, LP_X and LP_Y. These categories split under movement by (63a). In a first step, LP_{Y_3} would move, as in (65a); then LP_{X_3} moves, as in (65b).

(64)

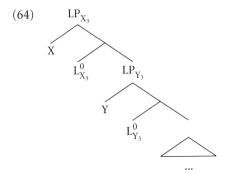

(65)   a.

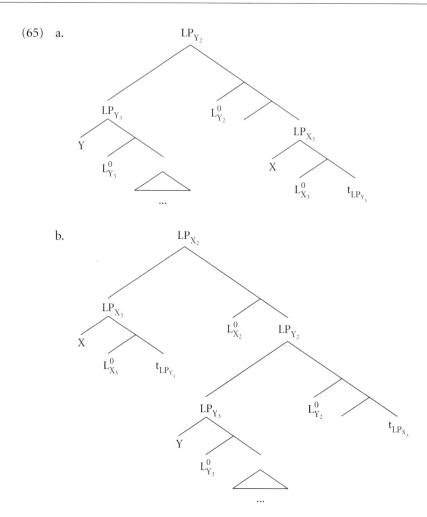

b.

After two further steps of movement, of which there are many in Koopman and Szabolcsi's model, the structure in (66) emerges.

(66)

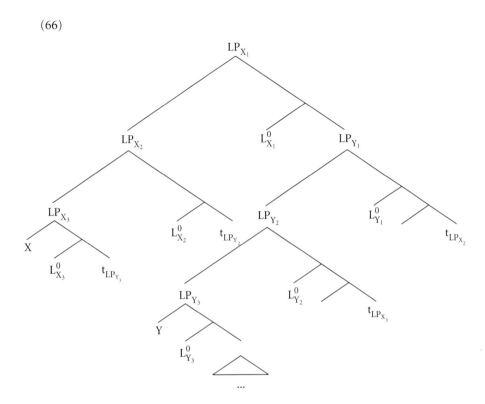

Two points are relevant here. First, as the careful reader will no doubt have noticed, the derivation currently under discussion violates the conjunction of (11a), (11b), and GenPIM – for the same reasons that the Nilsen-Bentzen derivations do. Second, (66) contains an inverse cross-serial dependency between the $L^0_{X_n}$s and the $L^0_{Y_n}$s. Again, these inverse cross-serial dependencies are simply a derivational by-product. There is no reason in the theory why they should be unpronounced. Theories that make unconstrained remnant movement available are too unrestrictive even if they stick to the seemingly severe linear restrictions imposed by the LCA, as Koopman and Szabolcsi (2000); Nilsen (2003); Bentzen (2005) do.[30] This drives home the point made in the introduction: Without a restrictive theory of operations, the strict S-H-C hypothesis has no empirical content.

In the next section I show that the conjunction of (11a), (11b), GenPIM, and the assumption that movement is always leftward rules out inverse cross-serial dependencies.

5.   The absence of inverse cross-serial dependencies

It should already be clear that in a system as the one entertained here, which dis-allows rightward movement, inverse cross-serial dependencies cannot be derived in a way totally symmetric to the derivation of straight cross-serial dependencies in Section 4.1. The relevant movement operation that maps (52a) onto (52c) will necessarily line up the moving elements in an order where scope corresponds to left-to-right order and never the other way around. The reason lies in the struc-tural rather than linear definition of order preservation, (54a) above, together with the assumption that movement is universally leftward. Another option might be a nesting derivation, but this is ruled out because Relativized Minimality im-poses crossing rather than nesting. This is good news: the restriction to leftward movement induces an asymmetry.

We need to see now how to block all remaining derivations for inverse un-bounded cross-serial dependencies. Under the assumptions made so far, there are two candidates: a head-movement derivation and a remnant-movement deriva-tion. I discuss them in turn.

5.1   Head movement

Head-to-head movement is problematic. Consider the structure in (67). This is a structure with a sequence of initial heads with their specifiers to the right. If we assume that the ban against rightward movement is the only linear asymmetry in syntax (see Abels and Neeleman (2006) for this view), then structures like (67a) can be base generated. Alternatively, if we adopt the LCA, then right specifiers are ruled out and must be derived through roll-up movement as in (67b) (see (2b) above). To make the structure in (67b) more easily readable, functional heads that are required by Kayne's LCA but irrelevant to the point under discussion are indicated as empty branches.

(67) a.

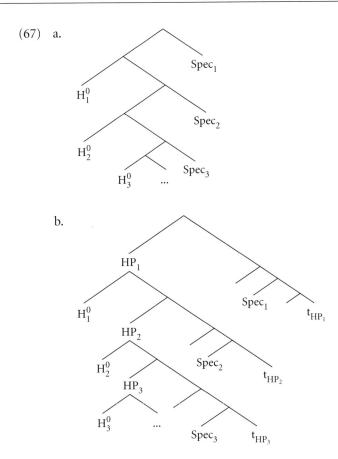

b.

Standard (left adjoining) head movement derives (68a) with an inverse cross-serial dependency from (67a). Similarly, head movement derives (68b) from (67b). If (67b) is to be ruled out, independent assumptions about locality have to be invoked. This is not impossible, but it shifts the explanatory burden from the strict S-H-C hypothesis even further to the theory of movement.

(68) a.

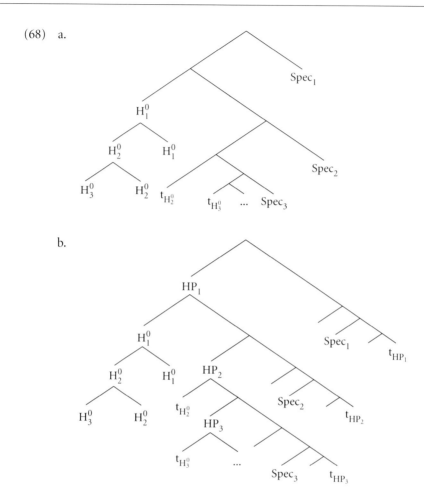

b.

Since inverse cross-serial dependencies are universally unattested, the derivations in (68) must be ruled out. These facts might then be interpreted as a new empirical argument against head movement as head adjunction (see Hinterhölzl (1997); Brody (2000); Koopman and Szabolcsi (2000); Boeckx and Stjepanovič (2001); Chomsky (2000, 2001a); Williams (2002, 2004); Stabler (2003); Abels (2003); Nilsen (2003); Müller (2004); Lechner (2005); Matushansky (2006) for recent discussion of head movement from various angles). The easiest way of banning head movement in the sense of head adjunction is to demand that all movement obey the extension condition.

5.2 Remnant movement

As discussed in the introduction to this section, the ban against rightward movement rules out derivations for inverse cross-serial dependencies which are fully
symmetrical to (52). However, we have also seen in Section 1 that any rightward movement analysis can be mechanically re-done in terms of remnant movement, (2c). It is therefore no surprise that remnant movement may lead to inverse
cross-serial dependencies, as was illustrated in Section 4.2.

In the discussion of Nilsen's and Koopman and Szabolcsi's theories I claimed
that it is a pure coincidence under their assumptions that audible inverse cross-
serial dependencies are unattested. I will illustrate this claim by giving a trivial
reformulation of the Nilsen-Bentzen account of cross-serial orders in Norwegian
which leads to inverse crossed orders.

(69)   Inverse Nilsen/Bentzen
    a.   Above every verbal element, there is a lifter head L_V^0, which lifts the
        closest $L_V P$ – if present – into its specifier.
    b.   Above every adverbial element, there is a lifter head L_{Adv}^0, which lifts the
        closest $L_{Adv} P$ – if present – into its specifier.

These assumptions give rise to derivations like those depicted in (70a–c). Remov-
ing unnecessary clutter from (70c) yields (70d), where we see the beginning of an
overt inverse cross-serial dependency emerging. The cycle of operations could be
repeated; it easily generates unbounded inverse cross-serial dependencies.

(70)   a.

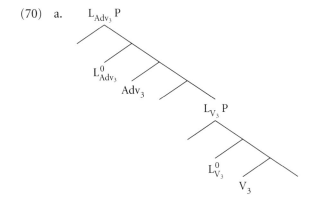

b.

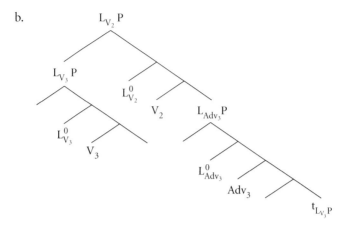

c.

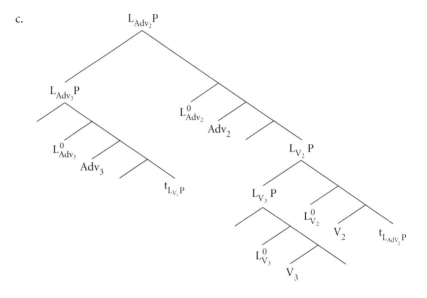

d.

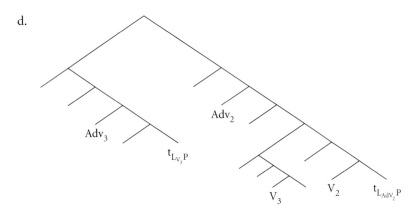

A theory that predicts the ban against inverse cross-serial dependencies must rule out such derivations. Fortunately we are already in a position to do this. If the operations moving $L_V P$ and $L_{Adv}P$ exist at all, then they fall under the perview of (11a) and (11b), that is, the two operations must be ordered with respect to each other. But once the operations are ordered with respect to each other, the symmetric feeding relations between them are disallowed by GenPIM. Thus, even if such operations exist, they can never give rise to inverse cross-serial dependencies.

5.3 Conclusion

If the empirical hypothesis from Section 3 is true and UG disallows inverse cross-serial dependencies, then syntactic theory must account for this. With assumptions (71i–iii) in place, we can rule out all derivations for inverse cross-serial dependencies except for the remnant movement derivation.

(71) (i)   Movement obeys the extension condition.
      (ii) Movement is uniformly leftward.
      (iii) Movement operations are order preserving in the sense of (53).

If we add to these assumptions the assumption that movement operations are ordered, (11a) and (11b), and apply this ordering as in GenPIM, (15), then inverse cross-serial dependencies are correctly predicted to be impossible. I take this section of the paper to be an informal proof-by-case of this claim.

6.   Conclusion

I opened the paper with the question of how existing linear asymmetries in language can be explained and made the trivial observation that constraints on structures (like the Cinque hierarchy and the LCA) might be necessary to explain such asymmetries, but that they are insufficient. I pointed out that giving up the Proper-Binding Condition and the freezing principle runs the risk of robbing the LCA of its empirical content. A restrictive theory of movement must accompany any theory (LCA or otherwise) which aims at deriving linear asymmetries in language from a ban against rightward movement.

Section 2 represents a step in this direction. It is standardly assumed that operations in syntax are ordered. I took this as a phenomenon rather than an epiphenomenon and formulated the assumption as UCOOL. UCOOL, however, is meaningless without an instruction of how to deploy it. I argued on the basis of mostly German data that assumptions at least as strong as (11) and GenPIM are necessary. The universal claim made in UCOOL remains to be verified. The system yields a flexible, fine-grained, and apparently correct framework for the analysis of phenomena in various domains: improper movement, effects of the freezing principle and exceptions from it, and remnant movement with immediate predictions of what is possible and what is impossible.

It emerged, table (36), that there is a nearly perfect match between the three conditions unified under GenPIM (identity, surfing paths, diving paths). It also emerged that the ordering of operations does seem to be a(nti)symmetric and total. This suggests that a whole range of important issues that were set aside in Section 2 warrant further study: Is UCOOL universally fixed? How can it be integrated into a derivational theory of syntax? Is the asymmetry in the formulation of Gen-PIM an eliminable feature of the theory? What is the relation between UCOOL and the Cinque Hierarchy? What is the exact set and order of movement types referenced in UCOOL? ...

Section 3 reviewed some well-known facts regarding cross-serial dependencies in Dutch and Swiss German. There exists a hitherto unnoticed linear asymmetry in this empirical domain: Inverse cross-serial dependencies are impossible, (51). I suggested a novel analysis of forward cross-serial dependencies, 4.1, and went on to show in Sections 4.2 and 5 that theories which derive cross-serial dependencies through remnant movement are incompatible with the main assumptions argued for here and fail to predict the impossibility of inverse cross-serial dependencies. It now remains to be seen whether insights gained in analyses that make unrestricted use of remnant movement (such as Haegeman (2000); Hinterhölzl (1997)) can be captured under a more restrictive theory of operations, such as the one proposed here.

This paper has been somewhat programmatic. I had to raise many issues that I could not resolve in the space of this paper and mention constructions that I could not discuss. These issues and constructions include the right-roof constraint and the ban against unbound intermediate traces in remnants, *tough*-movement, clefts, and relative clauses. Other potentially relevant constructions have not even been mentioned. It might be interesting, for example, to consider ECM under *wh*-movement in Romance languages and the locality bounds on control into adjuncts from the current perspective. Both constructions might yield an answer to the question whether the ordering of operations is asymmetric or antisymmetric. I am planning to take up these questions in future work.

Notes

* I would like to thank the participants of the Left-Right Seminar (Tromsø, Spring 2006), the Ph.D. course on remnant movement and left-right asymmetries (Leipzig, Summer 2006), the participants of the remnant movement reading group (Tromsø, Fall 2006 and Spring 2007), the audiences in Geneva (spring 2007) and Konstanz (GGS, spring 2007), and Andrew Nevins for invaluable comments, discussion, and challenges to the proposals made here and their predecessors. Among the aforementioned I am particularly indebted to Øystein Nilsen and Gereon Müller.

1. In addition to a restrictive theory of the architecture of individual phrases we also need to assume tight constraints on possible base-generated hierarchies of multiple phrases. I assume that some version of this hypothesis, variously called the *Hierarchy of Projections* Adger (2003), the Cinque hierarchy, the functional sequence (fseq in Starke (2004)), or Pollock-Cinque functional hierarchy (PCFH in Williams (2002)), is correct, although current formulations face a number of problems (see Bobaljik (1999) and Nilsen (2004: Chapter 1) for clear statements of the two most pressing issues). I will usually refer to this assumed fixed hierarchy of phrasal projections as the Cinque hierarchy.

2. It may appear that this treatment of right heads, specifiers, and adjuncts underestimates the actual differences between the structures on the left and on the right hand side in (2). For discussion of differences pertaining to derived c-command relations and the presence of additional functional structure, see Abels and Neeleman (2006).

3. Here and throughout I frame the discussion in terms of different types of movement operations and their sequencing: If $\sigma \ll \tau$ under UCOOL, then, once τ has applied to phrase P, σ can no longer apply to P. The anonymous reviewer cautions that this might be misread as a return to a construction specific view of movement. However, everything can easily be restated in terms of feature attraction. To do this, UCOOL can be construed as a feature hierarchy or as an extrinsically imposed ordering on feature checking. If we understand it as a feature hierarchy,

my formulation in terms of operational sequencing can be restated as follows: If $\sigma \ll \tau$ under UCOOL, then once τ has been attracted and phrase P pied-piped, σ contained in P can no longer be attracted and/or induce pied-piping of P. A similar, even more clunky reformulation is available in a probe-goal system with the activity condition and the general (EP)P-property driving movement. Nothing contentive is at stake here and my own formulation in terms of operational sequencing seems to me to be maximally transparent.

4. I know of no operation whose binding-theoretic fingerprint is the opposite of (10b), that is, where (i) and (iii) are unacceptable and (ii) is acceptable.

5. Asymmetry and antisymmetry are defined as follows (see Partee et al. (1993)):

(i)   a.   A relation R is asymmetric iff $\forall x, y[< x, y > \in R \rightarrow < y, x > \notin R]$
      b.   A relation R is antisymmetric iff $\forall x, y[[< x, y > \in R \wedge < y, x > \in R] \rightarrow x = y]$

6. Every now and then one or another of the assumptions in 11 are revoked or questioned. Thus Nilsen's (2003) account of cross-serial dependencies effectively revokes (11a), as I will show below; Müller and Sternefeld's (1993) principle of unambiguous binding revokes (11b); and Grewendorf's (2001) account of the lack of superiority effects only in short distance questions in German revokes (11c).

7. Williams' (2002) Representation Theory – and its partial translation into a derivational theory sketched in Nevins (2004: 298–301), also a few remarks in Nevins and Hornstein (2005) – can treat UCOOL as a constraint on entire derivations. Representation Theory is incompatible with root-extending merge, which I would like to hold on to because of the transparent relation between root-extending merge and compositional interpretation.

8. Chomsky's (2001b; 2001a) notion of the cycle, where information about what happened in the lower phase remains accessible during the higher phase until the next higher strong phase head is introduced, overcomes these problems only partly. The loophole created by cyclic phase-edge-to-phase-edge movement is just too large.

9. Grewendorf's (2003) constraint on remnant movement therefore falls out as a subcase of the general ban on improper movement.

10. See Frey (2000, 2005) for discussion and comparison to topicalization in English with German vorfeld topicalization. Frey discusses a number of interpretive differences between what is called "topicalization" in these languages. Below I show that German topicalization does not feed *wh*-movement. The anonymous reviewer reminds me that English topicalization – at least marginally – does (Lasnik and Saito 1992: 101–102), which suggests that English topicalization might be closer to what I call scrambling in German.

11. Similarly for Japanese, where the topic marker apparently does not attach to *wh*-phrases – see Kuroda (1965), Heycock (to appear) for a useful overview. This might be attributed to a semantic or pragmatic incompatibility (see already Bach (1971) for this suggestion).

12. Rizzi (2006: 122) treats D-linked *wh*-phrases as topics. The reasoning in the text suggests that this is not correct. Indeed, in many languages the morphosyntax of D-linked *wh*-phrases is different from that of topics. Japanese, see fn. 11, is typical in this respect. Presumably D-linking has more to do with restricted quantification than with topicality.

13. Similar facts are found in Czech (Pavel Caha and Lucie Medova, p.c.). Clause-bound scrambling and *wh*-movement do not give rise to weak crossover effects, but long *wh*-movement does, but only for binding into arguments in the higher clauses. Within the clause where the *wh*-phrase originates there are no weak crossover effects. This pattern of data is as expected under the current setup. The explanation for Czech would run exactly parallel to Wiltschko's explanation of the German pattern in terms of scrambling feeding *wh*-movement.

14. Chomsky (1973: 249–250); Kayne (1984: 169); Pesetsky (1982: 319); and for German Müller (1995: 390 fn. 26) find similar examples unacceptable; my informants disagree and find them only slightly degraded. One important difference between the present examples and Chomsky's original one is that Chomsky's example contained a non-D-linked *wh*-phrase. Chomsky (2004: ex. # 19) has recently claimed that PPs (with a D-linked *wh*-phrase) can be extracted from ECM subjects. For some speakers pied-piping of *of* seems to be necessary to make these examples acceptable.

15. This sentence is of course possible if we construe *Oscar* as the object of *ask* and *it* referentially.

16. These examples are not acceptable to all speakers.
The fact that many examples in the literature where scrambling is followed by subextraction are unacceptable is probably due to a specificity island (see Fanselow (2001: 413) for this suggestion and Pafel (1993) on the difficulty of delineating specificity effects precisely in German).

17. I would like to thank Eric Haeberli for pointing out some interfering factors with my original examples that made them worse than they needed to be.

18. It could be countered that the examples predicted to be bad under this interpretation of table (17) are ungrammatical simply because the putative second operation is clause-bound. This is true, but it is also question-begging. On usual assumptions clause-boundedness is described in terms of a prohibition against using [Spec, CP] as an intermediate landing site and that [Spec, CP] is not the right kind of landing site for the bounded movement. In other words, the explanation comes back to improper movement anyway.

Moreover, in the system of Chomsky (2001b) long movement does not need to pass through the phase edge as an escape hatch any more. The lower phase is only spelled out when the next higher phase head is introduced. This allows movement to proceed from phase-medial to phase-medial position (see Abels (2003: Chapter 2) for discussion), which makes even the description of clause-boundedness a tricky and unresolved issue.

Without a viable counterproposal, this objection has little force.

19. Williams (2002) suggests a solution to this particular problem in terms of what he calls mismapping, discussion of which would lead too far afield. If I understand Williams correctly, the examples discussed immediately below are not amenable to an analysis in terms of mismapping.

20. Non-obvious glosses are as follows:

PRES	present tense	SM	subject agreement marker
PERF	perfective	FV	final vowel
F	marker of focus and cyclicty		

21. The syntax, semantics, and morphology of the marker of focus and cyclicity glossed F is discussed in detail in Abels and Muriungi (2006a, to appear).

22. Although these particular constructions in Dutch, unlike Swiss German (for which see Huybregts (1984); Shieber (1985)), are recognizable by a context-free device when viewed as a string language, there can be very little doubt indeed that structurally, context sensitivity is needed here (Huybregts (1976); Bresnan et al. (1982); Kracht (2007); Steedman (2000)). Huybregts (1984) discusses a slightly different construction in Dutch which is even weakly context sensitive.

23. The claim made here is quite different from that in Bobaljik (2004), who wonders about the apparent absence of predicate clusters in VO-languages. As noted in Wagner (2005) Norwegian (SVO) examples like (48) seem to be a counterexample to Bobaljik's generalization. Tagalog (VSO) is another apparent counterexample.

24. A second reason for excluding rightward-movement as an analytic option is that such analyses invariably require a version of the right roof constraint, a constraint that, under a conception of the grammar with remnant movement and without rightward movement, ought to be derivable from constraints on remnant movement. The present formulation of UCOOL and GenPIM does not derive the right roof constraint. Eventually this should be changed.

Notice that if all superficial rightward movement is analyzed as remnant movement, then the right roof constraint bans movement of remnants containing traces of remnant creating movement which originate more than one clause deep inside the remnant. Stated this way, the right roof constraint becomes part of a larger generalization known to constrain remnant movement in Germanic: Movement of remnants containing unbound intermediate traces is impossible (see den Besten and Webelhuth (1987, 1990); Grewendorf (1994); Fanselow (1993); Bayer (1996); Müller (1998, 1999) for relevant discussion). What this generalized version of the constraint follows from remains unclear.

25. The constituent structure thus derived is not the one argued for in Bresnan et al. (1982) (see also Steedman (2000)). Bresnan et al.'s constituent structure can be derived if instead of lifting all arguments out of the verbal projections all verbs are lifted out of the initial structure in an order-preserving fashion with subsequent movement of the remnant of the tree in (52a). Such a derivation might indeed be called for. Nothing in the logic of this paper hinges on the choice. For reasons of expository simplicity, I assume the derivations given here.

26. Richards' (1997) mechanism of *tucking in* achieves the same result, but at the cost of violating the extension condition, a move that I would like to avoid.

27. A possible way forward on the issue of nesting dependencies is to make use of feature geometries. Thus, suppose there are two operations, Δ and Γ, which target the features α and β, respectively. Assume furthermore that β is a feature which depends on α in the sense that it is lower in the feature geometry than α. If Δ targeting α applies to the structure in (ia) followed by application of Γ targeting β a nesting configuration results, (ib). If the operations apply in the opposite order, Y will move first, (ic). Applying Δ to this structure will either move Y again or lead to a (defective) intervention effect. Either way, a nesting dependency is not derivable this way.

(i)   a. $[X_{[\alpha]} \ldots [\ldots Y_{[\alpha \,:\, \beta]} \ldots]]$
      b. $[Y_{[\alpha \,:\, \beta]} \ldots [X_{[\alpha]} [t_X \ldots [\ldots t_Y \ldots]]]]$
      c. $[Y_{[\alpha \,:\, \beta]} \ldots [X_{[\alpha]} \ldots [\ldots t_Y \ldots]]]$

Reversing the original arrangement of the features as in (iia), will give rise to movement of Y by Relativized Minimality whether Δ is applied first or Γ. If Δ is applied first, then Γ might move Y another step leaving X in place. If Γ is applied first, then Y will either move another step or give rise to a defective intervention effect and block movement of X. The only possible derivation where both X and Y move is the one in (ib), which yields the nesting path.

(ii) a. $[Y_{[\alpha \,:\, \beta]} \ldots [\ldots X_{[\alpha]} \ldots]]$
      b. $[Y_{[\alpha \,:\, \beta]} \ldots [t_Y \ldots [\ldots X_{[\alpha]} \ldots]]]$

This is Starke's (2001) logic for weak island phenomena and it might be applicable in the relevant cases.

28. Note that, since Norwegian allows positioning the subject in between the various adverbs, there is little if any evidence that the adverb-cluster constituent exists. This casts doubt on the adverb-cluster constituent hypothesized under the remnant movement analysis. For reasons of space I cannot pursue the issue further.

29. Even if operations are only antisymmetrically ordered, $F_{Adv}P$-movement and VP-movement cannot be of the same type, because in that case Müller's generalization still rules out the derivation. As we saw, Müller's generalization follows from closest attract even if operations are only antisymmetrically ordered.

30. As far as I can tell, the LFG account of the Dutch cross-serial dependencies in Bresnan et al. (1982) suffers from the same problem: there is no reason to expect a linear asymmetry in the realm of cross-serial dependencies. The same is true of Steedman's 2000 account in terms of type-lifting.

References

Abels, Klaus. 2002. On an alleged argument for the proper binding condition. In *Proceedings of HUMIT 2001. MIT Working Papers in Linguistics 43*, ed. Tania R. Ionin, Heejeong Ko, and Andrew Nevins, 1–16. Cambridge, MA.

Abels, Klaus. 2003. Successive cyclicity, anti-locality, and adposition stranding. Doctoral dissertation, University of Connecticut.

Abels, Klaus, and Peter Muriungi. 2006a. The focus particle in Kîîtharaka. In *Papers on information structure in African languages*, ed. Ines Fiedler and Anne Schwarz, volume 42 of *ZAS Papers in Linguistics*, 1–20. ZAS.

Abels, Klaus, and Peter Muriungi. to appear. The focus particle in Kîîtharaka: Syntax and semantics. *Lingua*.

Abels, Klaus, and Ad Neeleman. 2006. Universal 20 without the LCA. ms.

Adger, David. 2003. *Core syntax: A minimalist approach*. Oxford: Oxford University Press.

Adger, David, Daniel Harbour, and Laurel Watkins. 2007. Feature intervention, information structure and word order. In *GLOW Newsletter # 58*.

Alexiadou, Artemis. 1997. *Adverb placement: A case study in antisymmetric syntax*, volume 18 of *Linguistik Aktuell*. Amsterdam, Philadelphia: John Benjamins.

Bach, Emmon. 1971. Questions. *Linguistic Inquiry* 2:153–166.

Bayer, Josef. 1996. *Directionality and logical form. On the scope of focussing particles and wh-in-situ*. Dordrecht: Kluwer.

Beck, Sigrid. 1996. Quantified structures as barriers for LF movement. *Natural Language Semantics* 4:1–56.

Belletti, Adriana, ed. 2004. *Structures and beyond*, volume 3 of *Oxford studies in comparative syntax The cartography of syntactic structures*. Oxford: Oxford University Press.

Bentzen, Kristine. 2005. What's the better move? – on verb placement in Standard and Northern Norwegian. *Nordic Journal of Linguistics* 28:153–188.

den Besten, Hans, and Gert Webelhuth. 1987. Remnant topicalization and the constituent structure of vp in the germanic sov languages. *GLOW Newsletter* 18:15–16.

den Besten, Hans, and Gert Webelhuth. 1990. Stranding. In *Scrambling and barriers*, ed. Günther Grewendorf and Wolfgang Sternefeld, 77–92. Amsterdam and Philadelphia: Academic Press.

Bobaljik, Jonathan D. 1999. Adverbs: The hierarchy paradox. *GLOT International* 4:27–28.

Bobaljik, Jonathan D. 2004. Clustering theories. In *Verb clusters: A study of Hungarian and Dutch*, ed. Katalin e Kiss and Henk van Riemsdijk, 121–145. Philadelphia: John Benjamins.

Boeckx, Cedric, and Norbert Hornstein. 2003. Reply to "Control is not movement". *Linguistic Inquiry* 34:269–280.

Boeckx, Cedric, and Sandra Stjepanović. 2001. Heading toward PF. *Linguistic Inquiry* 31:345–355.

Bošković, Željko. 1994. D-structure, theta-criterion, and movement into theta-positions. *Linguistic Analysis* 24:247–286.

Bošković, Željko. 1999. On multiple feature checking: Multiple *Wh*-fronting and multiple head movement. In *Working minimalism*, ed. Samuel David Epstein and Norbert Hornstein, 159–188. MIT Press.

Bošković, Željko, and Daiko Takahashi. 1998. Scrambling and last resort. *Linguistic Inquiry* 29:347–366.

Bresnan, Joan W., R. Kaplan, Stanley Peters, and Annie Zaenen. 1982. Cross-serial dependencies in Dutch. *Linguistic Inquiry* 13:613–635.

Brody, Michael. 2000. Mirror theory. syntactic representation in perfect syntax. *Linguistic Inquiry* 31:29–57.

Chomsky, Noam. 1965. *Aspects of the theory of syntax*. Cambridge, MA: MIT Press.

Chomsky, Noam. 1973. Conditions on transformations. In *A festschrift for Morris Halle*, ed. Stephen R Anderson and Paul Kiparsky, 232–286. New York: Holt, Rinehart and Winston.

Chomsky, Noam. 1981. *Lectures on government and binding*. Dordrecht: Foris.

Chomsky, Noam. 1986. *Barriers*, volume 13 of *Linguistic Inquiry Monograph*. Cambridge, MA: MIT Press.

Chomsky, Noam. 1993. A minimalist program for linguistic theory. In *The view from building 20*, ed. Kenneth Hale and Samuel J. Keyser, 1–52. Cambridge, MA: MIT Press.

Chomsky, Noam. 1995. Categories and transformations. In *The minimalist program*, 219–394. Cambridge, MA: MIT Press.

Chomsky, Noam. 2000. Minimalist inquiries: The framework. In *Step by step: Essays on minimalism in honor of howard lasnik*, ed. Roger Martin, David Michaels, and Juan Uriagereka, 89–155. Cambridge, MA: MIT Press.

Chomsky, Noam. 2001a. Beyond explanatory adequacy.

Chomsky, Noam. 2001b. Derivation by phase. In *Ken Hale: A life in language*, ed. Michael Kenstowicz, 1–52. Cambridge, MA.: MIT Press.

Chomsky, Noam. 2004. On phases, December 2004.

Chomsky, Noam, and Howard Lasnik. 1995. *The minimalist program*, Chapter 1 The Theory of Principles and Parameters, 13–127. Cambridge, Mass: MIT Press.

Cinque, Guglielmo. 1996. The antisymmetric programme: Theoretical and typological implications. *Journal of Linguistics* 32:447–464.

Cinque, Guglielmo. 1999. *Adverbs and functional heads – a cross-linguistic perspective*. New York and Oxford: Oxford University Press.

Cinque, Guglielmo, ed. 2002. *Functional structure in DP and IP*. Oxford Studies in Comparative Syntax. Oxford University Press.

Cinque, Guglielmo. 2005. Deriving Greenberg's universal 20 and its exceptions. *Linguistic Inquiry* 36:315–332.

Cinque, Guglielmo. 2006. *Restructuring and functional heads*. Oxford studies in comparative syntax: The cartography of syntactic structures. Oxford and New York: Oxford University Press.

Collins, Chris. 1994. Economy of derivation and the generalized proper binding condition. *Linguistic Inquiry* 25:45–61.

Collins, Chris. 1997. *Local economy*. Cambridge, Mass.: MIT Press.

Collins, Chris. 2005. A smuggling approach to raising in English. *Linguistic Inquiry* 36:289–298.

Culicover, Peter W., and Ray Jackendoff. 2001. Control is not movement. *Linguistic Inquiry* 32:493–511.

Culy, Christopher. 1985. The complexity of the vocabulary of Bambara. *Linguistics and Philosophy* 8:345–351.

Davies, William D., and Stanley Dubinsky. 2004. *The grammar of raising and control*. Blackwell.

Dehdari, Jonathan. 2006. Crossing dependencies in Persian. MA-thesis, Brigham Young University.

Diesing, Molly. 1992. *Indefinites*. Cambridge, MA.: MIT Press.

den Dikken, Marcel. 1995. Extraposition as intraposition, and the syntax of english tag questions.

Epstein, Samuel David. 1999. Un-principled syntax and the derivation of syntactic relations. In *Working minimalism*, ed. Samuel David Epstein and Norbert Hornstein, 317–345. Cambridge, MA: MIT Press.

Epstein, Samuel David, Erich M. Groat, Ruriko Kawashima, and Hisatsugu Kitahara. 1998. *A derivational approach to syntactic relations*. Oxford: Oxford University Press.

Evers, Arnold. 1975. The transformational cycle in Dutch and German. Doctoral dissertation, University of Utrecht.

Fanselow, Gisbert. 1990. Scrambling as NP-movement. In *Scrambling and barriers*, ed. Gunther Grewendorf and Wolfgang Sternefeld, 113–142. John Benjamins.

Fanselow, Gisbert. 1991. Minimale syntax. Habilitationsschrift, Universität Passau.

Fanselow, Gisbert. 1993. The return of the base generators. *Groninger Arbeiten zur Germanistischen Linguistik* 36:1–74.

Fanselow, Gisbert. 2001. Features, θ-roles, and free constituent order. *Linguistic Inquiry* 32:405–437.

Fanselow, Gisbert. 2004. The MLC and derivational economy. In *Minimality effects in syntax*, ed. Arthur Stepanov, Gisbert Fanselow, and Ralf Vogel, volume 70 of *Studies in Generative Grammar*, 73–124. deGruyter.

Fiengo, Robert. 1977. On trace theory. *Linguistic Inquiry* 8:35–62.

Fox, Danny, and David Pesetsky. 2005. Cyclic linearization of syntactic structure. *Theoretical Linguistics* 31:1–46.

Frey, Werner. 2000. Über die syntaktische Position der Satztopiks im Deutschen. *ZAS Papers in Linguistics* 20:137–172.

Frey, Werner. 2005. Pragmatic properties of certain German and English left peripheral constructions. *Linguistics* 43:89–129.

Friederici, Angela D, Matthias Schlesewsky, and Christian J Fiebach. 2003. WH-movement versus scrambling: The brain makes a difference. In *Word order and scrambling*, ed. Simin Karimi, 325–344. Malden, Mass.: Blackwell Publishing.

Glushan, Zhanna. 2006. Japanese style scrambling in Russian: myth and reality. Master's thesis, Universitetet i Tromso.

Greenberg, Joseph. 1963. Some universals of grammar with particular reference to the order of meaningful elements. In *Universals of language*, ed. Joseph Greenberg, 73–113. Cambridge, Mass.: MIT Press.

Grewendorf, Günther. 1994. Variable binding and reconstruction.

Grewendorf, Günther. 2001. Multiple *wh*-fronting. *Linguistic Inquiry* 32:87–122.

Grewendorf, Günther. 2003. Improper remnant movement. *Gengo Kenkyu* 123:47–94.

Haegeman, Liliane. 2000. Remnant movement and OV order. In *The derivation of VO and OV*, ed. Peter Svenonius, volume 30 of *Linguistik Aktuell*, 69–96. Amsterdam and Philadelphia: John Benjamins.

Haegeman, Liliane, and Henk van Riemsdijk. 1986. Verb projection raising, scope and the typology of rules affecting verbs. *Linguistic Inquiry* 17:417–466.

Haider, Hubert. 1993. *Deutsche Syntax- generativ: Vorstudien zur Theorie einer projektiven Grammatik*. Tübingen: Gunter Narr Verlag.

Heycock, Caroline. to appear. Japanese -*wa*, -*ga*, and information structure.

Higginbotham, James. 1984. English is not a context-free language. *Linguistic Inquiry* 15:225–234.

Hinterhölzl, Roland. 1997. A VO-based approach to verb raising. In *Proceedings of NELS, McGill university*, ed. K Kusumoto, 187–202. GLSA.

Hiraiwa, Ken. 2002. Movement and derivation: Eliminating the PBC. In *Penn Linguistics Colloquium 26*. Philadelphia, PA.

Hornstein, Norbert. 1999. Movement and control. *Linguistic Inquiry* 30:69–96.

Hornstein, Norbert. 2001. *Move! A minimalist theory of construal*. Cambridge, USA: Blackwell.

Huybregts, Riny. 1976. Overlapping dependencies in Dutch. *Utrecht Working Papers in Linguistics* 1:24–65.

Huybregts, Riny. 1984. The weak inadequacy of Context-Free Phrase Structure Grammars. In *Van periferie naar kern*, ed. G de Haan, M Trommelen, and W Zonneveld, 81–99. Dordrecht: Foris.

Kayne, Richard. 1984. *Connectedness and binary branching*. Dordrecht: Foris.

Kayne, Richard. 1994. *The antisymmetry of syntax*. Cambridge, MA.: MIT Press.

Kayne, Richard. 1998. Overt vs. covert movement. *Syntax* 1:128–191.

Kayne, Richard. 1999. Prepositional complementizers as attractors. *Probus* 11:39–73.

Kayne, Richard. 2004. Prepositions as probes. In *Structures and beyond: The cartography of syntactic structures, volume 3*, ed. Adriana Belletti, 192–212. Oxford University Press.

Kayne, Richard. 2005. Antisymmetry and Japanese. In *Movement and silence*, ed. R. Kayne, 215–240. Oxford: Oxford University Press.

Kitahara, Hisatsugu. 1997. *Elementary operations and optimal derivations*. Cambridge, MA: MIT Press.

Koopman, Hilda, and Anna Szabolcsi. 2000. *Verbal complexes*. Cambridge, MA: MIT Press.

Kracht, Marcus. 2003. *The mathematics of language*. Studies in Generative Grammar 63. Berlin, New York: Mouton de Gruyter.

Kracht, Marcus. 2007. The emergence of syntactic structure. *Linguistics and Philosophy* 30:47–95.

Kuno, Susumu, and Jane J. Robinson. 1972. Multiple wh-questions. *Linguistic Inquiry* 3:463–487.

Kuroda, S.-Y. 1965. Generative grammatical studies in the Japanese language. Doctoral dissertation, MIT.

Kuthy, K. de, and Walt Detmar Meurers. 1999. On partial constituent fronting in German. In *Tübingen studies in head-driven phrase structure grammar*, ed. V. Kordoni, 22–73.

Landau, Idan. 2003. Movement out of control. *Linguistic Inquiry* 34:471–498.

Larson, Richard K. 1988. On the double object construction. *Linguistic Inquiry* 19:335–391.

Lasnik, Howard, and Mamoru Saito. 1991. On the subject of infinitives. In *Papers from the 27th regional Meeting of the Chicago Linguistic Society Part One: The General Session*, ed. Lise M. Dobrin, Lynn Nichols, and Rosa M. Rodriguez, 324–343. Chicago, Ill.: Chicago Linguistic Society, University of Chicago.

Lasnik, Howard, and Mamoru Saito. 1992. *Move α: Conditions on its application and output*. Cambridge, MA: MIT Press.

Lechner, Winfried. 2005. Interpretive effects of head movement, July 2005.

Maclachlan, Anna, and Owen Rambow. 2002. Cross-serial dependencies in Tagalog. In *Proceedings of the Sixth International Workshop on Tree Adjoining Grammar and Related Frameworks (TAG+6)*, 100–104.

Matushansky, Ora. 2006. Head-movement in linguistic theory. *Linguistic Inquiry* 37:69–109.

May, Robert. 1979. Must comp-to-comp movement be stipulated? *Linguistic Inquiry* 10:719–725.

Müller, Gereon. 1995. *A-bar syntax: A study of movement types*, volume 42 of *Studies in Generative Grammar*. New York: Mouton de Gruyter.

Müller, Gereon. 1998. *Incomplete category fronting: A derivational approach to remnant movement in German*. Dordrecht, Boston: Kluwer Academic Publishers.

Müller, Gereon. 1999. Imperfect checking. *The Linguistic Review* 16:359–404.

Müller, Gereon. 2001. Order preservation, parallel movement, and the emergence of the unmarked. In *Optimality theoretic syntax*, ed. Geraldine Legendre, Jane Grimshaw, and Sten Vikner, 279–313. MIT Press.

Müller, Gereon. 2004. Verb-second as vP-first. *Journal of Comparative Germanic Syntax* 7:179–234.

Müller, Gereon, and Wolfgang Sternefeld. 1993. Improper movement and unambiguous binding. *Linguistic Inquiry* 24:461–507.

Müller, Gereon, and Wolfgang Sternefeld. 1996. A'-chain formation and economy of derivation. *Linguistic Inquiry* 27:480–511.

Muriungi, Peter. 2005. Wh-questions in Kiitharaka. *Studies in African Linguistics* 34:43–104.

Nevins, Andrew Ira. 2004. Derivations without the activity condition. *MIT Working Papers in Linguistics* 49:287–310.

Nevins, Andrew Ira, and Norbert Hornstein. 2005. Representation Theory by Edwin Williams. *Language* 81:757–761.

Nilsen, Øystein. 2003. *Eliminating positions: Syntax and semantics of sentence modification*. Utrecht, NL: LOT.

Nilsen, Øystein. 2004. Domains for adverbs. *Lingua* 114:809–847.

Pafel, Jürgen. 1993. Ein Überblick über die Extraktion aus Nominalphrasen im Deutschen. In *Extraktion im Deutschen*, ed. Franz-Josef d'Avis, Sigrid Beck, Uli Lutz, Jürgen Pafel, and Susanne Trissler, Arbeiten des Sonderforschungsbereichs 340 34, 192–245. Universität Tübingen, Universität Stuttgart.

Partee, Barbara Hall, Alice ter Meulen, and Robert A. Wall. 1993. *Mathematical methods in linguistics*. Dordrecht, Boston, London: Kluwer Academic Publishers.

Pearson, Matthew. 2000. Two types of VO languages. In *The derivation of VO and OV*, ed. Peter Svenonius, Linguistik Aktuell, 327–364. Amsterdam and Philadelphia: John Benjamins.

Perlmutter, David M., and Paul M. Postal. 1983/1972. The relational succession law. In *Studies in relational grammar 1*, ed. David M. Perlmutter, 30–80. Chicago: University of Chicago Press.

Pesetsky, David. 1982. Paths and categories. Doctoral dissertation, MIT.

Pesetsky, David. 2000. *Phrasal movement and its kin*. Linguistic Inquiry Monograph 37. Cambridge, MA: MIT Press.

Polinsky, Maria, and Eric Potsdam. 2002. Backward control. *Linguistic Inquiry* 33:245–282.

Pollock, Jean-Yves. 1989. Verb movement, universal grammar, and the structure of IP. *Linguistic Inquiry* 20:365–424.

Postal, Paul M. 1971. *Cross-over phenomena*. New York: Holt, Rinehart, and Winston.

Postal, Paul M. 1974. *On raising: One rule of English grammar and its theoretical implications*. Cambridge, MA: MIT Press.

Pullum, Geoffrey K., and Gerald Gazdar. 1982. Natural languages and context-free languages. *Linguistics and Philosophy* 4:471–504.

Ramchand, Gillian. to appear. *Verb meaning and the lexicon: A first phase syntax*. Cambridge University Press.

Richards, Marc David. 2004. Object shift and scrambling in North and West germanic. Ph.d. thesis, University of Cambrdige.

Richards, Norvin W. III. 1997. What moves where when in which language? Ph.d. dissertation, MIT.

Rizzi, Luigi. 1990. *Relativized minimality*, volume 16 of *Linguistic Inquiry Monograph*. Cambridge, MA: MIT Press.

Rizzi, Luigi. 1997. The fine structure of the left periphery. In *Elements of grammar: Handbook in generative syntax*, ed. Liliane Haegeman, 281–337. Dordrecht, Netherlands: Kluwer.

Rizzi, Luigi. 2004a. Locality and left periphery. In *Structures and beyond: Cartography of syntactic structures*, ed. Adriana Belletti, volume volume 3, 104–131. New York: Oxford University Press.

Rizzi, Luigi, ed. 2004b. *The structure of CP and IP – the cartography of syntactic structures*, volume 2 of *Oxford studies in comparative syntax. The cartography of syntactic structures*. Oxford: Oxford University Press.

Rizzi, Luigi. 2006. On the form of chains: Criterial positions and ECP effects. In *Wh-movment: moving on*, ed. Lisa Lai Shen Cheng, 97–134. Cambridge, Mass.: MIT Press.

Rochemont, Michael S., and Peter W. Culicover. 1997. Deriving dependent right adjuncts in English. In *Rightward movement*, ed. Dorothee Beerman, David Leblanc, and Henk van Riemsdijk, volume 17 of *Linguistik Aktuell*, 279–300. John Benjamins.

Ross, John Robert. 1967. Constraints on variables in syntax. Doctoral dissertation, MIT.

Sakai, Hiromu. 1994. Derivational economy in long distance scrambling. In *Formal approaches to Japanese linguistics 1*, ed. Masatoshi Kozumi and Hiroyuki Ura, volume 24 of *MIT Working Papers in Linguistics*, 295–314. MITWPL.

Sauerland, Uli. 1996. The interpretability of scrambling. In *Formal approaches to Japanese linguistics 2*, ed. Masatoshi Koizumi, Masayuki Oishi, and Uli Sauerland, volume 29 of *MIT Working Papers in Linguistics*, 213–234. MITWPL.

Savitch, Walter J., Emmon Bach, William Marsh, and Gila Sfran-Naveh, ed. 1987. *The formal complexity of natural language*. Dordrecht: Reidl.

Shieber, Stuart. 1985. Evidence against the context-freeness of natural languages. *Linguistics and Philosophy* 8:333–343.

Stabler, Edward P. 1997. Derivational minimalism. In *Logical aspects of computational linguistics*, ed. Retore, 68–95. Springer.

Stabler, Edward P. 2003. Comparing 3 perspectives on head movement. In *Head movement and syntactic theory*, ed. Anoop Mahajan. UCLA/Potsdam Working Papers in Linguistics.

Stabler, Edward P. 2004. Varieties of crossing dependencies: Structure dependence and mild context sensitivity. *Cognitive Science* 28:699–720.

Starke, Michal. 2001. Move dissolves into merge: A theory of locality. Doctoral dissertation, University of Geneva.

Starke, Michal. 2004. On the inexistence of specifiers and the nature of heads. In *Structures and beyond: The cartography of syntactic structures*, ed. Adriana Belletti, Chapter 8. Oxford University Press.

von Stechow, Arnim, and Wolfgang Sternefeld. 1988. *Bausteine syntaktischen Wissens: ein Lehrbuch der generativen Grammatik*. Opladen: Westdeutscher Verlag.

Steedman, Mark. 2000. *The syntactic process*. MIT Press.

Sternefeld, Wolfgang. 1992. Transformationstyplogie und strukturelle Hierarchie.

Ura, Hiroyuki. 1994. Varieties of raising and the feature-based bare phrase structure theory. *MIT Occasional Papers in Linguistics* 7:1–150.

Wagner, Michael. 2005. Review of verb clusters: A study of Hungarian, German and Dutch. *Linguistlist* 16.

Wexler, Kenneth, and Peter Culicover. 1980. *Formal principles of language acquisition*. Cambridge, MA: MIT Press.

Williams, Edwin. 2002. *Representation theory*. Cambridge, Mass.: MIT Press.

Williams, Edwin. 2004. The structure of clusters. In *Verb clusters*, ed. Katalin e Kiss and Henk van Riemsdijk, 173–201. John Benjamins.

Williams, Edwin S. to appear. Subjects of different heights. In *Proceedings of FASL 14 – The Princeton meeting*, ed. Hana Filip, Steven Franks, James E. Lavine, and Mila Tasseva-Kurktchieve. Slavica.

Wiltschko, Martina. 1997. D-linking, scrambling and superiority in German. *Groninger Arbeiten zu germanistischen Linguistik* 41:107–142.

Wiltschko, Martina. 1998. Superiority in German. In *Proceedings of the sixteenth West Coast Conference on Formal Linguistics*, ed. E. Curtis, J. Lyle, and G. Webster, 431–445. Stanford, CA: CSLI Publication.

Wurmbrand, Susanne. 2006. Verb clusters, verb raising, and restructuring. In *The Blackwell companion to syntax*, ed. Martin Everaert and Henk van Riemsdijk, volume 5, Chapter 75, 229–343. Blackwell.

Author's address:

Department of Phonetics and Linguistics
University College London
Gower Street
London WC1E 6BT
United Kingdom

k.abels@ucl.ac.uk

Agreement with coordinated subjects
A comparative perspective

Marjo van Koppen
University of Utrecht/UiL-OTS & NWO

I discuss the variation concerning agreement with coordinated subjects in Dutch dialects. I show that a verb or a complementizer in several variants of Dutch agrees with the first conjunct of a coordinated subject and in other variants with the coordinated subject as a whole. I argue that this variation can be accounted for by the interaction between the syntactic derivation and the post-syntactic morphological component. More specifically, I argue that syntax establishes an agreement relation with both the coordinated subject as a whole and the first conjunct of the coordinated subject. Subsequently, during the post-syntactic morphological derivation, one of these agreement relations will be overtly expressed on the Probe. The decision as to which one of the two relations is spelled out depends on the affix inventory of the language or dialect. More specifically, the subset principle is extended in such a way that, confronted with the situation in which a Probe is related to two Goals, an affix is inserted for the relation which results in the most specific agreement morphology. The analysis is extended to the typologically unrelated languages Irish and Arabic.

Keywords: coordination, complementizer agreement, first conjunct agreement, agree

1. Introduction

Corbett (1983) shows that languages have different strategies to deal with agreement with coordinated arguments. Some languages agree with one of the conjuncts of the coordinated argument (so-called *partial agreement*), others agree with the "resolved" features of the coordinated argument as a whole (henceforth referred to as *resolved agreement*). The resolved feature set is a combination of the feature sets of the conjuncts. An illustration of these two strategies is provided in

Linguistic Variation Yearbook 7 (2007), 121–161.
ISSN 1568–1483/E-ISSN 1569–9900 © John Benjamins Publishing Company

(1a) and (1b) respectively (from Johannessen 1998: 31, who attributes the example to Van Oirsouw 1987).[1]

(1) a. **Gatal**   ˀ**el-walad** we-l-banaat   ˀel-bisse
         killed-$_{3SG.M}$ [the boy and-the-girls] the cat
     b. ˀ**el-walad** we-l-banaat   **gataluu**   ˀel-bisse
         [the boy and-the-girls] killed-$_{3PL.M}$ the cat
         'The boy and the girls killed the cat.'   [Palestinian Arabic]

In (1a) the finite verb agrees with the first conjunct of the coordinated subject. In (1b), however, the feature specification on the finite verb, which is [3PL.M], is not identical to either of the feature bundles of the conjuncts, which are [3SG.M] and [3SG.F] respectively. Rather, it carries a combination of these features. The resolved feature set of a coordination of DPs is formed systematically. Corbett (1983) shows that the value for number in the resolved feature set is always plural. The value for person in this phi-feature set is dependent on the specification for person in the feature sets of the conjuncts. When (at least) one of the conjuncts has the specification first person, the resolved feature set is also first person. When none of the conjuncts is first person, but (at least) one of them is second person, the resolved feature set is specified for second person. Finally, when none of the conjuncts is first or second person, the value for person in the resolved feature set is third person.

The same pattern can be found in dialects of Dutch. I illustrate this on the basis of examples displaying so-called complementizer agreement (henceforth CA, cf. among others Hoekstra & Smits 1997; Van Haeringen 1958; Haegeman 1992; Zwart 1993). CA is the phenomenon whereby a complementizer agrees in phi-features with the embedded subject. An example of CA is provided in (2) below (from Haegeman 1992).

(2) Kpeinzen **da-n**   zunder **goa-n** kommen.
     I.think   that-$_{PL}$ they   go-$_{PL}$ come
     'I think that they are going to come.'   [Lapscheure Dutch]

In this example, the complementizer *da* 'that' agrees with the embedded subject *zunder* 'they' as is indicated by the plural inflection on this complementizer. When the subject is coordinated, dialects differ as to whether they show partial agreement or resolved agreement (data in (3b) are from the SAND-project, cf. Barbiers et al. 2005).

(3) a. Ich dink **de-s**   **doow** en ich   ôs   kenne treffe.
         I   think that-$_{2SG}$ [you$_{SG}$ and I]$_{1PL}$ each.other$_{1PL}$ can-$_{PL}$ meet
         'I think that you and I can meet.'   [Tegelen Dutch]

    b.   **Oa-n Bart en Liesje**   nie ipletn ...
        if-$_{3PL}$ [Bart and Liesje]$_{3PL}$ not watch.out
        'When Bart and Liesje don't watch out...'   [Tielt Dutch]

In (3a) the complementizer *det* agrees with the first conjunct of the coordinated subject, *doow* 'you', resulting in the form *des*.[2] If the complementizer agrees with the resolved feature set of the coordinated subject, it should have shown [1PL]-agreement. In (3b) the complementizer *oa* 'if' shows plural agreement. This means that it does not agree with one of the conjuncts as they are both singular. Rather it agrees with the resolved feature set of the coordinated subject. In this paper, I show that whether agreement with a coordinated subject leads to partial agreement or resolved agreement is not a coincidence, but rather that this is systematically determined. I argue that this type of variation can be fully reduced to the lexicon. The syntactic derivation of examples (3a) and (3b) is exactly the same. The variation arises at the level of morphology, which I assume to be post-syntactic (cf. Halle & Marantz 1993). More in particular, I show that it is the affix inventory of the language which is responsible for this type of variation.

    This paper is organized as follows. In Section 2 I provide an analysis for the data concerning CA with coordinated subjects in Dutch dialects. In Section 3 I go into the agreement relation between the finite verb and the coordinated subject.[3] Finally Section 4 sums up the results of this paper.

2.   Complementizer agreement with coordinated subjects in Dutch dialects

2.1 Prerequisite: The analysis of complementizer agreement

Before I go into the analysis of CA with coordinated subjects, I will first make explicit the analysis of CA with non-coordinated subjects. Reconsider the example in (2), repeated here as (4).

(4)   Kpeinzen **da-n**   zunder **goa-n** kommen.
     I.think   that-$_{PL}$ they   go-$_{PL}$ come
     'I think that they will come.'   [Lapscheure Dutch]

I assume, following among others Van Craenenbroeck & Van Koppen (2002) and Carstens (2003), that the presence of an affix on the complementizer indicates the presence of phi-features on C°. These phi-features on C° are – just like the phi-features on T° – uninterpretable in the sense of Chomsky (1995), which means that they require syntactic checking. Feature checking takes place via the operation

Agree (Chomsky 2000). This mechanism relates the uninterpretable, or in more recent terminology unvalued, phi-features of a certain head (the Probe) to a set of interpretable (or valued) phi-features (the Goal) in the c-command domain of the Probe. In this analysis of CA there are (at least) two sets of unvalued phi-features in the extended VP-domain of dialects with CA: on T° and on C°. The former features are spelled out on the finite verb, the latter on the complementizer. This means that the agreement morphology on the finite verb is the result of a different agreement relation than that on the complementizer. As the affix on the complementizer and the one on the finite verb are not dependent on the same relation (as for instance argued by Zwart 1993, 1997), it should be possible that the affix on the finite verb spells out different features than the one on the complementizer. The example in (3a) illustrates this: the affix on the complementizer reflects a partial agreement relation, whereas the one on the finite verb indicates resolved agreement.

Consider the structure in (5). The subject has moved to Spec,TP.[4] Then C° is merged. C° has unvalued phi-features, which have to be checked. Agree searches the c-command domain of C° and finds the interpretable phi-features of the subject as a potential Goal. This agreement relation is spelled out as CA.

(5)

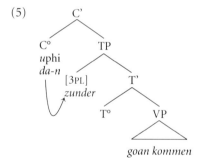

2.2 CA with a coordinated subject

In this subsection, I provide an account for the fact that in Tegelen Dutch the complementizer agrees partially with the coordination, whereas in Lapscheure Dutch it shows resolved agreement. Consider again the examples in (3a) and (3b), repeated here as (6a) and (6b) respectively.

(6) a. Ich dink **de-s**   **doow**   en   ich   ôs   kenne treffe.
         I   think that-$_{2SG}$ [you$_{SG}$ and I]$_{1PL}$ each.other$_{1PL}$ can-$_{PL}$ meet
         'I think that you and I can meet.'   [Tegelen Dutch]

b. **Oa-n Bart en Liesje**   nie ipletn...
     if-$_{3PL}$ [Bart and Liesje]$_{3PL}$ not watch.out
     'When Bart and Liesje don't watch out...'   [Tielt Dutch]

I propose that the locus of the variation found between Tegelen Dutch and Tielt
Dutch, lies in the post-syntactic lexicon rather than in the syntactic derivation. I
show that when Agree searches for a Goal in the c-command domain of Probe C°
and is confronted with a coordinated subject, it finds two equally local, matching
Goals: (i) the phi-feature set present at the maximal projection dominating both
conjuncts and (ii) the phi-feature set of the first conjunct. I propose that Agree
relates the Probe to these Goals simultaneously. The decision as to which one of
these Goals eventually determines the agreement morphology on the complementizer is postponed to the level of Morphology. It is made on the basis of the affix
inventories present in the language. When the relation with the phi-feature set of
the maximal projection determines the affix on the complementizer, the result is
resolved agreement. When, on the other hand, the relation with the first conjunct
is spelled out, the result is partial agreement. In short, I argue for an intricate interaction between Syntax and Morphology. During the syntactic derivation the
potential Goals for a certain Probe are identified. At the level of Morphology it is
decided which of these Goals determines the affix on the Probe.

In Subsection 2.2.1, I discuss the syntactic part of the derivation in detail.
This derivation is similar for Tegelen Dutch and Tielt Dutch. The morphological
part of the derivation will be provided in Subsection 2.2.2. Subsection 2.2.3 discusses a prediction concerning the relation between locality and agreement with
coordinated subjects. Finally Section 2.2.4 summarises this section.

2.2.1 *CA with a coordinated subject: Syntactic derivation*

Reconsider the examples in (6). The relevant part of the syntactic derivation of
these examples is provided in (7). The structure contains the phi-feature specification belonging to the example in (6a) from Tegelen Dutch. However, the same
structure could be used to represent the derivation of example (6b) from Tielt
Dutch, the only difference would be the phi-feature specification.

I assume coordinated subjects to be CoPs (cf. among others Kayne 1994; Johannessen 1998; Munn 1993 for argumentation). Furthermore, I assume that the
so-called 'resolved' features are present on CoP (the maximal projection dominating all conjuncts) (cf. also Soltan 2004).

(7)

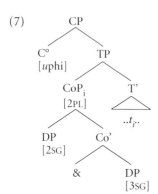

The structure in (7) represents the stage in the derivation where C° is merged with TP. The coordinated subject (CoP) has moved to Spec,TP. By assumption, C° in dialects with CA has uninterpretable phi-features. The mechanism Agree has to search for a matching Goal within the c-command domain of C°. This c-command domain contains (at least) three potential Goals with matching features,[5] i.e. CoP, the first conjunct and the second conjunct. Although all three Goals match the features of the Probe, the Probe ends up agreeing with either CoP or with the first conjunct. It never agrees with the second conjunct in the languages and dialects under discussion.[6] I argue this is the case because the second conjunct is never local enough to serve as a Goal. I define locality in terms of c-command. The definitions of respectively 'equally local' and 'more local' are provided in (8) and (9).

(8)   **Equally local**
      Y and Z are equally local to X iff,
      (i)   X c-commands both Y and Z
      (ii) the set of nodes that c-command Y is equal to the set of nodes that c-command Z.

(9)   **More local**
      Y is more local to X than Z iff,
      (i)   X c-commands both Y and Z
      (ii) the set of nodes that c-command Y is a proper subset of the set of nodes that c-command Z.

The definition of c-command is given in (10).

(10)   **C-command**
       X c-commands Y, iff
       (i)   X excludes Y[7]

(ii) the first node that dominates X, also dominates Y.[8]

For the structure in (7), this means that CoP and the first conjunct are more local to C° than the second conjunct, as the former two potential Goals are c-commanded by a proper subset of the nodes that c-command the second conjunct. CoP and the first conjunct are only c-commanded by C°, whereas the second conjunct is c-commanded by C° and by the first conjunct.[9]

CoP and the first conjunct, on the other hand, are equally local with respect to C°. They are c-command by the same set of nodes: namely only by C°. The question arises what happens if the c-command domain of the Probe contains two equally local Goals. Agree identifies an element as a suitable Goal when it meets certain requirements: it has to be local and it has to have matching features (cf. Chomsky 2000, 2001a, b).

In the configuration in (7), there are two potential Goals. They are equally local with respect to the Probe and they both have matching features. Normally, when the c-command domain of a Probe contains more than one suitable Goal, the more local Goal is selected over the other available Goal(s) (cf. Chomsky 2000, 2001a, b). As it is not the case that one of the Goals is more local to the Probe than the other, this does not work here. There are two ways to interpret the observation that Agree always relates the Probe to the more local Goal: either Agree 'sees' all available Goals in the c-command domain of the Probe, but only relates the most local Goal to the Probe or Agree only 'sees' the most local Goal with respect to the Probe. Although nothing really hinges on it, I assume that the latter interpretation of this statement is correct: Agree only 'sees' the most local Goal in the c-command domain of the Probe. When two Goals are equally local, they are found in the same application of the operation Agree. I assume that as they are identified as suitable Goals simultaneously, Agree establishes a relation between both these Goals and the Probe. The only thing the mechanism Agree can do is relate a Probe to a Goal, it cannot choose to not relate a certain Goal to the Probe. Arguably, it can also not select one Goal over the other when both are equally local. This means that the derivation as such, so with one Probe related to more than one Goal is sent off to PF and hence to Morphology. I would like to propose that it is only at this level that it is decided which one of these two Goals determines the agreement morphology on the Probe.

Concretely, this means that during the syntactic derivation of both example (6a) from Tegelen Dutch and example (6b) from Tielt Dutch, Probe C° is related to two Goals simultaneously: CoP and the first conjunct in Spec,CoP. The derivation of these two examples is exactly the same up until this point.

2.2.2 *CA with a coordinated subject: Morphological part of the derivation*
2.2.2.1 *Introduction*

When a Probe for phi-features agrees with one Goal, the agreement morphology on the Probe is determined by this Goal. Halle (1997) suggests that the insertion of affixes is regulated via the Subset Principle. The definition of this principle is provided in (11) (Halle 1997:428, cf. also Harley & Noyer 1999:5).

(11)   **Subset Principle**
   The phonological exponent of a Vocabulary Item is inserted into a morpheme in the terminal string if the item matches all or a subset of the grammatical features specified in the terminal morpheme. Insertion does not take place if the Vocabulary Item contains features not present in the morpheme. Where several Vocabulary Items meet the conditions for insertion, the item matching the greatest number of features specified in the terminal morpheme must be chosen.

When there is only one Goal for a certain Probe, the Subset Principle defines which affix is more suitable to replace the feature bundle on the Probe, i.e. which feature bundle matches most features of the Probe.

In (7), the Probe is not related to just one Goal, but to two Goals. The question arises what happens if Morphology is confronted with such a configuration. There are several logical possibilities:

i.   Both agreement relations are spelled out, resulting in two affixes on the Probe. Each affix reflects the feature specification of one Goal.
ii.   One of the agreement relations is spelled out, resulting in one affix on the Probe. The feature specification of only one of the two Goals is spelled out on the Probe.
iii. Both agreement relations are spelled out, resulting in one affix expressing (a subset of) the features of both Goals at the same time.
iv.   None of the agreement relations are spelled out, resulting in either a crashing derivation (Morphology is not able to cope with the situation) or in no agreement affix on the Probe.

I show that when this situation arises in the languages and dialects under discussion in this paper, only one of the two agreement relations is spelled out: Morphology selects one of the two available Goals to determine the agreement morphology on the Probe. I argue that in this case the Goal that determines the affix spelled out on the Probe is not selected randomly. Rather, the relation between the Probe and the Goal that results in the most specific agreement morphology will be spelled out. For the structure in (7), this means that the relation between C° and CoP takes precedence over that between C° and the first conjunct in Spec,CoP if the former relation results in more specific morphology on the Probe and vice versa.

More in particular, on the basis of the Subset Principle the most suitable affix for each of these two relations is selected, resulting in two affixes: each affix matches the features of the relation it replaces best. Next, one of these two affixes has to be inserted on the Probe. I assume that the mechanism responsible for this decision selects to insert the more specific of the two affixes, i.e. the affix expressing most features. Again this can be seen as an instance of the mechanism underlying the Subset Principle: a set of affixes is compared and the one expressing most features is selected.

This analysis is applied to Tegelen Dutch in Section 2.2.2.2 and Tielt Dutch in Section 2.2.2.3. In Section 2.2.2.4 I discuss the German dialect Bavarian. This dialect displays a combination of partial agreement and resolved agreement.

2.2.2.2 *Tegelen Dutch*
Recall the example in (3a), repeated here as (12).

(12) Ich dink **de-s**   **doow**   en   ich   ôs   kenne treffe.
      I   think that-$_{2SG}$ [you$_{SG}$ and I]$_{1PL}$ each.other$_{1PL}$ can-$_{PL}$ meet
      'I think that you and I can meet.'   [Tegelen Dutch]

At the level of Morphology, Probe C° is related to two Goals: the phi-feature set of CoP and that of the first conjunct in Spec,CoP. This configuration is given in (7) and repeated in (13).

(13)

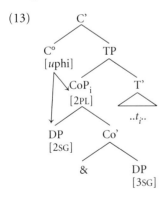

Now the question arises which of these Goals will eventually determine the agreement morphology on the Probe, i.e. on the complementizer. In order to determine this we have to investigate the complementizer agreement paradigm of this dialect.

(14)

	CA
1SG	det
2SG	de-s
3SG	det
1PL	det
2PL	det
3PL	det

This table shows that only with a [2SG]-subject, the complementizer carries an agreement affix. The other person/number combinations do not result in agreement on the complementizer. In the structure in (13) there is a choice: either the relation between C° and a [2SG]-Goal, or the relation between C° and the [2PL]-Goal has to be spelled out. The former relation leads to the s-affix on the complementizer, whereas the latter does not lead to an agreement ending at all.[10] What the example in (12) clearly shows is that in this case Morphology spells out the relation between C° and the first conjunct of the coordinated subject, resulting in partial agreement on the complementizer. This relation leads to more specific agreement morphology than the other available relation.

Given the assumptions on affix insertion, the configuration in (13) should not be able to lead to agreement on the complementizer with the coordinated subject as a whole. The reason for this is that this relation leads to less specific agreement morphology than the relation between C° and the first conjunct in Spec,CoP. This prediction is borne out by the ungrammaticality of the example in (15).

(15) *... det doow en ich ôs   treff-e.   [Tegelen Dutch]
     ... that [you$_{sg}$ and I]$_{1pl}$ each.other$_{1pl}$ meet-$_{pl}$

This analysis also predicts that when the second person pronoun does not constitute the first but the second conjunct, partial agreement is no longer possible. The reason for this is that in this case, the pronoun is not local enough to serve as a Goal for C°. As the example in (16) shows, this prediction is also borne out.

(16) ... det /*de-s   Marie en doow   uch   treff-e.
     that / that-$_{2SG}$ [Marie and you$_{SG}$]$_{2PL}$ each.other$_{2PL}$ meet-$_{PL}$
     '...that Marie and you will meet each other.'   [Tegelen Dutch]

2.2.2.3 *Tielt Dutch*

Now that we have established how partial agreement in dialects like Tegelen Dutch comes about, let's look at resolved agreement in the dialect of Tielt. First recall the example in (3b) repeated here as (17).

(17) **Oa-n Bart en Liesje** nie ipletn …
if-3PL [Bart and Liesje]3PL not watch.out
'When Bart and Liesje don't watch out…' [Tielt Dutch]

When the derivation of this example is passed on to the level of Morphology, Probe C° is related to two Goals: CoP with [3PL]-features and the first conjunct with [3SG]-features. This configuration is provided in (18).

(18)

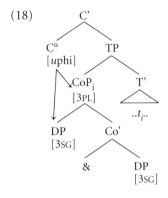

When this derivation reaches the morphological component, it has to be decided which one of these Goals determines the affix on the Probe. In order to do so, it first has to be determined which affixes belong to which Goals. Consider the paradigm of CA in Tielt Dutch below in (19). The forms provided in the second column represent the complementizer *oa* with the relevant clitic pronoun attached to them.

(19)

	CA
1SG	oa-kik
2SG	oa-je
3SG	oa-se
1PL	oa-me
2PL	oa-je
3PL	oa-n-ze

The only person/number combination with a clear agreement affix belonging to it is [3PL]. In all other persons there does not appear to be an agreement affix present. However, Haegeman (1992) argues for the dialect of Lapscheure (which is spoken in the same dialect area) that the first person plural also has an *n*-affix on the complementizer.[11] This affix is present in the surface form of the complementizer as it assimilates with the initial consonant of the pronoun. Assuming Tielt Dutch is not different from Lapscheure Dutch in this respect, this *n*-affix can be taken to either represent the feature specification [1PL] or [3PL]. The [2PL] in this dialect seems to behave like the [2SG]. For instance, the clitic pronoun for the [2SG] is equal to the one for the [2PL], as is clear from the table in (19). This is a common phenomenon in varieties of Dutch (cf. Maclean & Bennis 2005; also Goeman 1999:250 for an overview of the literature on the second person plural in Dutch dialects). Therefore, I assume that the *n*-affix has the feature specification [PL]. It is not inserted in the second person plural, as the plural feature is not present or active in this case.[12] This means that the relation between C° and CoP in (18) results in the presence of an *n*-affix on the complementizer, whereas the relation between C° and the first conjunct does not result in agreement morphology. Again it is the relation resulting in an agreement affix that takes precedence over the relation which does not result in an agreement affix.

2.2.2.4 *Bavarian*

In the preceding subsections, two cases where discussed of the configuration in which there is one Probe related to two Goals. In both these cases, one of the Goals did result in an affix on the Probe and the other one did not. I have shown that in both these cases it is the Goal resulting in an affix on the Probe that determines the Probe's agreement morphology. The only difference between these two cases is that in Tegelen Dutch it is the relation with the first conjunct that gets realized on the complementizer, resulting in partial agreement, whereas in Tielt Dutch it is the one with CoP, resulting in resolved agreement. In this subsection, I discuss a dialect in which both relations result in an affix on the complementizer, namely Bavarian.

Bavarian, like Tegelen Dutch, has CA with [2SG]-subjects. Interestingly, this German dialect also displays CA with [2PL]-subjects. This is illustrated in example (20) (cf. Bayer 1984:233).

(20) a. ... **daß-st du**   kumm-st.
          that-$_{2SG}$ you$_{SG}$ come-$_{2SG}$
          '...that you are coming.'

b.   … **daß-ts   ihr   kumm-ts.**
    that-_{2PL} you_{PL} come-_{2PL}
    '…that you are coming.'   [Bavarian]

In Bavarian, the subject can also be coordinated, resulting in the same configuration as discussed above for Tegelen Dutch and Tielt Dutch, in which the C°-Probe has both CoP and the first conjunct as its Goals. As this dialect not only shows agreement with [2SG]-subjects, but also with [2PL]-subjects, it is particularly interesting for the current investigation. It provides a case in which both the relation between C° and CoP and that between C° and the first conjunct in Spec,CoP results in CA. This is represented in the structure in (21).

(21)

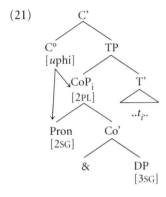

The question arises which Goal, i.e. the one with [2sg]-features or the one with [2pl]-features, determines the affix on the complementizer. Consider the table in (22) displaying the CA-paradigm in Bavarian (cf. Bayer 1984:233).

(22)

feature specification subject	affix on the complementizer
1SG	
2SG	-st
3SG	
1PL	
2PL	-ts
3PL	

This table shows that there are two agreement affixes in the CA-paradigm; one appears with [2SG]-subjects, the other with [2PL]-subjects. This means that the feature inventory of Bavarian can be represented as in (23).[13]

(23)   [2SG] → -st
         [2PL] → -ts

With this feature inventory in mind, consider the examples in (24).

(24)   a.   ... **daß-sd du**   **und d'Maria**   **an Hauptpreis gwunna**
                    that-$_{2SG}$ [you$_{SG}$ and the Maria]$_{2PL}$ the first.prize   won
              hab-ds.
              have-$_{2PL}$
         b.   ... **daβ-ds du**   **und d'Maria**   **an Hauptpreis gwunna**
                    that-$_{2PL}$ [you$_{SG}$ and the Maria]$_{2PL}$ the first.prize   won
              hab-ds.
              have-$_{2PL}$
              '...that Maria and you have won the first prize.'   [Bavarian]

In both the a- and the b-example, the 'resolved' feature specification of the coordinated subject is [2PL], as illustrated by the agreement affix on the finite verb habds
'have'. The coordinated subject contains a [2SG] first conjunct. The affix on the
complementizer can either reflect the resolved [2PL]-features of CoP, or the [2SG]-
features of the first conjunct. Put differently, both Goals are able to determine the
agreement affix on the Probe.

    This is expected given the fact that both affixes express person and number:
they are equally specific. The mechanism responsible for choosing which Goal
determines the affix on the Probe makes this decision on the basis of which affix spells out most features. In this case the affixes spell out an equal amount of
features and hence both affixes can appear. The mechanism under consideration
randomly picks one or the other affix.[14]

2.2.3   Locality and CA with coordinated subjects
One prediction the analysis of CA with coordinated subjects makes, concerns
modification of the coordinated subject. When CoP is more local with respect
to C° than the first conjunct in Spec,CoP, the first conjunct is no longer a Goal
and partial agreement should be impossible. This situation arises when the coordinated subject is modified by a focus particle. Consider the schematic representation of this configuration in (25).

(25)

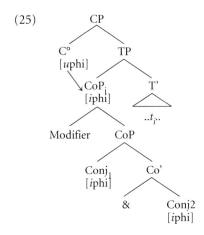

Reconsider the definition of c-command and locality provided in (8)–(10). In the configuration in (25), the first conjunct is c-commanded by the modifier and by C°. CoP is only c-commanded by C°. This means that CoP is more local with respect to C° than the first conjunct. In other words, the first conjunct is a potential Goal for C°, but as it is not local enough, C° cannot enter into an agreement relation with this Goal. This means that when there is an element modifying CoP, CA reflecting the features of the first conjunct in Spec,CoP should not be possible. With this reasoning in mind, consider the data in (26) from Tegelen Dutch.[15]

(26)   ... det / $^?$de-s   auch doow en   Anna   komm-e
          that / that-$_{2SG}$ also [you$_{SG}$ and Anna]$_{2PL}$ come-$_{PL}$
          '... that you and Anna will also be coming.'   [Tegelen Dutch]

Two things have to be noted about this example. First of all, both the complementizer with CA and the complementizer without CA are possible in this example. This is remarkable as in example (15) from Tegelen Dutch, repeated here as (27), only the variant with the inflected complementizer is possible.

(27)   ... de-s   / *det doow en   ich   ôs   treff-e.
          that-$_{2SG}$ / that [you$_{SG}$ and I]$_{1PL}$ each.other$_{1PL}$ meet-$_{PL}$
          '...that you and I will meet each other.'   [Tegelen Dutch]

The second thing that has to be noted about the example in (26) is that the use of the complementizer with CA results in a more degraded sentence than the use of the non-inflected complementizer. However, the prediction introduced above is not fully met by these data. In the example from Tegelen Dutch, CA reflecting the agreement relation with the first conjunct of the coordinated subject only leads

to a degraded but not to a fully ungrammatical sentence. I would like to argue
that this is caused by the fact that the modifier, in this case the focus particle *auch*
'also', can be either modifying the coordinated subject as a whole or just the first
conjunct. When it modifies the coordinated subject as a whole, it modifies CoP
and in this case the focus particle c-commands the first conjunct. This is illustrated
in (25). If, on the other hand, the focus particle modifies just the first conjunct,
then it is still equally local to C° as CoP. The latter configuration is reflected in the
structure in (28).

(28)

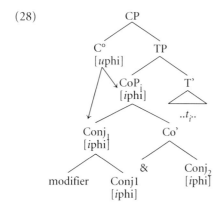

In (28), the modifier is not c-commanding the first conjunct. CoP and Conj1 are
equally local with respect to C° as the set of nodes c-commanding CoP is equal to
the set of nodes c-commanding Conj1. This means that C° can agree with both
CoP and the first conjunct and hence that the complementizer can show partial
agreement.

   In other words, the the example in (26) is syntactically ambiguous. We can
disambiguate this example in the following way. Consider the example in (29).

(29)   Context: I think that not only HE and Marie will have to dance, but

     ... de-s   auch **DOOW** en   Marie   zulle moete   danse.
     that-$_{2SG}$ also   [YOU$_{SG}$ and Marie] will   have.to dance
     '...that YOU and Marie also have to dance.'   [Tegelen Dutch]

In this example, stress is put on the first conjunct, forcing the interpretation in
which the focus particle modifies just the first conjunct. In this case, the use
of the inflected complementizer results in a fully grammatical sentence. The informant notes however that the non-inflected complementizer can also occur in
this example.

This analysis makes two further predictions. First of all, modification of the subject by a focus particle should not have this effect when the subject is not co-ordinated. In this case, the focus particle is merged with the maximal projection of the pronominal projection. However, this does not have any influence on the locality of the phi-features of the pronominal projection to C°. As a consequence, the complementizer should be able to agree with a modified subject pronoun. This prediction is borne out by the example in (30).

(30)   ... de-s   / $^{?*}$det   auch **doow** kum-s.
          that-$_{2SG}$ /   that also   you$_{SG}$ come-$_{2SG}$
          '...that you too will come.'   [Tegelen Dutch]

Secondly, in a dialect in which CA reflects the agreement relation with CoP, rather than the one with the first conjunct, modification of the subject by a modifier should not have any influence on the appearance of CA. The reason for this is that no matter where the focus particle attaches, CoP will always be local enough to serve as a Goal. In Lapscheure Dutch, like in Tielt Dutch, the complementizer agrees with CoP as illustrated in example (31) (from Haegeman 1992).

(31)   ... da-n   /*da **Valère en Pol**   morgen   goa-n.
          that-$_{3PL}$ / that [Valère and Pol]$_{3PL}$ tomorrow go-$_{PL}$
          '...that Valère and Pol will go tomorrow.'   [Lapscheure Dutch]

As expected, CA has to appear when the coordinated subject is modified by a focus particle, as is illustrated by the example in (32) (Liliane Haegeman p.c.).

(32)   ... da-n   /*da zelfs **Valère en Pol**   morgen   goa-n.
          that-$_{3PL}$ / that even [Valère and Pol]$_{3PL}$ tomorrow go-$_{PL}$
          '...that even Valère and Pol will go tomorrow.'   [Lapscheure Dutch]

Although more thorough investigation into modification of coordinated subjects and the appearance of partial agreement on the complementizer should be carried out, the data point into the direction predicted by the analysis of partial agreement on the complementizer provided in the previous subsections.

2.2.4 *Conclusion*
The analysis put forth in this section for CA with coordinated subjects claims that the variation attested in this construction results from differences in the lexicon. This result is in line with the assumptions about the locus of micro-variation advocated in the Minimalist Program: micro-variation should be reduced to variation in the lexicon (cf. Chomsky 1995: 169–170). The syntactic part of the analysis is

exactly the same for all three dialects under consideration here: Bavarian, Tegelen Dutch and Tielt Dutch. A Probe encounters two Goals at the same time and enters into an agreement relation with these two Goals. The question whether a Probe ends up showing partial agreement or resolved agreement is entirely dependent upon which of these two agreement relations results in more specific agreement morphology.

3.   Verbal agreement with coordinated subjects in Dutch dialects

In this section, I discuss agreement between the finite verb and the subject. The agreement morphology on the finite verb is a reflex of the agreement relation between the clausal head T° and the subject. The question arises if this Probe behaves similar with respect to coordinated subjects as C°. Put differently, the question arises if the finite verb also shows either partial agreement or resolved agreement.

I show that given the current assumptions on the interaction between Syntax and Moprhology, T° is expected to enter into an agreement relation with both Goals, resulting in either partial agreement or resolved agreement on the finite verb. Counter to these expectations the finite verb cannot agree with the first conjunct or the coordinated subject in the SVO- and the CSOV-order. Consider the structures in (33) and (34), representing the stage of the derivation in which respectively T° and C° are merged.

(33)

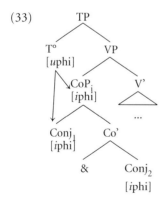

(34)

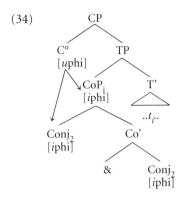

According to the assumption concerning locality and c-command provided in (8)–(10), it is the case that in both (33) and (34), the Probe (T° and C° respectively) encounters two equally local Goals: CoP and the first conjunct in Spec,CoP. In the preceding section, I have shown that this configuration leads to a situation in which the complementizer (on which the features of C° are spelled out) can show resolved agreement or partial agreement. Given the similarity between the configuration in (33) and (34), one would expect that the finite verb (on which the features of T° are spelled out) also has both options. This expectation is not borne out by the data, however. In the dialects of Dutch and German discussed here, the finite verb cannot agree with the first conjunct of the coordinated subject in the SVO- and CSOV-word order. This is exemplified by the examples in (35) and (36) for Tegelen Dutch and Bavarian respectively.

(35) Doow   en   Marie   *ontmoet-s / ontmoet-e uch.
      [you_SG and Marie]_2PL meet-_2SG / meet-_PL each.other_2PL
      'You and Marie will meet each other.'   [Tegelen Dutch]

(36) Du   und d'Maria   *ho-sd   / hab-ds an Hauptpreis gwunna.
      [you_SG and the.maria]_2PL have-_2SG / have-_2PL the first.prize won
      'You and Maria have won the first prize.'   [Bavarian]

In the next subsection, I go into the difference between verbal agreement and CA with respect to their behaviour concerning coordinated subjects. I show that the difference is caused by the fact that the coordinated subject moves out of the c-command domain of T°, whereas it does not move out of C°'s c-command domain.

3.1 Movement and its consequences for agreement

The question that has to be answered is why C° entertains a relation with the first conjunct in Spec,CoP at the level of Morphology, whereas T° does not. The only property distinguishing T° from C° with respect to the relation with the subject is that the coordinated subject moves out of the c-command domain of T° during the syntactic derivation, while it does not move out of the c-command domain of C°. This is depicted in the structures in (37) and (38).

(37)

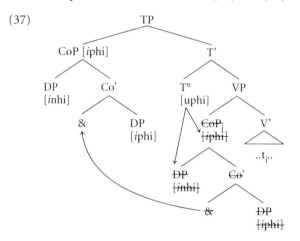

(38)

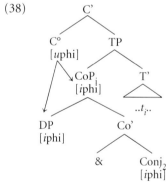

In (38), the coordinated subject containing C°'s Goals, CoP and the first conjunct in Spec,CoP, does not (necessarily) move out of the c-command domain of Probe C°. In (37), on the other hand, the coordinated subject does move out of the c-command domain of T° to Spec,TP necessarily in order to fulfill T°'s EPP requirement. The fact that movement of the coordinated subject past the Probe leads to the bleeding of partial agreement on that Probe has also been observed for other languages. Consider, for instance, the data in (39) from Polish (cf. Citko 2004: 1–2).

(39) a. Do pokoju **weszła**   **młoda kobieta** i   chłopiec
           to   room   entered$_{F.SG}$ [young woman and boy]
           'Into the room walked a young woman and boy.'

      b. młoda kobieta i   mały chłopiec weszli   /*weszła   do
           [young woman and small boy   ] entered$_{PL}$ / entered$_{SG}$ to
           pokoju
           room
           'A young woman and a small boy entered the room.'   [Polish]

In this example, the finite verb agrees with the first conjunct of a coordinated post verbal subject, but it cannot agree with the first conjunct of a coordinated pre-verbal subject. This effect has not only be noted for Polish, but also for – for instance – Arabic as shown in example (1) (cf. Soltan 2004; Aoun et al. 1994; Munn 1999), Russian (cf. Babyonyshev 1996), modern and biblical Hebrew (cf. Doron 2000) and Brazilian Portugese (cf. Munn 1999).[16] The impossibility of partial agreement with movement thus seems to be a more common characteristic. The question is how movement of the coordinated subject out of T°'s c-command domain affects the agreement relations T° entertains. In order to account for this, I make two assumptions: (i) the mechanism Agree takes place at Spell Out (cf. among others Chomsky 2000: 13–14, Van Craenenbroeck & Van Koppen 2002) and (ii) copies of movement are inaccessible for operations like Agree (cf. also Van Koppen 2005, 2006a).[17] There are two ways to implement the idea that the internal structure of copies is not available for these kinds of relations. The first one is to assume that copies do not have internal structure at all, but rather only contain the features present on the maximal projection of the moved item. I refer to this type of copies as reduced copies. Reduced copies are very much comparable to traces, i.e. items left behind by the moved item that only serves as a placeholder or marker of the moved item. As the copy does not have internal structure, there cannot be a relation with an item that is part of this internal structure. This way of looking at copies of movement provides a natural explanation for the fact that spelled out copies of movement are always reduced in the sense that they spell out only the functional features of the moved item (cf. also Van Koppen 2005, 2006a). However, current analyses of reconstruction (cf. among others Chomsky 1993; Sauerland 1998), which assume that reconstruction takes place via copies, form a problem for assuming reduced copies or traces. As the reduced copy only contains the features of the maximal projection, it is unclear how reconstruction should be analysed. Although there are ways to deal with reconstruction without making use of copies of movement,[18] I will leave this hypothesis as a subject for further research (cf. Van Koppen 2006a).

Another, potentially somewhat less controversial, way to implement the idea that the internal structure of copies is not accessible for agreement relations is to assume that copies of moved items are in fact similar to these moved items, but that they are for some (yet to be uncovered) reason opaque for agreement relations.[19] As copies of movement are similar to the moved item, reconstruction can be analysed via the – by now – standard way, making use of the copy theory of movement (cf. among others Chosmky 1993; Sauerland 1998). Extending the copy-metaphor, one could think of copies as PDF-documents: the internal structure of the document is visible, but not accessible. The copy is so to say 'frozen' (cf. also Uriagereka 1999). The internal structure is present, but cannot be accessed.

Given these two assumptions, the difference between verbal agreement with coordinated subjects and CA with coordinated subjects can be analyzed as follows. Consider the structures in (37) and (38), repeated here as (40) and (41) respectively. As the subject necessarily moves out of the c-command domain of T° (to check T°'s EPP-feature), T° always agrees with a copy of the moved subject, as illustrated in example (40). The internal structure of this copy is inaccessible, represented by the box, agreement with the first conjunct is never possible, represented by the arrow bouncing off. This means that partial agreement on the verb does not occur, as probe T° has never entered into an agreement relation with the first conjunct. It only agrees with CoP. As a result, the verb always shows resolved agreement. C° can show both partial agreement and resolved agreement, as the subject does not necessarily move out of its c-command domain. It does not agree with a copy of the subject, which means that the internal structure and hence the first conjunct in Spec,CoP is visible.

(40)

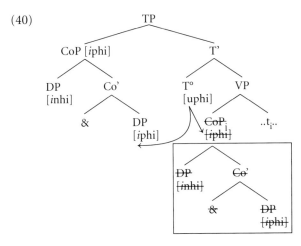

(41)

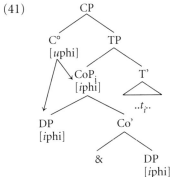

3.2 Predictions of the analysis

The analysis provided in the preceding subsections makes a number of interesting predictions. First of all, if a coordinated subject does not move out of VP, partial agreement is expected to occur on the finite verb. This prediction should not only hold for the dialects of Dutch discussed here, but should be a more general characteristic of language. When it is indeed the case that a Probe has the ability to agree with both CoP and the first conjunct in Spec,CoP because both are equally local, partial agreement is expected to occur in the VS-order in more languages than Dutch dialects. However, there are two requirements a language has to meet in order for partial agreement to appear on the finite verb in the VS-order: first of all, it has to be the case that the VS-order is the result of the subject staying lower than the head containing phi-features. In other words, when the VS-order is derived from movement of the subject to the specifier of the inflectional head and concomitant movement of the inflectional head to a higher functional head, partial agreement is not expected to occur on the finite verb. The reason for this is that in the latter case the subject has moved out of the c-command domain of the phi-Probe and hence that the phi-Probe agrees with the copy of the moved item. As a consequence, partial agreement is impossible. Secondly, given the assumption that the relation resulting in the most specific agreement morphology is spelled out on the complementizer, the agreement paradigm has to be such that the relation with the first conjunct results in more specific agreement morphology on the verb. When this is not the case, resolved agreement rather than partial agreement is expected to appear on the finite verb. As I have already mentioned above, there are indeed many languages that allow for partial agreement in the VSO-order but that do not have partial agreement in the SVO-order. In this section, I demonstrate this on the basis of agreement between coordinated subjects and finite verbs in VSO-languages like Irish and Arabic.[20] A second prediction is that partial agreement on the complementizer is not compatible with extracted subjects, whereas resolved agreement on the complementizer is.

3.2.1 *First conjunct agreement in Irish and Standard Arabic*
I have proposed that the absence of partial agreement on the finite verb is the result of movement of the coordinated subject out of the c-command domain of $T°$. The subject leaves behind a copy of movement. The internal structure of this copy is not accessible for agreement relations. As a consequence, Agree cannot establish an agreement relation between $T°$ and the first conjunct in Spec,CoP. If the subject does not move out of this domain, however, the situation arises in which partial agreement on the finite verb is expected to be able to arise. In this case the subject is not a copy of movement, it is not inaccessible and the agreement relation between $T°$ and the first conjunct in Spec,CoP can be established and spelled out on the finite verb. This situation is schematically represented by the structure in (42).

(42)

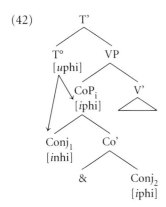

When the derivation in (42) is sent off to the interfaces without any further move-ment of the subject, one of these two relations has to be spelled out at the level of Morphology. When the relation between T° and the first conjunct in Spec,CoP is spelled out, partial agreement appears on the finite verb. I argue that this is exactly what happens in Irish and Standard Arabic. First consider the example in (43) (from McCloskey 1986: 248).[21]

(43) Bhíos   *pro*-féin   agus Tomás   ag   caint   le   chéile
      be-~PAST~1SG~ [*pro*-EMPH and   Thomas] talk PROG. with each.other
      'Thomas and I were talking to one another.'   [Irish]

This example shows the customary VSO-word order in Irish: the finite verb pre-cedes the subject which in turn precedes the rest of the clause. McCloskey (1996) argues convincingly that in the VSO-order in this language the verb is in T° and the subject stays in Spec,VP. What is striking about this example, is that affix on the finite verb *bhíos* 'be' does not show resolved agreement, but rather partial agree-ment. As such, this example from Irish corroborates the prediction made by the analysis for the absence of partial agreement on the finite verb in varieties of Dutch discussed in the previous section: it shows that partial agreement can occur on the finite verb if the subject does not move out of the c-command domain of T°.[22] Furthermore, a closer inspection of the Irish agreement pattern shows that the ap-pearance of partial agreement on the finite verb instantiates another case in which the relation resulting in the most specific agreement morphology is spelled out. To see this, consider the derivation in (44) of the example in (43).

(44)

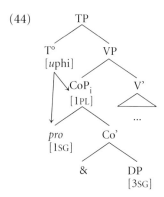

Just as in the varieties of Dutch discussed above, Probe T° has unvalued phi-features and is confronted with two potential Goals, CoP and the first conjunct in Spec,CoP. At the level of Morphology, one of these two available relations has to be spelled out on the finite verb. In order to see which relation results in richer agreement morphology on the finite verb, a closer look at the agreement system of Irish is required. As McCloskey & Hale (1984) show, Irish has two verbal forms: (i) an analytic form which is invariant and used with overt subjects and (ii) a synthetic form that inflects for person and number, but that is not compatible with overt subjects. These two forms are in complementary distribution: either the analytic form is used with an overt pronoun, or the synthetic form is used without an overt pronoun. If there is a synthetic form available, then this form has to be used. The analytic form results in ungrammaticality in that case. This illustrated in the examples in (45) (from McCloskey & Hale 1984: 490–491).

(45) a. Chuirfinn   isteach ar an phost sin.
         put$_{\text{CONDIT.ISG}}$ in   on the job   that
         'I would apply for that job.'
     b. *Chuirfinn   mé insteach ar an phost sin.
         put$_{\text{CONDIT.ISG}}$ I   in   on the job   that
     c. *Chuirfeadh   mé insteach ar an phost sin
         put$_{\text{ANALYTIC}}$ I   in   on the job   that
     d. Chuirfeadh   Eoghan insteach ar an phost sin
         put$_{\text{ANALYTIC}}$ Owen   in   on the job   that
         'Owen would apply for that job.'   [Irish]

The contrast in grammaticality between the example in (45a) and the one in (45c) shows that if there is a synthetic form available, it has to be used: using the analytic form leads to ungrammaticality. In (45d) the analytic verb form can occur, as there is no synthetic form available. Furthermore, comparison of the example in (45a) with the one in (45b) shows that a synthetic form is not compatible with an overt subject pronoun.

In the derivation in (44), Morphology is confronted with an inflectional head T° that entertains two agreement relations, one with CoP and one with pro in Spec,CoP. If the relation between T° and CoP would be spelled out, the verb would show up in its analytic or non-inflected form, as the coordination as a whole is an overt subject and hence cannot be combined with a synthetic verb form. If on the other hand the relation between T° and the first conjunct in Spec,CoP is spelled out, the verb appears in the synthetic form, as the first conjunct of this subject is non-overt pro. So, as the relation between T° and the first conjunct in Spec,CoP results in more specific agreement morphology on the finite verb, it is this relation which is spelled out.

The same reasoning can be applied to Standard Arabic. Consider the examples in (46) (from Harbert & Bahloul 2002: 50–51).

(46) a. **xaraj-at al-bintu** wa ʔal-waladu
           left-$_{3SG.F}$ [the girl and the boy]
           'The girl and the boy left.'
      b. **xaraj-a** ʔ**al-waladu** wa   al-bintu
           left-$_{3SG.M}$ [the boy   and the girl]
           'The boy and the girl left.'   [Standard Arabic]

These examples show that in the VSO-order in Standard Arabic, the verb agrees with the first conjunct of the coordinated subject. The example in (46a) shows that when the first conjunct is feminine, the agreement on the finite verb is also feminine. When the first conjunct is masculine – as in the example in (46b) – the agreement on the finite verb is also masculine.[23] One dominant point of view concerning VSO-clauses in Arabic is that the finite verb occupies the head of the inflectional projection and the subject stays inside the VP (cf. among others Fassi-Fehri 1993; Bahloul & Harbert 1992; Harbert & Bahloul 2002; Mohammad 2000; Soltan 2004).[24,25] The situation in Standard Arabic is – given this view – parallel to that in Irish. The verb is in the inflectional projection. It searches its c-command domain and finds two equally local suitable Goals to agree with, i.e. CoP and the first conjunct in Spec,CoP. It agrees with the first conjunct of the coordinated subject.[26] Interestingly, in Standard Arabic, in contrast to Irish, the coordinated subject can move past the finite verb, resulting in an SVO-clause. In these types of clauses partial agreement is not possible to appear on the finite verb, as predicted by the analysis. Consider the examples in (47) (from Mohammad 2000: 112).

(47) a. **al-waladu wa ?al bintu** xaraj-aa
          [the boy   and the girl] left-_{M.DUAL}
          'The boy and the girl left.'
     b. **al bintu wa ?al-waladu** xaraj-aa
          [the girl and the boy]   left-_{M.DUAL}
          'The girl and the boy left.'   [Standard Arabic]

The agreement on the finite verb in these examples necessarily reflects masculine dual features, regardless of the order of the conjuncts. It cannot show partial agreement. This is expected under the analysis of partial agreement put forth in the previous subsection. The subject in these examples moves to the specifier of the inflectional projection, out of the c-command domain of the inflectional head. The internal structure of the copy which the coordinated subject leaves behind by movement is inaccessible for agreement relations. This means that when Agree takes place, the inflectional head has no other option than to agree with CoP. This results in resolved agreement on the finite verb.

To summarise, in contrast to finite verbs in Dutch dialects, finite verbs in Irish and Standard Arabic agree with the first conjunct of a coordinated subject. Partial agreement on the finite verb in these languages is possible because – in contrast to the varieties of Dutch – the coordinated subject has the option not to move out of the c-command domain of T°. As predicted, movement of the coordinated subject out of the c-command domain in Standard Arabic leads to bleeding of partial agreement on the finite verb in this language.

Partial agreement in Irish and Standard Arabic can be analysed in exactly the same way as partial agreement on the complementizer in varieties of Dutch. In all cases, a Probe is confronted with two equally local Goals. The Probe enters in an agreement relation with both Goals. Morphology has to spell out one of these agreement relations. The features of the relation resulting in the most specific agreement morphology are spelled out on the Probe.

3.2.2 *Subject extraction in CA-dialects*

I have argued that partial agreement cannot occur on the finite verb in SVO- and CSOV-clauses due to movement of the coordinated subject out of T°s c-command domain. The prediction this analysis makes is that if the coordinated subject moves out of C°s c-command domain, partial agreement should no longer be a possibility on the complementizer either. This prediction is borne out by the example in (48) from Tegelen Dutch.[27]

(48)   Doow en   Marie denk ik,
        [You_SG and Marie] think I

    a. *... **de-s**   het spel   zull-e winnen.
             that-_2SG the game will-_PL win

    b. ?... det het spel   zull-e winnen.   [Tegelen Dutch]
             that the game will-_PL win

The examples in (48) show that the complementizer cannot be inflected when the subject is extracted. The relevant part of the derivation of the example in (48) is represented by the tree structure in (49).

(49)

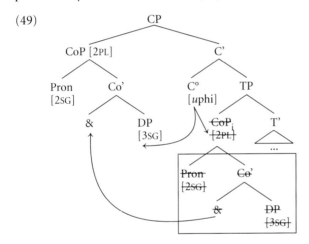

The subject CoP has moved from Spec,TP to Spec,CP in the derivation represented in (49). Specifically, it has moved to the edge of the strong CP-phase so that it is available for further movement. By moving, it has left a copy in Spec,TP. The internal structure of this copy is inaccessible for agreement relations. Agree takes place when the derivation is sent off to PF. As a consequence, the agreement relations of C° are established with the copy of the moved subject and not with the moved subject itself. In other words, when Agree takes place, no agreement relation between C° and the first conjunct in Spec,CoP can be established. Agree relates the unvalued features of C° to those of CoP. This relation has to be spelled out on the complementizer. As the [2PL]-features of this Goal do not correspond to an agreement affix that can appear on the complementizer, the non-inflected complementizer has to be inserted.

    This analysis in turn makes two further predictions concerning CA with extracted subjects. First of all, if a non-coordinated [2SG]-subject moves to the matrix clause, CA is expected to be maintained. Secondly, if a coordinated subject is extracted in a dialect that agrees with the coordinated subject as a whole, like Lapscheure Dutch, CA is expected to be possible. The first prediction is borne out by the example in (50) from Tegelen Dutch (for similar data from Frisian cf. De Haan 1997).

> (50)   Doow denk ik de-s   de wedstrijd zal-s   winnen.
>   You   think I   that-₂ₛɢ the game   will-₂ₛɢ win
>   'YOU, I think will win the game.'   [Tegelen Dutch]

This example shows that when a simplex [2SG]-subject is extracted, the complementizer is inflected. The relevant part of the derivation of this example is given in (51).

(51)

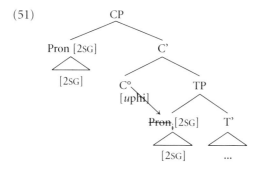

The subject of the embedded clause doow 'you' has moved to Spec,CP, the edge of the strong phase level. It has left behind a copy in Spec,TP. The internal structure of this copy is not available for agreement relations. When the subject does not move out of the c-command domain of C°, Morphology spells out the relation between C° and the maximal projection of this pronoun. When the subject has moved, Morphology can still spell out this relation, as the maximal projection of the copy of the moved pronoun is available for agreement relations, although its internal structure is not. As expected, the complementizer shows CA even when the [2SG]-subject is extracted in this dialect.

   The second prediction is corroborated by Lapscheure Dutch (Liliane Haegeman p.c.).[28] As already illustrated in example (31) repeated here as (52a), Lapscheure Dutch – on a par with Tielt Dutch – shows resolved agreement on the complementizer. Interestingly, when this coordinated subject is extracted, as in (52b), the agreement morphology does not disappear, as expected.

(52) a. … **da-n** **Pol en Valère** morgen goa-n kommen
           that-₃ₚₗ [Pol and Valère]₃ₚₗ tomorrow go-ₚₗ come
           '…that Pol and Valère will come tomorrow.'

     b. ?**Pol en Valère** peinzen-k **da-n** morgen goa-n kommen
          [Pol and Valère]₃ₚₗ think-I that-₃ₚₗ tomorrow go-ₚₗ come
          'Pol and Valère, I think that will come tomorrow.' [Lapscheure Dutch]

The crucial part of the derivation of this example is given in (53).

(53)

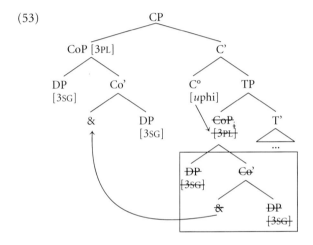

The coordinated subject has moved from Spec,TP to the edge of the strong phase-level, in order to move further into the matrix clause. In (53), T° cannot agree with the first conjunct, as the internal structure of the copy of the moved subject is opaque for agreement relations. At the spell out point to PF, Agree relates C° to CoP only. Consequently, CoP determines the affix on the complementizer. In this dialect it is the case that both when the subject moves out of the c-command domain of C° and when it does not move out of this domain, the relation with CoP is spelled out on the complementizer. Extraction of the subject out of the c-command domain of C° therefore has no effect on CA.

The same point can be made on the basis of data from Bavarian. Recall that Bavarian complementizers show agreement in the second person singular and in the second person plural. Agreement between a complementizer and a [2PL]-coordinated subject with a [2SG]-first conjunct can result in either partial agreement or resolved agreement on the complementizer. This is illustrated in the examples in (24), repeated as (54).

(54) a. … **das-sd du**   und d'Maria   an Hauptpreis gwunna
          that-$_{2SG}$ [you$_{SG}$ and the Maria]$_{2PL}$ the first.prize   won
          hab-ds
          have-$_{2PL}$

      b. … **das-ds du**   und **d'Maria**   an Hauptpreis gwunna
          that-$_{2PL}$ [you$_{SG}$ and the Maria]$_{2PL}$ the first.prize   won
          hab-ds
          have-$_{2PL}$
          '…that Maria and you won the first prize.'   [Bavarian]

Given the analysis presented above, the complementizer in Bavarian should still
show [2PL]-agreement after extraction of the coordinated subject, but not [2SG]-
agreement. This prediction is borne out by the data in (55).

(55)
          Du   und d'Maria   glaub'e
          [you$_{SG}$ and the Maria]$_{2PL}$ believe.I
      a. *__das-sd__ an Hauptpreis gwunna hab-ds
          that-$_{2SG}$ the first.prize   won   have-$_{2PL}$
      b. **das-ds** an Hauptpreis gwunna hab-ds
          that-$_{2PL}$ the first.prize   won   have-$_{2PL}$
          'You and Maria I think that have won the first prize.'   [Bavarian]

This example once again shows that when the coordinated subject is extracted,
partial agreement is no longer possible, but resolved agreement is, as expected.

4.   Summary

I have shown that a Probe for phi-features with a coordinated subject in its c-
command domain encounters two equally local Goals: namely CoP and the first
conjunct of the coordinated subject occupying the specifier of CoP. This configuration is represented in the structure in (56).

(56)

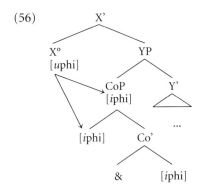

I have shown on the basis of hitherto undiscussed data from Germanic dialects that when the Probe is C°, either the agreement relation with CoP or that with Conj1 can be spelled out on the complementizer: resulting in resolved agreement on the complementizer or partial agreement respectively. I have shown that these two 'strategies' for agreement with coordinated subjects identified by Corbett (1983) are actually two sides of the same coin: partial agreement arises when the relation with the first conjunct results in more specific agreement morphology, and resolved agreement when the relation with CoP does. Furthermore, partial agreement is possible on the complementizer (in dialects which display CA), but never on the finite verb in CSOV- and SVO-clauses. The agreement morphology on the finite verb reflects the phi-features of T°, the complementizer those of C°. There is no straightforward reason why C° can, but T° cannot agree with the first conjunct of a coordinated subject. I have argued that the inability of T° to agree with the first conjunct of a coordinated subject is related to the movement of the coordinated subject out of the c-command domain of T°. In other words, I have shown that partial agreement can only arise when the coordinated subject is within the c-command domain of the Probe, otherwise the Probe necessarily shows resolved agreement. I have argued that T° cannot agree with the first conjunct, because T° – in contrast to C° – agrees with the copy of the moved subject. By assumption, the internal structure of this copy is unavailable for agreement relations. I have shown that this analysis of agreement with coordinated subjects can be applied to the Germanic dialects under discussion, as well as to Arabic and Irish.

Notes

1. I come back to this example and also to the difference in word order in Subsection 3.2.1.

2. Interestingly, the agreement ending on the complementizer and the one on the finite verb do not reflect the same feature specification in example (3a). The one on the complementizer reflects second person singular features, the agreement ending on the finite verb, however, shows second person plural features. This state of affairs is interesting in view of recent ideas concerning feature inheritance (cf. Chomsky 2005, 2006). In short, the idea is that only the phase head, i.c. C°, has phi-features. These phi-features are inherited by T° upon merger of C°. As the feature set of T° originates in C° one might expect the agreement ending on the complementizer, which I assume to spell out C°'s phi-features, and the one on the finite verb, spelling out T°'s phi-features, to spell out the same agreement relation. This is not necessarily the case, however, as is illustrated in example (3a). For discussion of the relevance of these data in light of these new proposals, I refer the reader to Van Koppen (2006b), Van Craenenbroeck & Van Koppen (2007).

3. In this paper I restrict myself to verbal agreement with coordinated subject in SVO- and CSOV-contexts. For a discussion of agreement with coordinated subjects in VSO-contexts in Dutch dialects, I refer the reader to Van Koppen (2005).

4. It is standardly assumed that once the subject has checked its case features against T° it can no longer be used as a Goal since it is not active anymore (cf. Chomsky 2000). However, Carstens (2003) argues that the subject is still active upon merger of the complementizer.

5. 'Matching features' are features that are of the same type (for instance phi-features). They do not necessarily have to have the same values.

6. In this paper, I restrict myself to the interaction between resolved agreement and partial agreement with the first conjunct. Although Second Conjunct Agreement is not possible in the languages and dialects under discussion in this paper, it is in languages like Swahili (cf. Johannessen 1998). I refer the reader to Van Koppen (2005) for a short discussion of Second Conjunct Agreement in relation to the proposal provided in this paper.

7. X excludes Y if no segment of X dominates Y.

8. I do not assume the derived notion of dominance (May 1985; Chomsky 1986) in which X dominates Y iff all segments of X dominate Y. Rather, I assume the primitive notion of domination in which X dominates Y iff X is higher up the tree than Y such that you can trace a line from A to B going only downwards (cf. Lexicon of Linguistics).

9. An anonymous reviewer wonders what happens when there are more than two conjuncts. The short answer to this question is that still only the first conjunct or the CoP are available for agreement. Because of space limitations, I cannot go into this question in more detail here. The reader is referred to Van Koppen (2005) for an in depth discussion of agreement with coordination containing more than two conjuncts. It is shown there that also in this case it holds that the first conjunct and CoP are the only two available Goals for the Probe.

10. It is of course possible that in the person/number combinations that do not trigger overt agreement on the complementizer, there is actually a zero affix present. If this is the case, this zero affix is presumably less specific than the *s*-affix, as the latter singles out a specific person/number combination: second person singular, whereas the latter behaves more like an elsewhere affix: it is inserted in all sorts of different phi-feature environments.

11. In the dialect of Lapscheure (cf. Haegeman 1992) there is also an *n*-affix present in the first person singular. This affix cannot appear in Tielt Dutch. Furthermore, Haegeman (1992) provides some evidence in favour of the idea that there is an underlying *t*-element in the third person singular and the second person in Lapscheure Dutch. I refer to Van Koppen (2005) for an in depth discussion of CA in this dialect and also for arguments showing that this *t*-element is indeed present, but should not be considered an affix.

12. The question arises at this point how the fact that the second person plural behaves like a second person singular should be implemented in the system. One way of implementing it would be to stipulate an impoverishment rule (cf. Bonet 1991) that states that in the environment of the feature specification second person, plural is not active.

13. At this point the question arises if the feature value singular should be present in the feature inventory. Harley & Ritter (2002) for instance argue that negative feature values, expressing the default value of a feature, are not present in the feature inventory. However, I do assume that the default values of features are present in the affix inventory (cf. also Vanden Wyngaerd 1994; Rooryck 2000; Van Koppen 2005).

14. Halle & Marantz (1993) also discuss cases in which it is impossible to establish which affix should be inserted on the basis of the feature specifications of the competing affixes. They suggest that in this case one affix should be stipulated as the winner '...*by imposing an extrinsic order of precedence between the two Vocabulary entries in question...*' (Halle & Marantz 1993: 120). This mechanism is clearly not at work in the case of Bavarian. In Bavarian it is not the case that one affix is stipulated as the winner, but rather that either one of the competing affixes is inserted.

15. For argumentation in favour of the claim that focus particles are adjuncts, rather than projecting there own category, cf. Barbiers (1995:71). Furthermore, I refer the reader to Barbiers (2003) for argumentation in support of the idea that focus particles are adjuncts attached to the projection they are modifying, rather than being clausal adverbs as argued for by Büring & Hartmann (2001).

16. Inversion of subject and verb seems to have a more general effect on agreement. Samek-Lodovici (2002), among others, argues that agreement impoverishes under subject inversion. He provides examples from among other languages Standard Arabic (cf. also Bahloul & Harbert 1992 for similar observations), Trentino and Fiorentino (cf. also Brandi & Cordin 1989).

17. There are several other potential analyses for the fact that movement leads to the impossibility of partial agreement. For instance, the fact that the subject is in a Spec,Head-relation with Probe T°, but not with Probe C° might be relevant for the impossibility of partial agreement in the former case. For arguments against this view, cf. Van Koppen (2005).

18. First of all, the question should be raised if reconstruction should get a syntactic analysis at all. In the literature (cf. among others Sharvit 1999; Sharvit & Guerzoni 1999; Van Craenenbroeck 2004) it has been argued that reconstruction does not always involve a lower copy of movement. In these cases a syntactic analysis of reconstruction does not suffice to account for the data. These constructions raise the question if reconstruction should be given a syntactic analysis at all. If reconstruction should be given a syntactic analysis, there are other analyses available that do not make crucial use of the copy-theory of movement. Epstein et al. (1998), for instance, argue that LF looks into the derivation after every Merge operation, immediately establishing the semantic relations. This means that copies of movement do not have to be addressed in order to account for reconstruction.

19. Note that both interpretations of the copy theory of movement view the moved item and the copy as distinct items, as the characteristics of the copy are different from those of the moved item (one is inaccessible to agreement relations, the other one is not). Another interpretation of the copy theory of movement is that a copy and the moved item are actually two occurrences of one and the same entity appearing in two places (cf. among others Gärtner 2002). As these items are actually one item, they have the same characteristics. This latter view on copies is not compatible with the accessibility asymmetry discussed above.

20. This prediction cannot be tested in varieties of Dutch, as in these varieties the subject usually moves to Spec,TP (i.e. it moves across the inflectional projection). The only context in which the subject does not move across the inflectional head is in expletive constructions. However, given that these constructions usually have indefinite subjects, and given that the agreement on the finite verb with coordinated indefinite DPs differs from that with coordinated definite DPs, it is not so clear what predictions the current analysis would make. An anonymous reviewer suggests that a potential way to test this prediction would be to look at locative inversion in Dutch. Roughly speaking, two analyses of locative inversion can be distinguished. The first one assumes that the locative phrase moves to Spec,TP instead of the subject (cf. among others Coopmans 1989; Hoekstra & Mulder 1990). According to this analysis the subject does not move past the inflectional head. Given the assumptions made in this paper, this would predict that the verb has the option of agreeing with the first conjunct. Another approach to locative inversion (cf. among others Rochemont & Culicover 1990) is that the locative phrase topicalizes to Spec,CP. In this analysis, the subject also moves, namely to Spec,TP. As in regular topicalisation clauses the verb moves to C°. Given this approach, locative inversion is not expected to feed agreement with the first conjunct. Consider the example in (i).

(i)   Voor het huis *heb / hebb-en jij   en Piet gezoend.
      For the hous have / have-pl [you and Pete] kissed
      'You and Pete have kissed in front of the house.'

The example is only grammatical if the verb agrees with the subject as a whole, not when it agrees with the first conjunct. We can interpret these data in various ways: (i) FCA is not possible in this example because the relevant configuration is not there. Put differently, the analysis of Rochemont & Culicover (1990) is correct and the subject has moved to Spec,TP allowing only agreement with the coordination as a whole. (ii) FCA is not possible in (i) because the relation between T° and CoP is more specific than that with the first conjunct of the coordinated subject. More research is necessary to resolve this issue. I will leave that to future research.

21. Abbreviations: EMPH = emphatic, PROG = progressive, PAST = past tense.

22. A prediction this analysis makes is that partial agreement on the finite verb in Irish is not possible if the subject is extracted, as in this case the subject is no longer within the c-command domain of T°. The subject leaves behind a copy. The internal structure of this copy is inaccessible, so that the relation between T° and the first conjunct of the subject is no longer visible at PF. Unfortunately, this prediction cannot be tested, as synthetic verbs cannot be combined with subject extraction. Consider the examples in (i) and (ii) (Brian O'Curnáin p.c.).

(i) Túféin   aL   bhí mé ag ceapadh aL *chuirfeá / chuirfeadh isteach ar an bpost
     you$_{emph}$ that was I   think   that put$_{2p.sg}$ / put$_{analytic}$ in   on the job
     sin.
     that
     'It was you that I was thinking would apply for that job.'

(ii) Méféin   agus Tomás   a   deir tú   a   bhí   ag caint   le   chéile
     [me$_{emph}$ and Tomás] that say   you that were$_{analytic}$ at talking with each.other
     'Me and Thomas you said that were talking to one another.'   [Irish]

In (i) a non-coordinated subject pronoun is extracted and the embedded verb has to appear in
the non-inflected analytic form. The same holds for the coordinated subject in (ii). The coordinated subject is extracted and the verb in the embedded clause does not show partial agreement.
In both cases the subject the embedded verb would agree with if it was not extracted appears as
an overt pronoun, instead of a *pro*-subject. This pattern might be related to the fact that in Irish
inflected verbs only occur with *pro*-subjects, but that *pro*-subjects cannot be extracted. I leave
this issue open as a topic for further research.

23. Mohammad (2000) and Van Gelderen (1996) argue that the agreement morphology on
the finite verb in VSO-clauses in Arabic is the result of agreement between an empty expletive
in the specifier of the inflectional projection and the inflectional head, rather than between
the inflectional head and the subject in VP. Following among others Fassi-Fehri (1993), Aoun,
Benmamoun & Sportiche (1994) and Soltan (2004) I assume that agreement in these examples
is not mediated by an empty expletive in the specifier of IP.

24. Aoun, Benmamoun & Sportiche (1994) argue that the finite verb in VSO-clauses actually
moves to a higher postion than the inflectional position. The main reason for this is that they
assume that agreement always takes place via the Spec,Head-configuration.

25. Aoun, Benmamoun & Sportiche (1994) argue that partial agreement in Moroccan, Lebanese
and Standard Arabic is actually not an instance of partial agreement. Rather, they propose that
there is clausal coordination with conjunction reduction. The finite verb agrees with only one of
the conjuncts as it is in a clause with only one of the conjuncts. The structure they propose for
the example in (46) can be represented as in (i).

(i) [left-$_{3p.sg.mj}$ [$_{IP}$ the boy ...]] and [e$_j$ [$_{IP}$ the girl ...]].

In the literature, many arguments against this point of view can be found (see among others Munn 1999; Soltan 2004). Furthermore, Harbert & Bahloul (2002) argue that at least for
Standard Arabic the arguments of Aoun et al. (1994) do not seem to hold.

26. More research into the verbal paradigm of Standard Arabic is necessary in order to establish
that in this language too it is the relation with the Goal resulting in the most specific agreement
morphology that is spelled out. It also has to be noted at this point that in other dialects of
Arabic, like Moroccan Arabic and Lebanese Arabic not only partial agreement but also resolved
agreement is possible in these contexts. It is clear that more research is necessary in order to
capture the complex agreement system of the variants of Arabic. This research unfortunately
does not fall within the scope of this paper.

27. The example in (48) is somewhat degraded, due to the fact that the informants find subject extraction, especially of coordinated subjects, not fully acceptable.

28. Although the informant accepts this sentence, she does indicate that she would prefer the one in (i).

(i)   Pol en   Valère   peinzen-k goan morgen   kommen.
      [Pol and Valère]$_{3pl}$ think-I   go   tomorrow come
      'Pol and Valère I think will come tomorrow.'   [Lapscheure Dutch]

References

Aoun, J., E. Benmamoun & D. Sportiche (1994). 'Agreement, word order, and conjunction in some varieties of Arabic'. In *Linguistic Inquiry* 25, 195–220.

Babyonyshev, M. (1996). *Structural connections in syntax and processing: Studies in Russian and Japanese*. Dissertation, MIT

Bahloul, M & W. Harbert (1992). 'Agreement asymmetries in Arabic'. In *Proceedings of WCCFL* 11.

Barbiers, S. (1995). *The syntax of interpretation*. Dissertation, Leiden University. LOT-dissertations 14.

Barbiers, S. (2003). *Generalized focus particle doubling*. Handout of a talk presented at CGSW 18, Durham, September 18–20, 2003.

Barbiers, S. et al. (2005). *Syntactic Atlas of the Dutch Dialects, part 1*. Amsterdam University Press, Amsterdam.

Bayer, J. (1984). 'COMP in Bavarian syntax'. In *The Linguistic Review* 3, 209–274.

Bonet, E. (1991). *Morphology after syntax*. Dissertation, MIT.

Brandi, L. & P. Cordin (1989). 'Two Italian dialects and the Null Subject Parameter'. In O. Jaeggli & K. Safir (eds.). *The null subject parameter*. pp. 11–142.

Büring, D. & K. Hartman (2001). 'The syntax and semantics of focus-sensitive particles'. In *Natural Language and Linguistic Theory* 19:2, 229–281.

Carstens, V. (2003), 'Rethinking Complementizer Agreement: Agree with a Case checked Goal.' In *Linguistic Inquiry* 34:3, 393–412.

Chomsky, N. (1986). *Barriers*. MIT Press, Cambridge/MA.

Chomsky, N. (1995). *The minimalist program*. MIT Press, Cambridge/MA.

Chomsky, N. (2000). 'Minimalist inquiries: The framework'. In R. Martin et al. (eds.). *Step by step: Essays on minimalist syntax in honour of Howard Lasnik*. MIT press, Cambridge/Mass.

Chomsky, N. (2001a). 'Derivation by Phase'. In M. Kenstowicz (ed.). *Ken Hale: A life in language*. MIT Press, Cambridge/MA. pp. 1–52.

Chomsky, N. (2001b). *Beyond explanatory adequacy*. Manuscript, MIT.

Chomsky, N. (2005). *On phases*. Ms. MIT.

Chomsky, N. (2006). *Approaching UG from below*. Ms. MIT.

Citko, B. (2004). 'Agreement asymmetries in Coordinate structures'. In *Proceedings of FASL* 12.

Coopmans, P. (1989). 'Where stylistic and syntactic processes meet: locative inversion in English'. *Language* 65: 728–751

Corbett, G. (1983). 'Resolution rules: Agreement in person, number, and gender'. In G. Gazdar, E. Klein & G. Pullum (eds.). *Order, Concord and Constituency.* pp. 175–206.

Craenenbroeck, J. van (2004). *Ellipsis in Dutch dialects.* Dissertation, Leiden University. LOT-dissertations 96.

Craenenbroeck, J. van & M. van Koppen (2002). *The locality of agreement and the CP-domain.* Handout Glow 2002, Amsterdam.

Craenenbroeck, J. van & M. van Koppen (2007). *Feature inheritance and multiple phase boundaries.* Handout Glow 2007, Tromsoe.

Doron, E. (2000). 'VSO and left-conjunct agreement: Biblical Hebrew vs. Modern Hebrew'. In A. Carnie & E. Guilfoyle (eds). *The syntax of verb initial languages.* Oxford Studies in Comparative Syntax. pp. 75–96.

Epstein, S., E. Groat, R. Kawashima & H. Kitahara (1998). *A Derivational Approach to Syntactic Relations.* Oxford University Press, Oxford.

Fassi Fehri, A. (1993). *Issues in the structure of Arabic clauses and words.* Kluwer, Dordrecht.

Gärtner, H-M. (2002). *Generalized Transformations and Beyond. Reflections on Minimalist Syntax.* Akademie-Verlag.

Gelderen, E. van (1996). 'Parametrizing Agreement Features'. In *Linguistics* 34.4, 753–767.

Goeman, T. (1999). *T-deletie in de Nederlandse dialecten, Kwantitatieve analyse van structurele, ruimtelijke en temporele variatie.* Dissertation, Vrije Universiteit van Amsterdam. LOT-dissertations 26.

Haan, G. de (1997). 'Voegwoordcongruentie in het Fries'. In E. Hoekstra & C. Smits (eds.). *Vervoegde voegwoorden.* Amsterdam, Cahiers van het P.J. Meertensinstituut 9. pp. 50–67.

Haegeman, L. (1992). *Theory and description in generative syntax, A case study in West Flemish.* Cambridge University Press, Cambridge.

Haeringen C. van (1958). 'Vervoegde voegwoorden in het Oosten'. In C. van Haeringen. *Gramarie, Keur uit het werk van zijn hoogleraarstijd.* Van Gorcum, Assen.

Halle, M. (1997). 'Distributed Morphology: Impoverishment and fission'. In B.

Halle, M. & A. Marantz (1993). 'Distributed Morphology and the pieces of inflection'. In K. Hale & S.J. Keyser (eds.). *The view from building* 20. MIT Press, Cambridge/MA. pp. 111–176.

Harbert, W. & M. Bahloul (2002). 'Postverbal subjects in Arabic and the theory of agreement'. In J. Ouhalla & U. Shlonsky (eds.). *Themes in Arabic and Hebrew syntax.* Kluwer Academic publishers, Netherlands. pp. 45–70.

Harley, H. & E. Ritter (2002). Person and number in pronouns: A feature geometric analysis. In *Language* 78.3, 482–526.

Harley, H. & R. Noyer (1999). 'Distributed Morphology'. In *Glot International* 4:4, 3–9.

Hoekstra, T. & R.Mulder. 1990. Unergatives as copular verbs; locational and existential predication. In *The Linguistic Review* 7:1–79.

Hoekstra, E. & C. Smits (1997). 'Vervoegde voegwoorden in de Nederlandse dialecten'. In E. Hoekstra & C. Smits (eds.). *Vervoegde voegwoorden.* Cahiers van het P.J. Meertensinstituut 9, Amsterdam. pp. 6–30.

Johannessen, J. (1998). *Coordination.* Oxford University Press, New York/Oxford.

Kayne, R. (1994). *The Antisymmetry of Syntax.* Linguistic Inquiry Monograph 24.MIT Press, Cambridge/MA.

Koppen, M. van (2005). *One Probe-two Goals: Aspects of agreement in Dutch dialects.* Dissertation, Leiden University. LOT-dissertations 105.

Koppen, M. van (2006a). *Agreement with (the internal structure of) copies of movement.* Manuscript, University of Utrecht. http://www.let.uu.nl/~Marjo.vanKoppen/personal/

Koppen, M. van (2006b). *Complementizer agreement and the relation between T° and C°.* Manuscript, University of Utrecht. http://www.let.uu.nl/~Marjo.vanKoppen/personal/

Maclean, A. & H. Bennis (2005). *Variation in verbal inflection: Dutch dialects.* Handout Variflex workshop, Amsterdam 19–20 December 2005.

May, R. (1985). *Logical form.* MIT Press, Cambridge/MA.

McCloskey, J. (1986). 'Inflection and Conjunction in Modern Irish'. In *Natural Language and Linguistic Theory* 4, 245–28.

McCloskey, J. (1996). 'On the scope of verb movement in Irish'. In *Natural Language and Linguistic Theory* 14, 47–104.

McCloskey, J. & K. Hale (1984). 'On the Syntax of Person-Number Inflection in Modern Irish'. In *Natural Language and Linguistic Theory* 1, 487–533.

Mohammad, M. (2000). *Word order, agreement and pronominalization in Standard and Palestinian Arabic.* John Benjamins, Amsterdam/Philadephia.

Munn, A. (1993). *Topics in the Syntax and Semantics of coordinate structures.* Dissertation, University of Maryland.

Munn, A. (1999). 'First conjunct agreement: Against a clausal analysis'. In *Linguistic Inquiry* 30, 643–668.

Oirsouw, R. van (1987). *Th syntax of coordination.* Crrom Helm, London.

Pollard, C. & I. Sag (1994). *Head-Driven Phrase Structure Grammar.* The University of Chicago Press, Chicago.

Rochemont, M. & Culicover, P. 1990. *English focus constructions and the theory of grammar.* Cambridge: CUP.

Rooryck, J. (2000). 'On two types of underspecification: Evidence from agreementin relative clauses'. In J. Rooryck (2000). *Configurations of sentential complementation: Perspectives from Romance languages.* Routledge, London.

Samek-Lodovici, V. (2003). 'Agreement Impoverishment under Subject Inversion'. In G. Fanselow & C. Féry (eds.). *Resolving Conflicts in Grammar.* Linguistiche Berichte Sonderheft 11:49–82.

Sauerland, U. (1998). *The meaning of chains.* Dissertation, MIT.

Sharvit, Y. (1999). 'Connectivity in specificational sentences'. In *Natural language Semantics* 7, 229–339.

Sharvit, Y. & E. Guerzoni (1999). 'Reconstruction and its problems'. In P. Dekker & R. van Rooy (eds.). *Proceedings of the 14th Amsterdam Colloquium.* University of Amsterdam.

Soltan, U. (2004). *An argument for AGREE and Multiple Spell-Out: standard Arabic agreement asymmetries revisited.* Handout of the Workshop on Minimalist Theorizing, Indiana University. June 26, 2004.

Uriagereka, J. (1999). 'Multiple Spell-Out'. In S. Epstein & N. Hornstein (eds.). *Working minimalism.* MIT. pp. 251–282.

Wyngaerd, G. Vanden (1994). *PRO-legomena: Distribution and reference of infinitival subjects.* Mouton de Gruyter, Berlin/New York.

Zwart, J-W. (1993). *Dutch syntax: A minimalist approach.* Dissertation, University of Groningen. Groningen dissertations in linguistics 10.

Zwart, J-W. (1997). *A minimalist approach to the syntax of Dutch.* Kluwer, Dordrecht/Boston/London.

Author's address:

Universiteit van Utrecht/UiL-OTS
Janskerkhof 13a
3512 BL Utrecht
Netherlands

Marjo.vanKoppen@let.uu.nl

The Brythonic Reconciliation

From verb-first to generalized verb-second

Mélanie Jouitteau
CNRS, UMR 7110 LLF*

I argue that despite their traditional verb-first vs. verb second partition, Welsh and Breton both instantiate a ban on verb-first and I present an analysis of these two languages as fundamentally verb second. In this view, so-called verb first orders prototypically illustrated by Welsh result from inconspicuous strategies to fill in the preverbal position, whereas traditional verb second prototypically illustrated by Breton results from conspicuous strategies to fill in the preverbal position. I show that both conspicuous and inconspicuous verb second orders are present in both Welsh and Breton. The difference in word order between Welsh and Breton is reduced to (i) a lexical parameter, that is availability of a free preverbal expletive particle in Welsh, and (ii) a syntactic parameter: Breton allows for the creation of expletives by short movement, a parameter shared with Icelandic and other languages instantiating stylistic fronting.

Keywords: Verb-first, verb-second, stylistic fronting, expletives, Breton, Celtic, Welsh, Brythonic, Icelandic, EPP

Introduction

The aim of this article is threefold: I wish to (i) propose the new generalization that Brythonic word orders obey a ban on verb-first, (ii) properly define the parameters responsible for intra-Brythonic variation and (iii), show how the Breton data can be exploited for the inquiry about the EPP Principle and its technical implementations. The article is organized as follows.[1]

First, I propose a new generalization for basic word orders in Welsh and Breton, both Celtic languages of the Brythonic branch. Welsh is traditionally described as a VSO language, in opposition with Breton described as V2. In contrast, I propose that both languages uniformly illustrate a ban on verb-first. They

Linguistic Variation Yearbook 7 (2007), **163–200**.
ISSN 1568–1483 / E-ISSN 1569–9900 © John Benjamins Publishing Company

are fundamentally V2. In Section 1, I show that a preverbal topic or focus triggers conspicuous V2 in both languages. In Section 2, I turn to wide focus sentences: I show that Welsh word order is more accurately described as C-VSO or expletive-VSO. I present new data from Breton also showing C-VSO orders and expletive-VSO orders in wide focus sentences. I consequently reject the traditional VSO/V2 opposition between the two languages because in both languages the preverbal position has to be filled. So-called 'VSO' orders result from *inconspicuous* strategies to fill in the preverbal position, whereas prototypical V2 orders result from *conspicuous* strategies to fill in the preverbal position.

In Section 3, I concentrate on the locus of variation between Welsh and Breton. I reduce the variation between them to (i) a lexical parameter and (ii) a syntactic parameter. Welsh has a lexical *inconspicuous* free expletive available, triggering so-called 'VSO' orders preceded by an *inconspicuous* preverbal element. Breton, in contrast, typically resorts to a syntactic operation, 'light expletive fronting', that brings a *conspicuous* material into the preverbal position, leading to prototypical V2 orders. Welsh does not have this syntactic *inconspicuous* movement available. Breton 'light expletive fronting' targets the closest postverbal element in the derivation and fronts it before the inflected verb. I carefully show that whatever the given numeration of a Breton wide focus sentence, *the chain of the moved preverbal element contains the immediate postverbal position*. I show that this generalization correctly obtains (i) the correct information packaging for V2 orders (ii) the restriction of V-frontings to wide focus sentences, (iii) the complementary distribution of 'light expletive fronting' with topicalization, *wh* movement, matrix C heads or merge of an expletive, and (iv) the precise set of ungrammatical preverbal elements in wide focus sentences (long extracted XPs and long extracted verbal heads, but also any internal IP element if there is a closer element).

In Section 4, I propose that the ban on verb-first orders illustrated by Welsh and Breton is best understood as an EPP effect. I discuss the different technical implementations of the EPP available in the literature in view of the Brythonic data. Building on the parallel with Icelandic 'Stylistic fronting', I build on the proposal of Holmberg (2000, 2005) that movement can create expletives from any postverbal category, regardless of its X vs. XP status. The closest postverbal element splits its features, obtaining a *light expletive* that fronts as a last resort strategy to fill in the preverbal position. I show how the Breton data provides arguments for movement of more material than a phonological matrix, forcing a syntactic account of the EPP. I review different implementations of the EPP and show how the Breton data reveals their limits.

1.   The word orders represented in both Welsh and Breton

Welsh and Breton are the two main Modern Celtic languages of the Brythonic branch. Descriptive grammars as well as the generativist literature traditionally oppose the two with respect to their basic word orders (see Roberts 2005 for Welsh; Jouitteau 2005b for Breton and references therein). Welsh illustrates a VSO language with typical V to C movement in main clauses and embedded, like Irish or Scottish Gaelic.

(1)   Fe/Mi glywes   i'r   cloc.   *Welsh*
      C   heard-1sɢ the clock
      'I've heard the clock'.

The image for Breton is somewhat more complicated. Embedded Breton sentences seem uniformly of the Welsh CVSO type, but main clauses show a V2 pattern interrupted by a lexically restricted verb-first paradigm, or else the fronting of a verbal head across the auxiliary (so-called "Long head Movement" paradigms).

   In this section, I present the comparative Welsh and Breton data that illustrate well-known similarities. I close with a discussion of the V2 characterization of Breton.

1.1   Topic and focus

Focalisation strategies give rise to identical V2 orders in Breton and Welsh. In (2) to (4) below, the focalized constituent uniformly moves into the preverbal position and receives narrow focus reading.

(2)   **Y   plentyn** a   redodd _t_Subject__ adref   *Welsh*
      Ar   bugel a   redas   _t_Subject__ d'ar gêr   *Breton*
      the child   ® ran   home
      '(It was) the child (that) ran home'.

(3)   **Ceffyl** a   brynodd y   dyn _t_Object__   *Welsh*
      Ur marc'h a   brenas   an   den _t_Object__   *Breton*
      a   horse ®   bought the man
      '(It was) a horse (that) the man bought'.

(4)   **Ar y pren**   y canai   'r aderyn _t_PP__   *Welsh*
      War ar wezenn e kane   al labous _t_PP__   *Breton*
      on the tree   ® sang-ɪᴍᴘꜰ the bird
      '(It was) on the tree (that) the bird sang.'

Sentences in (2) to (4) are easily derivable by movement of an XP into a Focus projection, presumably to check a Focus feature in FocP. I assume a derivation where the inflected verb is located in the highest inflexional head (in the line of Harlow 1981; Rouveret 1990, 1994 for Welsh; and Diesing 1990 for Yiddish). In the latest cartography developments, this inflectional head is Fin, the lowest head of an articulated CP domain. The preverbal particle glossed '®' is also located in Fin (see Jouitteau (2005b) for Breton and Roberts (2005) for Welsh). Preverbal topics in Breton show the same XP-VSO orders as the above preverbal focus. I derive them by merge of the preverbal XP in a TopP projection, a position from which they bind an IP internal pronoun (see Jouitteau2005b: Chapter 2). I assume that Brythonic orders with narrow reading (either topic or focus) are uniformly XP-VSO.

1.2 Preverbal C heads

Welsh and Breton also present the same word orders in embedded and in yes-no questions: C-VSO. Examples (5) and (6) illustrate C-VSO orders in embedded sentences, and examples in (7) and (8) illustrate C-VSO orders in yes-no questions in both languages.

(5) Dw I 'n   meddwl Ø y dylech chi ddeud wrtho fo.   *Welsh*
     am I Asp think   C ® ought you say   to-3sg he   Roberts (2005)
     'I think you ought to tell him.'

(6) Me a soñj din   Ø e laro   dit   ar wirionez.   *Breton*
     I ® think to-1sg C ® will.tell to-2sg the thruth
     'I think s/he will tell you the truth.'

(7) **A** ddarllenodd Siôn y   llyfr ?   *Welsh*, Sadler (1988)
     Q read.3sg   John the book
     'Did John read the book?'

(8) **Hag** eo gwir an dra-se ?   *Breton*, Jouitteau (2005b)
     Q   is true the thing-here
     'Is that true?'

I add preverbal negation illustrated in (9) into the inventory of C-VSO orders in Breton. I analyze preverbal negation in Breton as a C head triggering that-trace effects. In the example illustrated in (10), the prenegation subject is coreferent with a resumptive subject pronoun that triggers rich agreement.[2]

(9) Ne glev   ket mat ar stlejviled an tonoiù uhel.   *Breton*
     NEG hear.3SG NEG good the reptiles   the sounds high
     'The reptiles do not perceive high frequencies.'

(10) Ar stlejviled ne   glev**ont** ket mat an tonoiù uhel.
     the reptiles   C-NEG hear.3PL NEG good the sounds high
     'The reptiles[+Foc] do not perceive high frequencies.'

The word orders examined so far are thus of two types, each of them represented
in both Welsh and Breton: (i) XP-VSO in matrix sentences whose derivation contain Move or Merge of an XP in a focus or topic position, and (ii) X-VSO where
X is semantically imposed by the numeration (C, Q, Neg). The word order variation between Breton and Welsh is thus restricted to affirmative matrix *wide focus*
sentences. In the following, we will investigate affirmative matrix sentences lacking
narrow focus or topic reading, typically sentences that can answer to a '*what happened*' type of question. This so-called 'unmarked order' is traditionally described
as VSO in Welsh, and as V2 in Breton (Urien 1982; Schapansky 1992, 1996, 1999).

1.3   The 'extra V2 step'; Further toward the locus of variation

Stated as a VSO/V2 opposition, the difference seems large. Welsh and Breton thus
appear to illustrate different types of languages. However, this opposition is weakened by an analysis that obtains Breton V2 via an intermediate VSO step. Movement of the verb over the subject triggers VSO orders in both Breton and Welsh,
and an additional 'extra V2 step', restricted to Breton, further moves a constituent
into the preverbal position (Anderson & Chung 1977; Anderson 1981; Stump
1984; Hendrick 1988, 1990; Borsley & Stephens 1989; Timm 1989, 1991; Schafer
1992, 1995 among others). The key variation between Welsh and Breton, in this
scenario, is the presence *vs.* absence of the second step in the derivation, this 'extra
V2 step' that Welsh lacks.

   The 'extra V2 step' is a stipulation that has the weight of a good generalization
if: (i) its presence can predict correct word orders in Breton, and (ii), its absence
can predict correct word order in Welsh. I claim that neither (i) nor (ii) are correct.

   With regard to Breton, the 'extra V2 step' would trigger the wrong results with
regard to the data previously illustrated here, or would have to be reformulated at
high theoretical costs. An 'Extra V2 step' must first be blocked in matrix sentences
with filled topic or focus positions as in (2), (3) and (4). It means that a particular
syntactic operation (anteposition of a preverbal element) applies only in derivations where there has been or will be no other anteposition of any XP preverbal

element. The correct word orders thus is obtained only if we rely on a last resort status for the 'extra V2 step'. Now, this last resort operation has to be set such as to target only assertive affirmative matrix sentences with wide focus information packaging, as it should not apply in embedded sentences (C-VSO in (6)), in negative matrices (C-VSO in (9)) or in matrix yes-no questions (Q-VSO in (8)). The last resort 'extra V2 step' should thus be sensitive to the presence of preverbal XPs, but also to preverbal heads: it must be blocked by the presence of any XP, but also of any preverbal head (C, Q, Neg). Borsley and Kathol (2000) state with reason that this result is a challenge for a derivational model. They propose that Breton word orders illustrate 'linear V2': the generalization is blind to the XP/head distinction because it applies on linear order. Note however that this generalization, absolutely accurate for Breton, is not less accurate for Welsh, as there is always either a head or an XP in the preverbal domain.

The attractive result of the 'extra V2 step' seems, at first sight, to be the reduction of the differences we have to postulate between Welsh and Breton. In fact, it is based on the generalization that Brythonic wide focus sentences illustrate a V2/VSO contrast, a generalization which proves inaccurate for both languages. In the following section, I will show that Welsh matrix wide focus sentences do show a preverbal element: a matrix C head. Welsh matrix wide focus sentences are thus more accurately described as C-VSO instead of VSO. I will also show that Breton does instantiate the same C-VSO orders. I consequently reject the idea that the 'extra V2 step' is the key distinction property of Breton.

2. Welsh and Breton C-VSO orders in wide focus sentences

Breton and Welsh both show grammatical C-VSO orders in *wide focus* sentences. Welsh unmarked surface order is C-VSO as in (1), repeated in (11), where the preverbal zone is filled by a merged C head (*mi* or *fe*, here in bold characters).[3]

(11) **Fe/Mi** glywes   i'r   cloc.
      C   heard-1SG the   clock
      'I've heard the clock'.

The sentence is fine in 'out of the blue' contexts and the preverbal element has no semantic impact, other than making the wide focus reading possible. Occurrence of the *Mi/Fe* particles in Welsh is restricted to matrix sentences. The inventory of matrix C particles in Welsh also includes particles that appear integrated in the verbal compound as in the Modern Welsh pattern illustrated in (12) (see Roberts

2005:120). This particle is lexically restricted to the present and imperfect of the verb 'to be'.[4]

(12) R-oedd Pwyll yn   arglwyd   *Welsh*, Sainz (2001)
      C-was   Pwyll asp. Lord
      'Pwyll was lord'.

The difference between Welsh and Breton does not lie, as usually assumed, in Breton lacking matrix C-VSO orders, but in the statistic number of sentences in which Breton has it, compared to Welsh. Merging a free preverbal matrix C head is the common option in Welsh (11), whereas it is always lexically restricted in Breton, like in the Welsh example (12). Matrix C head compounds are found in the locative and progressive form of 'to be' (13),[5] in future progressive constructions in the verb 'to go' (14), and, at least in the Gwened dialect, with the verb 'to come' (15).[6]

(13) a. Emañ Maijo el   levraoueg.   *Standard Breton*
          C-is   Maijo in-the library
      b. E oar   o hadañ   an ed.   Favereau (1997:272)
          C [were+ IMP] at plant-INF the wheat.
          'We were planting the wheat'.

(14) a. Han   me da laret deoc'h. . .   *Standard Breton*
          C-go.1SG I to tell   to-you
          'I'm going to tell you. . .'
      b. Eh a   da goueza.   *Treger dialect*, Gros (1996:32)
          C go.3SG to to.fall
          'S/He is going to fall.'

(15) a. É tan   a laret. . .   *Gwened dialect*
          C come-1SG P to-say   Guillevic and Le Goff (1986:97)
          'I've just said. . .'
      b. E ta   brezel.   *written Gwened dialect*,
          C come war   Herrieu (1994:11)
          'The war came.'

The Breton preverbal C heads above exclusively appear incorporated into the verbal compounds. The association of a verbal root with a given C head seems lexically parameterized. In syntax, the verbal root in *Fin* moves further up and incorporates into the higher C head. In Jouitteau (2005b:Chapter 2), I analyse the Breton incorporated particle as a topic head, a stipulation meant to predict that only hanging topics and scene setting adverbs can appear before an incorporated

C head. Interestingly, Rouveret (1996) and Roberts (2005:33) consider that the [Particle-V] compound in the Welsh 'to be' paradigms is also higher in the structure than the canonical site for the inflected verb.

It is obvious that availability of the particle is tied at core to word order: the sentences from (13) to (15) exhaustively illustrate the restricted set of matrix 'verb-first' sentences type in Breton.

To summarize the patterns of preverbal matrix C heads exposed so far: both Breton and Welsh show a pattern of matrix C heads incorporated into the verbal root, whose availability is lexically restricted. Welsh is unique in resorting also to a dummy matrix C head (*Mi/Fe*). This particle is directly responsible for the statistic importance of C-VSO orders in Welsh. In contrast to Welsh, Breton did not develop dummy matrix C heads that would be freely available in all *wide focus* sentences. Consequently, Breton matrix C-VSO orders are proportional to the lexical restriction of the Breton expletives C heads illustrated in (13) to (15).

Breton however developed another dummy preverbal element that is also restricted to matrix sentences. In (16)a, b and c, I show that this dummy element is obligatory when no other element precedes the inflected verb. In (16)a', b' and c', I show that the dummy element is ungrammatical when the preverbal position is already filled. From dialect to dialect, the morphology of the expletive is based on the morphology of the corresponding infinitive form of the verb 'to be'.[7] Some speakers appear to allow only (17), where the inflected verb is identical in root with the infinitive-expletive.

(16) a. *(**bez**') e ra   glav   a'. Glav (*bez)   a ra   *Standard Breton*
     b. *(**bout**) e ra   glav   b'. Glav (*bout) e ra   *Gwened dialect*
     c. *(**bit**) ë ra   glav   c'. Glav (*bit)   ë ra   *Poher dialect*
         to-be ®-does rain.   rain **to-be** ®-does
         'It rains'.

(17) *(**Bez**') eo   unan hag a c'hellfe   skoazellañ ac'hanomp, a gav
     to-be ®.is one C   ® could-he help   P-us,   ® find
     din.
     to-me
     'He is one who could help us, I think'.

The preverbal expletive *Bez'* in Breton prevents a verb-first order, but is not associated at all with the notion of subjecthood. Its morphologically takes from a shortening of the infinitive form of *bezañ* 'to be', and it does not show any sign of association with the postverbal subject. In this sense, it is a preverbal *free* expletive, in contrast with expletives like *there* in English. The examples from (18) to (20) below show successively that the preverbal Breton expletive triggers no definiteness effect on the postverbal subject, is not restricted to unaccusative constructions and is compatible with first, second and impersonal person.

(18) **Bez**   e   yelo   (**al** lein   / **ur** gastelodenn) war an
      EXPL ® will-go (the breakfast / a   pan)   on   the
      tan.   *Standard Breton*
      fire
      'Someone will put (the breakfast / a pan) on heat.'

(19) **Bez'** e   laz-it   bopred ma lapined!
      EXPL ® kill-2PL always my rabbits
      'You always kill my rabbits!'

(20) **Bez'** e   c'hell-er kavet   tokoù e gallaoueg.   Mantell (2000)
      EXPL ® can-IMP to.find accents in Gallo
      'We can find accents in Gallo.'

The X vs. XP status of *bez* is far from clear, and uneasy to test, as any manipulation into the preverbal area – to whom it is restricted – makes it disappear. As it is a free dummy preverbal element restricted to matrix sentences where nothing else fills in the preverbal position, I treat it on a par with the Welsh free matrix particle *Mi/Fe*. Diachronic arguments certainly do not oppose to their uniform expletive treatment, as illustrated below in a late Middle Welsh transitive expletive construction illustrated in (21). The preverbal pronominal expletive *Ef* is not available in Modern Welsh anymore. It is this particular element that has been later reinterpreted as the matrix C head *Fe* (see Borsley, Tallerman and Willis 2007:297) for the evolution of the contexts where preverbal *Ef* could be found in Middle Welsh).

(21) **Ef**   a   danuon Duw... taryan itt.   *Middle Welsh,* cited in Willis (2005)
      It PRT send   God   shield to-you
      'God will send a shield to you.'

I uniformly analyse the Breton and Welsh free dummy preverbal elements as expletives satisfying a syntactic ban on verb-first. This proposal is designed in accordance to their restricted distribution (matrix preverbal areas that are not filled by anything else), as well as their null semantic impact. The proposal that the Welsh *mi*-VSO and *fe*-VSO matrix sentences are instances of expletive-VSO orders has far reaching theoretical consequences, in particular for the traditional typology of expletives, which considers only XP elements as opposed to functional heads. I wish to take this step, and I assume that the crosslinguistic typology of expletives includes elements, XP or heads, which are semantically empty, and whose sole function is to prevent verb-first orders. I leave the discussion about the syntactic rule that forces their presence to Section 4. For the moment, I send the difference between Welsh and Breton, the one using matrix C heads as expletives, the other using the expletive *bez*, 'to be', to a lexical parameter due to different diachronic developments both aiming to create elements that could satisfy a ban on verb-first.

The typological image developed here so far shows a complete congruence of word orders in both Breton and Welsh. Both languages show similar XP-VSO orders with a preverbal XP narrow topic or focus reading, both languages have C-VSO orders in embedded sentences and yes-no questions, and both languages have C-VSO and expletive VSO orders in wide focus sentences. Breton and Welsh however do have contrasting word orders. In the following section, I will concentrate on the main locus of variation in Brythonic word order: Breton has a movement expletive strategy available, whereas Welsh has not.

3.   The locus of variation

Breton wide focus sentences are not restricted to *bez*-VSO orders. In this section, I will show that the preverbal position can be filled by either a subject, an agent oriented adverb, a past-participle, a passive participle, an infinitive, or an aspectual particle. These frontings are usually assumed to be completely free. I assume that this is far from being the case, and I will argue for the generalization in (22).

(22)   In Breton wide focus sentences derived by movement, the preverbal element originates from the immediate postverbal position.

In other words, the wide variety of possible fronted elements in Breton wide focus sentences is exactly proportional to the wide variety of elements that can be found in the immediate postverbal position, depending on the particular numeration/derivation of each sentence. The situation is schematically illustrated below: the inflected head stands in Fin, the lowest head of an articulated CP domain. Y is the immediate postverbal element, which fronts by a very short syntactic movement as an expletive strategy.

(23) $[_{\text{TopP}} \ [_{\text{FocP}} \ [_{\text{FinP}} \ Y_j \ [_{\text{Fin}} \ \circledR\text{-V} \ ] \ [_{\text{IP}} \ \bcancel{Y}_j$

Movement of Y across the inflected head is semantically equivalent to merging an expletive, and does not trigger any narrow reading effect on Y. I call this very short movement, which has no impact on information packaging, 'expletive' movement. Under the expletive movement hypothesis, Breton and Welsh show the same word orders (VSO) at the relevant level of semantic interpretation. Expletive movement provides a unified derivation of the wide focus orders of Breton despite the diversity of the elements targeted (diversity in category; D, V, Adv, Asp, etc., and diversity in syntactic status; X and XPs).

I will now go through the different possible values of Y in (23), showing for each possible value of Y that (i) Y is fronted from the immediate postverbal position, (ii) only Y, the closest postverbal element, can be fronted by expletive movement. Moreover, I will check the predictions induced by the last resort status of expletive movement: for each value of Y, I will make sure that no operation obeying the generalization in (22) is ever available if verb-first is avoided by other means.

3.1   The fronted argument of an existential construction

In the example in (24), the '*what happened*?' type question ensures that the answer in B constitutes a wide focus sentence. All information is new and the fronted element does not receive any focus or topic reading.

(24)   A: – Petra nevez 'zo   e   Breizh ?   *Ar Paper Timbr*, traditional song
              What   new   ®is in   Brittany
              'What is new in Brittany?'
       B: – [Trouz ha   moged] 'zo __ a-leiz
              noise and smoke   ®is   abundantly
              'There is a lot of noise and smoke.'

The sentence in (25), where an expletive is merged in the preverbal position, also constitutes a correct answer to (24) A. It shows the argument of the existential construction appearing in the immediate postverbal position.

(25)   [_EXPL_ Bout'] 'zo trouz ha   moged a-leiz.
              EXPL   ®is noise and smoke abundantly
       'There is a lot of noise and smoke.'

The example in (26) shows that when negation is merged into the preverbal domain, an expletive cannot be merged and the argument of the existential construction receives an obligatory narrow reading.

(26)   (Trouz ha   moged/ *Bout) n'   eus ket   a-leiz.
       (noise and smoke / EXPL)   NEG is   NEG abundantly
       'There is not a lot of NOISE AND SMOKE.'   focus
       'It is noise and smoke that there isn't abundantly.'   contrastive focus

'Noise and smoke, there is not a lot of.'   topic
'As for noise and smoke, there is not a lot of it.'   hanging topic

3.2 DP Subject

The generalization in (22) predicts that Breton has wide focus sentences with
SVO orders if the derivation brings it as the closest postverbal element. Stephens
(1982), Timm (1991) and Schapansky (1996) have already noted that Breton SVO
orders are not restricted to a narrow focus reading on the subject, and that focus movement cannot exhaustively account for SVO orders. Timm (1991:281)
and Schapansky (1996) have concordant results for SVO occurrences in both oral
and written corpus of Modern Breton : a large proportion of conspicuous V2 orders are SVO. Breton SVO orders as illustrated in (27) can be interpreted either
with a narrow topic/focus reading on the subject, or with wide focus reading of
the sentence.

(27)   Anna a lenn ____ al   levr.
       Anna ® reads   the book
       'Anna reads the book.' / 'It is Anna that reads the book.'

Below, I check that SVO unmarked orders are banned when another element already occurs in the preverbal position. The examples in (28) show that expletive
movement of the immediately postverbal subject is ungrammatical when a matrix
C head is available.[8]

(28)   a.   (*Me) **han** (me) da laret deoc'h.
            I   C-go I   to tell to-you
            'I'm going to tell you.'
       b.   (*Me) **é**   tan (me) a   laret...
            I   C-come I   to   tell
            'I'm going to tell you.'
       c.   (*Manon) **emañ** (Manon) el   levraoueg.
            Manon   PRT-is Manon   in-the library
            'Manon is in the library.'

Unmarked subject fronting is also incompatible with negation as in (29), with *Wh*
movement as illustrated in (30), or in embedded sentences as in (31).

(29)   (*Manon)   **n'**   he doa ket (Manon) kuzhet ar   c'hazh
       Manon-Foc   NEG had   NEG Manon   hidden the cat
       'Manon had not hidden the cat.'

(30)   Petra (*Tom)   a   wele   (Tom)   t_WH ?
       what   Tom^-Foc   ®   saw-3SG.M   Tom
       'What did Tom see?'

(31)   Goulenn a ra   m' (*Manon) he doa (Manon) kuzhet ar   c'hazh.
       ask   ® does if   Manon   she has   Manon   hidden the cat
       'S/He ask if Manon had hidden the cat.'

The generalization in (22) further correctly predicts that long extracted preverbal subjects are restricted to narrow reading (see Section 3.7)

3.3 Verb fronting

Verb Fronting is preverbal movement of a verbal head (an infinitive, a past participle or a passive participle), across an inflected auxiliary. This word order type illustrated in (32) is mostly known in the literature on Breton as the 'Long Head Movement' paradigm. The wide focus answer illustrates fronting of a passive participle across the auxiliary 'be'.

(32) A: – Petra 'zo   c'hoarvezet a newe?   *Gwerz Lezobre*, traditional song
              what ®-is happened   of new
              'What new happened?'

      B: – **Lavaret** 'zo   __   d'ac'h-c'hui, Lezobre, dont d' gombati maurian
              told   ®-is   to-2PL-2PL   Lezobre, come to combat moor
            ar   roue.
            the king
            'It is ordered to you, Lezobre, to come combat the Moor of the king.'

Alternatively, an expletive can be inserted (33), or focus fronting can take place (34). In both cases, the past-participle appears as the closest postverbal element, showing that movement of the passive participle in (32) takes place from the closest postverbal site.

(33) [_EXPL Bout] 'zo **lavaret** d'ac'h-c'hui, Lezobre, dont d' gombati maurian
              EXPL   is told   to-2PL-2PL Lezobre come to fight   moor
            ar   roue.
            the king
            'It is ordered to you, Lezobre, to come combat the moor of the king.'

(34)   [$_{VP}$ Dont d' gombati maurian ar   roue]$^{+ Foc}$ 'zo **lavaret** d'ac'h-c'hui,
      come to fight   moor   the king   is told   to-2PL-2PL
Lezobre _t^{VP}_.
Lezobre
'It is ordered to you, Lezobre, to come combat the moor of the king.'

However, the image is not always that clear: subject fronting and V-fronting some-times seem to be equivalent options. The optionality in fronting illustrated in (35) seems at first sight to go against the generalization that expletive movement targets the closest, and only the closest postverbal element.

(35)   (Manon / kuzhet) he doa   (Manon) (kuzhet) ar   c'hazh
    Manon   hidden   have.3SGF   Manon   hidden   the cat
'Manon has hidden the cat.'

However, I argue this optionality is in fact instantiated in the postverbal area. This is illustrated below in (36), taken from Rezac (2004) citing Kervella (1995).

(36)   Dec'h   en   devoa (ar merour) gwerzhet (ar merour) leue e
    yesterday ® 3SG.M had   the farmer   sold   the farmer   calf his
    vuoc'h ruz.   Kervella (1995:373)
    cow   red
'Yesterday the farmer had sold the calf of his red cow.'

I assume that there is an optional short head movement of the past participle into the middle field that can move the past-participle head over the subject and con-sequently make it the closest target for expletive movement (Rezac 2004; Jouitteau 2005b). Breton speakers vary as to their preference for postverbal placement of the subject with respect to the past-participle head.

    Favereau (1997:326–7) discusses this variation and attributes these opposite parameterizations to different speech-levels (see also Gerven 2002, and the discus-sion in *Tír na nÓg* 2000, 321:79, 322:97). I leave two scenarios open. One option is that the short movement of the verbal head is a syntactic option available for all speakers. In this case, some socio-linguistic factor rejects overt Aux-V-S or-ders, and all speakers should get complete optionality in fronting as illustrated in (35). An alternative scenario is that some speakers syntactically disallow short movement of the verbal head into the middle field. In this case, the prediction is that these speakers should allow for verb-fronting only when the subject does not intervene, that is only in sentences with incorporated pronominal subjects. These particular speakers should disallow V-fronting in (35). Interestingly, Ler-oux (1957:466) notes a preference for V-fronting in sentences with (incorporated) pronominal subjects. He estimates that, in ninety percent of cases, constructions involving infinitive fronting over the auxiliary *ober,* 'to do', arise with pronominal subjects in Middle Breton and Modern Breton. Further research is needed to choose between the two above mentioned scenarios.

Concerning the generalization in (22), I maintain that V-fronting arises in environments where the verbal head comes from the closest postverbal site. I will now show that V-fronting has the last resort status of an expletive strategy. V-fronting is incompatible with negation (37) or in a C-VSO embedded sentence (39), where the inflected head is already preceded by another head.[9]

(37) (*Kuzhet) **n'** he doa ket (kuzhet) ar   c'hazh
      hidden NEG had   NEG hidden   the cat
      'She had not hidden the cat.'

(38) Goul a ra ganit (*kuzhet) m' he doa (kuzhet) ar   c'hazh
      to-ask ® do to-me   hidden   if she has hidden   the cat
      'S/He asks me if she had hidden the cat.'

Wh movement is incompatible with expletive movement of a verbal head as illustrated in (39).

(39) Petra (*lennet) en   deus (lennet) Tom ~~petra~~ ?
      what   read   ®-3SG has read   Tom
      'What did Tom read?'

All instances of verb-fronting seem to violate the Head Movement Constraint (HMC) because the head is moved across the auxiliary, that is across another c-commanding head. My implementation of the syntactic operation at play will account for this (see Section 4).

3.4 Unmarked fronting of an object

Fronted objects with a wide focus reading are difficult to find in a corpus. Their rarity, I assume, is proportional to the restriction of environments that make them the closest postverbal element. For an object to be the immediate postverbal element, the numeration of the sentence must combine the different following factors: a synthetic verb, a pronominal incorporated subject, and the absence of intervening adverb. Such a case is illustrated in (40), and restriction to narrow focus by an intervening subject in (41).

(40)   A: – Petra   a   c'hoarvezo?
             what   ®   happen.FUT.3SG
             'What will happen?'
       B: – Va   lein   e   tebrin   ~~va lein~~.
               my   breakfast   ®   eat.FUT.1SG   my breakfast
             'I will eat my breakfast.'

(41)   Va   lein   e   tebro   an   diplodokus   ~~va lein~~   bemdez.
       [my   breakfast]$^{+Foc}$ ®   eat.FUT.3SG   the   diplodocus   my breakfast   everyday
       'The diplodocus will eat MY BREAKFAST everyday.'

OVS orders in Breton are generally assumed to be restricted to an obligatory narrow focus reading, and I consider it is an important result of the generalization
in (22) that it predicts the precise rare environment where OVS unmarked orders
are possible.

3.5   The problem of the aspectual particle 'bet'

Phillips (1996: 250) notes that verbal heads can move preverbally across the *bet* aspectual particle, and states it is a case of long distance V-fronting. The observation
is repeated in Kathol & Borsley (2000: 695) with the data in (42). The example with
a fronted PP in (42)a illustrates the normal postverbal word order. In (42)b, the
particle *bet* is not an intervener for V-fronting, but the example in (42)c shows that
this aspectual particle is not invisible for expletive movement: *bet* is the fronted element in (42)c. Finally, (42)d ensures that the two previous examples are really
cases of expletive movement as they are shown to be complementary.

(42)   a.   [Er   gegin]   meus   bet   kavet   ul levr
             in.the   kitchen   have.1SG   been   found   a   book
             ~~er   gegin~~.   Kathol & Borsley (2000: 695)
             in.the kitchen
             'I have found a book in the kitchen.'

       b.   kavet   meus   bet   ~~kavet~~   ul levr
       c.   bet   meus   ~~bet~~   kavet   ul levr
       d.   *[bet   kavet]   am eus   ~~bet kavet~~   ul levr
             been   found   have.1SG   been   found   a   book
             'I have found a book.'

The problem here for the generalization in (22) is that fronting of the verbal head
in (42)b seems to show that *bet* does not count as an immediate postverbal ele-

ment, whereas it seems to be able to count as the immediate postverbal element in (42)c. I propose that the postverbal *bet* does not count as an intervener for V-fronting (not does it for subject fronting or any expletive movement) because it is cliticized to the inflected head. The preverbal occurrence of *bet* is not a case of expletive movement: the preverbal *bet* is directly merged as an expletive. This analysis would be perfectly ad hoc if the two types of *bet* couldn't be found in the same sentence, but they are, which is impossible for any other postverbal element. The example in (43) shows the doubling of the particle *bet*. The sentence in (44) illustrates the occurrence of the postverbal aspectual particle *bet* alongside the merged preverbal expletive *bout* (dialectal alternative form of *bez*).

(43) **Bet** zo **bet**   un amzer, un amzer tremenet, e karen o kariñ   hag
      been is been a   time   a   time   passed   ® loved P to-love &
      e vezen karet.   *An teir seizenn*, traditional song
      ® was   loved
      'There has been a time, a time past, I loved to love and I was loved.'

(44) **Bout** zo **bet**   un amzer e tougen   teir   seizenn.
      to-be is been a   time   ® wear.PAST three silk.SINGULATIVE
      'There has been a time I used to wear three silk ribbon.'

It is hard to find any contrast between preverbal *bout* and *bet* here, since their semantic impact is null in both sentences. Moreover, the fact that both preverbal *bet* and *bout* are found in the very same song suggests that the variation is superficial.

In some uses, however, the aspectual particle *bet* seems to have a semantic impact in accordance with its perfective morphology. In the example in (45), the preverbal *bet* cannot be an expletive; quite the contrary, the *bet* particle here introduces the only new information of the sentence: the endpoint of the accomplishments, that is their realisation, happened before utterance time.

(45) 'Nn aotro 'r Vurwenn 'n euz komandet / ma vije   'c'hane
      the mister the Bourblanc has   ordered   / that would-be of-it
      distaget; ha war ar chafot lakaët **Bet** eo ac'hane distaget, ha
      detached, & on the scaffold put   been is of-it   detached and
      war ar chafot lakaët.   Luzel (1971)
      on   the scaffold put
      'Mister de Bourblanc has ordered that she would be detached from it (the gibbet) and so has it been done.'

The derivation of (45) does not run into the intervention effect problem, because *bet* is here semantically motivated.

I distinguish two different types of *bet* particles. The first type, illustrated in (42), is just a superficial morphological variant of the preverbal expletive *bez* or *bout* and serves as pure expletive that can be merged preverbally. The second, illustrated in (45), is a perfective particle, which can bring new information into the sentence. In postverbal position, the *bet* particle undergoes a cliticization process. *Bet* particles consequently never trigger intervention effects for expletive movement.[10]

3.6   Agent oriented adverb and intervening effects

Agent oriented adverbs such as *voluntarily, probably* or *by chance* have scope over the subject and are presumably merged higher than *v*P.[11] Whenever an agent oriented adverb is merged into the structure, it becomes the closest target for expletive movement. The example in (46) is taken from an advertisement for a spellchecker in Breton. The adverb *a-ratozh* modifies the passive participle head. Both narrow and wide focus reading are available in the sentence. However, pragmatics favours the wide focus reading, as illustrated in the glosses.

(46)   **A-ratozh**   eo bet   graet evit labourat gant meziantoù burevek
      intentionally is been done for to-work with office   software
      M***.
      M***
      'It has been created in order to work with the software of M***.'
      '??? It is intentionally that it has been created to work with the software of
      M***.'

The fact that the adverb can be fronted without a narrow focus/topic reading is a sign of its fronting by expletive movement. Accordingly, whenever an agent oriented adverb is present in the numeration, neither a subject nor a verbal head can front by expletive movement. In (47), an agent oriented adverb bans any other expletive movement: an intervening agent oriented adverb blocks expletive movement of a verbal head in (50b) or of a subject in (50c).

(47)   a.   Dre chañs   he doa   _____   Manon   kuzhet   ar   c'hazh.
          by   chance   have.3sG.F   Manon   hidden   the   cat
    b.   *Kuzhet   he doa   dre-chañs   Manon   ~~kuzhet~~   ar   c'hazh.
        hidden   have.3sG.F   by chance   Manon   hidden   the   cat
    c.   [Manon$^{+\text{FOC}}$]   he doa   dre-chañs   ~~Manon~~   kuzhet   ar   c'hazh.
        by chance   have.3sG.F   by chance   Manon   hidden   the   cat
        'Luckily, Manon had hidden the cat.'

3.7 Unavailable targets

Finally, I briefly check that elements that never reach the immediate postverbal position remain unavailable targets for expletive movement. Long distance extracted Adverbs (48) and long distance extracted Subjects (49) cannot front without a narrow focus reading. These long extraction patterns can only be derived by topicalization movements.

(48) **Dre-zegouezh** [am eus   klevet [he deus __ Anna desket   he
      By chance   have.1SG heard   have.3SG.F Anna learned her
      c'hentelioù
      lessons
      *'I've heard that Anna had learned her lessons by chance.'
      'It is by chance that I've heard that Anna had learned her lessons.'

(49) **Anna** [am eus   klevet [he deus __ desket   he   c'henteliou.
      Anna   have.1SG. heard   have.3SG.F learned her lessons
      *'I've heard that Anna had learned her lessons.'
      'It is Anna that I've heard that she had learned her lessons.'

Topicalization is not a syntactic operation available for a head, and verb fronting, which is achieved by expletive, short movement, is consequently clause-bound. This restriction for V-fronting is well known since Stephens (1982) and Borsley, Rivero and Stephens (1996). A past participle can be extracted from a matrix position as in (50) but not from an embedded clause as in (51):

(50) **Desket** he deus   __ Anna __ he   c'henteliou.
      learned have.3SG.F   Anna   her lessons.
      'Anna has learned her lessons'.

(51) *Desket [am eus   klevet [he deus   Anna __ he   c'henteliou]].
      Learned have.1SG. heard   have.3SG.F Anna   her lessons
      'I've heard that Anna had learned her lessons.'

I hope I have convincingly shown that preverbal elements in wide focus sentences obey the generalization in (22). In the coming section, I will expose and discuss the different technical solutions proposed in the literature that could account for such a generalization.

4. Brief history of the EPP and discussion of its formalisation

As we are concerned here with expletive movement, which I take to be an EPP effect, I briefly lay out the different traditions of analyses of the EPP, before entering into the different formulations of the EPP that the Brythonic paradigm requires.

The Extended Projection Principle emerges in Chomsky (1982) as a rule ensuring contrast between DPs and sentences: sentences need a subject whereas DPs do not. In Chomsky (1986), EPP is formulated as to ensure that a subject is present in sentences at surface structure. In early Minimalism (Chomsky 1995), the EPP is implemented by an uninterpretable [D/N] nominal feature on T. This theoretical step opens a way for divorcing the notion of the EPP and the notion of subjecthood. This marks the first drastic extension of EPP paradigms. EPP effects can potentially extend to all DP-V orders: quirky subjects, accusative fronting in impersonal adversatives, dative experiencers, OVS orders with objects in A position, etc. Preverbal adverbs of Locative inversion or the expletive *there* enter the EPP paradigm so long as an interpretable [D] feature can be postulated on them.

The movement towards an extension of the paradigms accounted for by the EPP continues in later versions of Minimalism. The field splits in (at least) two principal traditions of analysis. Both traditions can be characterized by a constant extension of the paradigms of EPP effects, but the direction of this extension is different in each tradition. The first tradition extends the paradigms of EPP effects in postulating EPP effects lower than T. In short, the hypothesis of EPP on T consisting of an uninterpretable [D] is taken to find its mirror image in *v*P, triggering object-shift which becomes an EPP effect. In the late 90's, extension of the sites where the EPP is postulated drastically increases: as the theory postulates that any syntactic relation can be established at a distance, overt movement becomes redundant and EPP implements the superficial requirement on overt movement. At this stage of the theory, any overt movement becomes an EPP effect. A reductionist tradition develops in a reaction to this EPP spreading, and various authors attempt to reduce entirely the EPP to the Inverse Case Filter (Bošković 1997, 2002; Miyagawa 2003 among others), or to a φ-feature sharing relation (Boeckx 2000). In substance, the reductionist approach tends to reintroduce the notion of non-redundant movement and works out solutions that would do without the notion of the EPP.

A separate tradition of analysis also starts from Chomsky's (1995) formulation of [–D] on T and extends the paradigm of EPP effects, but in another direction. The central idea is not to postulate EPP effects lower than T, but to enlarge the set of elements targeted by EPP.[12] The intuition is that a formulation of the EPP that

would do without the restriction to [+D] targets should be able to account for
V2 effects, as well as preverbal possessive PPs and Locative Inversion. Represen-
tatives of the 'final EPP' tradition are, among others, Holmberg (2000, 2005) for
Icelandic, Roberts and Roussou (2002) for V2 languages, Bury (2002, 2003, 2005),
Bailyn (2004) with the Generalized inversion proposal, Rezac (2004) for Breton
and Jouitteau (2005b) for Celtic languages. The generalization we have examined
so far in Brythonic clearly falls under the second tradition of EPP analysis. Any formulation of the EPP that will account for the paradigms of Celtic is immune to the
reductionist approach: verbal heads or matrix C heads cannot serve as discharging
Case and the presence of preverbal heads cannot be enforced by the Inverse Case
Filter. Moreover, the Inverse Case Filter and the EPP make predictions for different
sites in Brythonic: if the Inverse Case Filter is active in Breton or Welsh, it enforces
distribution of Case to the subject in its canonical position, that is on the right
of the inflected head. EPP effects, by contrast, show up on the left of the subject,
showing again that EPP cannot dissolve into the Inverse Case Filter.

   I will argue for a scenario such as the one illustrated below. This scenario is
also a working program for the formulation of the EPP. The structure in (52) triggers ungrammatical orders because the EPP is not satisfied in verb-first orders.
In case no expletive is merged directly into the preverbal position, the expletive
strategy illustrated in (53) arises. The closest postverbal element with a phonological matrix ([Phon]) is moved preverbally, together with the categorial features
([CAT]), without pied-piping its semantic features ([SEM]) that remain in the
postverbal position.

(52)

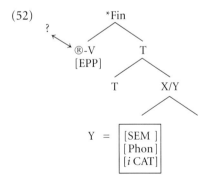

(53)

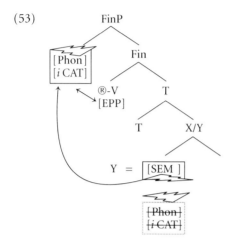

The syntactic operation illustrated in (53) indifferently targets heads and XPs. The last resort nature of EPP effects is obtained because expletive movement is triggered only in situations like (52), where the EPP is not satisfied by any other preverbal element. The semantic impact is null, that is it is equivalent to the merge of a free preverbal expletive. The fronted element is an expletive created in syntax by movement (Holmberg 2000). The preverbal element in (53) is a *light syntactic element* in the sense that it consists of a subset of features of the postverbal element Y. It is important to note that this derivation implies a view of grammar which is incompatible with the Lexical Integrity Hypothesis (Lapointe 1980) or the Atomicity Thesis (Di Sciullo & Williams 1987): the preverbal element in (53) is created by splitting the features of Y over two different (but local) syntactic positions.[13] In this sense, the preverbal element in (53) is a *light expletive* created in syntax by a local movement operation.

In the following sections, I will first examine and explain the splitting feature hypothesis first proposed by Holmberg (2000). I will next discuss and justify the hypothesis of the movement of a phonological matrix in syntax and point out the contrast with a PF operation. Finally, I will justify the hypothesis of the categorial features first proposed by Rezac (2004). I will show that the phonological matrix hypothesis and the categorial feature hypothesis are not redundant, and I will expose the technical problems that still arise. The section closes on a discussion of alternative analyses.

4.1 Feature splitting and [−P] feature

As noted by Schafer (1995), the possible fronting of a past participle across the auxiliary in Breton recalls the facts of Stylistic Fronting in Icelandic and Faeroese, as illustrated in (54).

(54) Hver heldur þú að **stolið** hafi ___ hjólinu *Icelandic,* Holmberg (2005)
      Who think you that stolen has   the-bike
      "Who do you think has stolen the bike?"

Stylistic Fronting in Icelandic has been extensively explored in the literature, and it is tempting to find parallels with Breton. The main difference between the two paradigms is that Stylistic Fronting occurs in subject gap positions or preverbal sites of impersonals, as illustrated in (58a) and (59a). Breton immediately contrasts with Icelandic because: (i) the canonical position of the Breton subject is postverbal, and Breton V-fronting is thus not related to subject gap positions (ii) the landing site of V-fronting is not SpecTP but SpecFinP, (iii) V-fronting is incompatible with high C heads as is not the case in (56).

(55) a. Hverju heldur þú ad **hann** hafi *stolid*
          What   think you that he   has stolen
          'What do you think he has stolen?'

      b. *Hverju heldur þú ad **hann** *stolid* hafi ____ ?
          What   think you that he   stolen has
          'What do you think he has stolen?'

(56) a. Ef **gengið** er eftir   Laugaveginum...   *Icelandic,* Holmerg (2005)
          if walked is along the-Laugavegur
          'If one walks along Laugavegur...'

      b. Ef **það** er **gengið** eftir Laugaveginum...
          if EXPL is walked along the-Laugavegur
          'If one walks along Laugavegur...'

Except for (iii), Breton and Icelandic paradigms both fall under the generalization that V-fronting occurs to prevent verb-first orders. The examples above show that V-fronting, as in Breton, is incompatible with a preverbal subject as in (58b), and that it is incompatible with the merge of the expletive *það* in impersonal constructions as in (59b). Moreover, Maling (1980) followed by Holmberg (2000, 2005) shows that Stylistic Fronting is not a process restricted to verbal heads, but a more general process that targets the closest postverbal element, irrespective of its X/XP status. Whenever an agent oriented adverb is merged in (57), this closest postverbal element becomes the sole possible target for expletive movement, triggering an intervention effect that bans V-fronting, as we saw was the case in Breton.

(57) a. sá sem **sennilega** hefur ~~sennilega~~ skrifað Þessa bók.
       he that probably has probably written this book
     b. sá sem **skrifað** hefur (*sennilega) ~~skrifað~~ Þessa bók.
       he that probably has probably written this book

Holmberg (2000:450)

Holmberg (2005) reviews the properties of Stylistic Fronting, all recalling those of Breton previously exposed: (i) absence of narrow focus reading on the fronted element, (ii) complementary distribution with topicalization, (ii) complementary distribution with the merge of a preverbal expletive, (iv) the targeted element can be either a head or an XP, and (v) Stylistic Fronting fronts specifically the immediate postverbal element.

The feature splitting hypothesis has been developed by Holmberg (2000, 2005) in order to account for V-fronting paradigms in Icelandic and Faroese. It accounts for information packaging as well as for the fact that V-fronting is not filtered by the Head Movement Constraint (HMC). The Head Movement Constraint (Travis 1984) requires that no head moves across another c-commanding head in syntax. The feature splitting hypothesis illustrated in (53) does not counter to the HMC because the moved element is never a head, but merely a subset of features of a head. The semantic features of the immediate postverbal element remain postverbal, as a separate subset of the features move into the preverbal position. This accounts for the null impact of expletive movement in information packaging. The fronted element is interpreted as if it had not moved because its semantic features really have not moved. It further predicts that this movement can target postverbal heads. Languages vary as to they allow for the splitting feature operation.

The following step is to identify the particular subset of features that compose a 'light expletive' and to propose a motivation for movement. Holmberg (2000, 2005) notes the extreme diversity of the fronted syntactic elements. He notes that the only property that preverbal elements seem to have in common is a phonological matrix. This generalization is encoded under an uninterpretable phonological feature [–P] on T. Strict locality of the movement is obtained by the Minimal Link Condition (MLC; Chomsky 1995), illustrated below.

(58) MLC: K attracts α if and only if there is no β,
         β closer to K than α, such that K attracts β.

This formulation of the EPP is designed to target any element that provides the required phonological matrix. This targets indifferently heads or XPs, and excludes PRO, *pro*, traces as well as operators.[14] The [-P] hypothesis correctly predicts that the trace of the verb in T in (53) is not an intervener for Y. By parity of argument, a trace of an incorporated subject wouldn't count as an intervener for fronting.

4.2 The phonological matrix and PF

The [P-] hypothesis is workable only as far as we assume that phonological matrices of syntactic elements are accessible during the derivation, an assumption which is not theoretically neutral. I wish to distinguish this hypothesis with a phonetic requirement. I show below that the abstract phonological matrix available during the derivation for EPP satisfaction can subsequently undergo phonological erasure. The sentence in (59) shows that a matrix particle satisfying the EPP in Welsh can remain unpronounced (see Awbery 2004, for other examples of unpronounced matrix particles in Welsh). In the Breton examples in (60), an element, if made salient in the previous discourse, can undergo topic-drop, without any additional expletive strategy.

(59) (Y) mae Siôn yn   palu'r   ardd.   *Welsh*, Sainz (2001)
      PRT is   Siôn Prog. dig-the garden
      'Siôn is digging the garden'.

(60) a.   ...ø a oa   gwir !   *Breton*, Favereau (1997:272)
          ® was right
          '..., which was right'.

      b.   ... ø e   veze tennet plouz berr.   *Breton*, Gros (1996:32)
          ® was pullen straw short
          '...(then) we used to draw lots'.

My conclusion is that the phonological matrix targeted by [–P] can be absent at PF.[15] The relevant level at which the EPP is active is syntax, and EPP should not be understood as a PF requirement (contra Rivero 1999, 2000 among others). The Breton paradigm offers more evidence that EPP satisfaction has to be a syntactic effect, in contrast to a PF requirement. Going back to the topic-drop examples in (60), the preverbal element absent from PF triggers different morphological realizations of the preverbal particle, which is realised as *a* in (63a) and as *e* in (63b). The following section shows that such an alternation can only be handled for in syntax.

4.3 Unvalued and underspecified categorial feature

The presence of categorial features in the preverbal element are evidenced by the behaviour of the preverbal particle *rannig* labelled '®' in my gloses, that shows morphological variation with respect to the syntactic category of its preceding element (see Anderson 1981; Urien 1989, 1999 among others). The morphological alternation of the *rannig* sheds light on the syntactic dimension of the relation between a preverbal element and the verbal complex. In the topic-drop examples above, the preverbal element has satisfied the EPP from the topic position at a level where syntactic categories are relevant, arguably no later than syntax.

The morphological alternation of the preverbal particle with respect to the category of the fronted element is also telling in wide focus sentences: it offers evidence that expletive movement fronts more than a phonological matrix. In my proposal in (53), a light expletive is constituted of a phonological matrix together with its categorial features. In any examples involving expletive movement in the above Section 3, it can be verified that light expletives created from postverbal DPs trigger the *a* realization of the *rannig*, whereas light expletives created from non-nominal targets trigger the *e* realization of the preverbal particle.[16] Since the verbal complex is sensitive to the category of its preverbal element derived by expletive movement, there is evidence that, at least in Breton, light expletives created by expletive movement do contain an interpretable categorial feature. This categorial feature is pied-piped with the phonological matrix subsequent to feature splitting. Note that this is another sign that EPP effects are syntactic, and do not take place at PF: if EPP was to be treated as a PF phenomena, the PF interface would have to handle a [+/– D] distinction, and presumably an agreement phenomenon.

Rezac (2004) notes the morphological alternations of the Breton preverbal particle and proposes to formulate this alternation in terms of Agree. The morphological realization of the preverbal particle is the result of an agreement relation with the category of the preceding element (that is, in my analysis, the immediate postverbal element previous to movement). The Probe consists of an uninterpretable feature, unvalued for category, that requires checking from any element having an interpretable category. Like the [–P] feature, the [–CAT] feature uniformly finds its corresponding interpretable feature on the closest postverbal element. Could we reduce the EPP effects to an uninterpretable unvalued categorial feature and derive EPP effects without the hypothesis of a [–P] feature? I argue this is not the case because only the [–P] feature accounts for the fact that traces of movement are not eligible targets for the EPP.

The hypothesis of an unvalued categorial feature is not unproblematic. First, it relies on the notion of syntactic category. It is not clear to me if syntactic categories are a property of human language or merely the fruit of human linguists categorizing from a range of testable properties instantiated by syntactic elements. Aside from this theoretical point, implementation of the *rannig* variation in Standard Breton by agreement would call for a rather delicate derivational morphology. In (61), the fronted element is the nominal predicate whose denoted properties are applied to the subject via the copula. The form of the *rannig* is the *e* non-nominal form despite the nominal origin of the predicate. In terms of Agree; nominal features of the noun root *medecin*, 'doctor', must be invisible for the Probe in Fin.

(61) [Medisin] **ez eo** / *a zo Myriam
      doctor   e-is   / *a-is Myriam
      'Myriam is a doctor'

In the same line of argumentation, (62) shows fronting of a past participle together with its genitive proclitic. The verbal root of the fronted element could lead to think that the realization of the *rannig* would design a nominal category, as is the case for infinitive heads. However, the morphology of the *rannig* shows up in the *e* non-nominal form.

(62) [O   lipet] em   eus   o̶—————l̶i̶p̶e̶t̶
      CL-3PL.GEN leaked ®.1SG have   CL-3PL.GEN leaked
      'I have leaked them.'

In (61) and (62), the category of the minimal morphological root (both [+D]) have to become invisible in the process of the morphological derivation of the root. In terms of Agree, this means that we could not make the economy of postulating the intervening presence in (61) and (62) of a non-nominal categorial feature being interpretable in the fronted element. The null head that turns the DP into a predicate must have an interpretable categorial feature. Finally, any formulation of the EPP in terms of agreement has to stipulate that the type of agreement described can never be made at a distance, which designs it as a very peculiar Agree relation.

I consider in my schematized proposal in (53) that the preverbal light expletive of XP-VSO orders of Breton wide focus sentences consists at least of a phonological matrix and a categorial feature. The trigger for movement of the light expletive can be the sole [–P] feature that pied-pipes categorial features, deriving the fact that postverbal traces of movement are not interveners.

I will now point on two other technical problems that any version of the feature-checking hypothesis has to face.

4.4 Two challenges for feature checking implementations of the EPP

Scenarios that obtain EPP effects by a feature checking mechanism, be it [–P], [–CAT], etc. all face the same problem: they have to assume a long-sighted effect. The problem is the following: the uninterpretable feature postulated on the inflected head must be able to find its corresponding interpretable feature in any postverbal element. Its corresponding interpretable feature crucially has to be found in any type of syntactic element (hence categorial feature or phonological feature). However, the uninterpretable feature seems blind to the interpretable features already present on its own site: the head on which it is encoded. Feature-checking scenarios for the EPP cannot avoid the stipulation that the uninterpretable feature is blind to the interpretable features of its own head.

The second challenge for any formulation of the final EPP is that EPP is not site dependent. The landing site of expletive movement is crosslinguistically far from clear. I assume that the Icelandic and Breton paradigms derive from the same effect, but Icelandic shows expletive movement in SpecTP, whereas Breton shows expletive movement in SpecFinP. The expletive movement landing site is dependent on the finite element, irrespective of its particular location in a given language. Another problem concerning the landing site of expletive movement shows up in the Icelandic paradigm. The Icelandic light expletive is restricted to subject gap positions, and consequently appears in environments where the trace of the subject is supposed to be. It is thus far from clear that the landing site of expletive movement is a specifier. Identification of the preverbal landing site as a specifier would also be complicated by the fact that light expletives merely consist of subsets of features of a head in case of V-fronting. The Icelandic paradigm and the matrix C-VSO Brythonic orders independently show that the EPP effect cannot be equated with the projection of a preverbal specifier (contra Chomsky 2000; Lasnik 2001 or Bailyn 2004).

The crosslinguistic formulation of 'Final EPP' effects also has to account for the fact that EPP effects are not crosslinguistically site-dependent (contra the idea that EPP crosslinguistically affects SpecTP).

4.5 Some alternative accounts and their problems

Roberts and Roussou (2002) propose that the EPP consist of a variable in T that must be bound by either a realisation of the subject or an XP, triggering V2 order. V2 languages have a Fin head whose phonological realization is obligatory (noted Fin*). This forces the verb to move into Fin and the Tense variable in T needs to be bound by any pronounceable element in a Specifier. Recourse to binding is elegant because it subsumes the different pre-tense positions (SpecTP in Icelandic vs. SpecFinP in Brythonic). If the inflected head needs to be bound by a c-commanding element, the precise landing site is of no importance, as well as the particular syntactic status of the preverbal element (X vs. XP). Robert and Roussou's proposal recalls a similar intuition in Rivero (1994) or Borsley, Rivero and Stephens (1996) who consider that past participle fronting in Breton is a last resort process of licensing Tense, applying if nothing else has moved preverbally. However, I do not follow this proposal. First, I have shown that the PF realization of the EPP satisfier is not a relevant key factor (60), and second because it lacks the precise predictions that feature splitting makes for information packaging.

Bury (2002, 2003, 2005) proposes another scenario. He proposes that the bottom-up construction of the tree basically proceeds by iterative verbal reprojections and the verb is inserted fully inflected (Koeneman 1995, 2000). The verb can move higher by two processes: either it incorporates into a higher head, or it reprojects and self-attaches to the structure, creating ambiguity on the spine of the tree. This is illustrated in (63), adapted from Bury (2002). In (66a), the non-labelled v has moved out of the vP and is dominated by its v reprojection, a verbal category whose status is structurally ambiguous: it could be either an adjunction to vP or a maximal projection. In (66b), the structure has been disambiguated via projection of a preverbal specifier, yielding a V2 structure.

(63)   a.   Verbal reprojection and ambiguity for Linearization

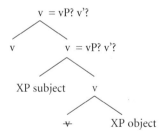

b. Projection of a specifier

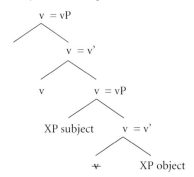

The intuition of the proposal is similar to that of Chomsky (2000), Lasnik (2001), or Bailyn (2004) whose versions of the EPP basically enforce the projection of a specifier. However, Bury's proposal also accounts for the absence of EPP effects in Celtic C-VSO orders, because incorporation of the inflected head into a matrix C head will not trigger reprojection of the verb and thus not trigger a desambiguization strategy. In this proposal, the absence of site-dependency for EPP effects nicely follows. I do not follow this hypothesis because, like the binding account, it fails to account for derivations where the preverbal head is not merged but moved, as is the case in V-fronting paradigms.

5. Conclusion

Welsh and Breton do not represent two different types of languages. Breton is a prototypical case of conspicuous V2, whereas Welsh is a prototypical case of inconspicuous V2. Both languages show a ban on verb-first that recalls an EPP effect. The key difference between the two languages is exhaustively sent to (i) a lexical parameter (Welsh as a matrix C particle available for expletive insertion, whereas Breton has some C particles restricted to a closed set of verbs, and a preverbal expletive spelled out *bout*, *bet* or *bez*), and to (ii) the feature splitting parameter. Breton can resort to light expletives created by expletive movement whereas Welsh cannot.

The expletive movement hypothesis presents a typological advantage in providing a coherent and motivated picture of the derivation for Brythonic word orders. It also identifies the same syntactic effect in two different languages, namely

Breton and Icelandic as described by Holmberg (2000, 2005). Advantages of the EPP analysis are also language internal: I have shown that the EPP accurately predicts pure verb-first sentences to be ungrammatical in Brythonic. Moreover, the EPP as developed here predicts exactly the preverbal element occurring in *wide focus* sentences in Breton for each derivation.

Finally, expletive movement resolves two paradoxes of Breton syntax. With regard to the derivation of V-fronting orders, all properties already observed in the literature are accounted for (wide focus reading, clause-boundedness, complementary distribution with Negation, topicalization and -Wh movement) and as well as new properties such as what element can intervene in the postverbal domain and consequently ban V-fronting. SVO unmarked orders are correctly predicted to instantiate exactly the same set of properties as V-fronting. The mysterious A properties of preverbal subject in the typical A-bar area are also accounted for: a preverbal subject in a Breton wide focus sentence answers positively the tests for A properties because its semantic features really are in an A position (the postverbal canonical A position of the subject). The literature is unclear about the qualification of the Breton preverbal site as an A position, because the A properties vanish for long extracted subjects. In the present proposal, preverbal A subjects in wide focus sentences are assumed without postulating a preverbal A position that would be available for long extracted subjects.

Further research is needed to find a correct implementation of the Extended Projection Principle that would account for the Brythonic ban on verb-first.

Notes

* Various versions of this work have benefited from the precious comments of Hamida Demirdache, Milan Rezac, Johan Rooryck, Javier Ormazabal, Olaf Koeneman, Aritz Irurtzun, Joseph Aoun, Nicolas Guilliot and two anonymous *Lingua* reviewers. I also wish to thank the audiences of *the Fourth Celtic Linguistic Conference* in Cambridge, the *First Workshop on Syntax and Semantics* at the University of the Basque Country and the *Syntax Group* of the LLING laboratory in the University of Naoned/Nantes.

1. The following abbreviations are used in the glosses: CL – Clitic, IMPF – Imperfect, SoADV – subject oriented adverb. Matrix C heads are glossed PRT, in contrast to the preverbal particles (*ranning-verb*) *a, e, y* glossed '®'. I assume that ® is a realised Fin head into which the verb incorporates.

2. Schafer (1995) proposes that negation is an A-bar projection banning A-bar movement of the subject as a Relativized Minimality effect. Her proposal obtains the desired result that prenegation subjects appear with a resumptive trace internal to IP. However, the proposal is too strong

as it predicts that any A-bar movement should trigger a resumptivity effect, which is never the case for non-subject XPs (see Jouitteau 2005b: Chapter 3).

3. Grammaticalization of the matrix particles in Welsh is documented: *Mi/Fe* have been lexicalised from the reinterpretation of preverbal subject or expletive pronouns in a V2 state of the language (Willis 1998, 2005; Bury 2000; Sainz 2002). This is illustrated below with the *Mi* particle in (i–a): the (i–b) glosses shows that Middle Welsh allowed for preverbal pronominal subjects together with coreferential rich agreement on the verb. The preverbal element *Mi* has been reanalyzed as a *dummy* particle. Welsh being a *pro*-drop language, rich agreement has been reanalyzed as illustrated in (x–b'), as identifying a postverbal *pro*.

(i)   a.   **Mi**   welais   gaer
      b.   1SG   saw-1SG   fort
      b'. C   saw-1SG *pro* fort
           'I saw a fort.'

      c.   **Mi**   a   ddygaist   fy   nghaws   i.
           C   ®   stole-2SG *pro* my   cheese   me
           'You stole my cheese'.   Willis (1998: 226)

(i–c) fully illustrates the next coming step of the evolution where the new particle appears with a verb marked for other persons than 1SG. The anaphoric disjunction with the historically [1SG.] feature of *Mi* marks the end of the process: a matrix particle becomes available in all matrix sentences. Willis 1998 claims that the VSO order of Brythonic languages is tied to a lexical parameter: the availability of a matrix particle. I share the intuition of this conclusion, but I do not share its formulation. The Merge of preverbal C heads does not trigger VSO orders, but C-VSO orders, which I analyze as a subcase of expletive-VSO orders. However, in the same line of thought, I propose that the matrix particles *Fe, Mi* retained their ability to satisfy the EPP from their respective origins. See Roberts (2005: 120) for a complete inventory of Welsh C particles.

4. Sainz (2001) considers that the affix *(y)r* is a particle historically created by the reanalysis of the perfect potential *ry/yr* in Middle Welsh.

5. Kervella (1995: §744) suggests that the particle could be analysed as a preverbal adverb that would have been reinterpreted as part of the verb.

6. '*E ta Brezel*' could also be reanalyzed as a case of narrative fronting, as it stands as the title of the first paragraph of Herrieu's book. However, I have found no other example of verb-first narrative fronting effects.

7. The preverbal '*bez*' is not restricted to wide focus. It cannot trigger focus on the inflected verb, but it can serve for 'verum focus'. The particle '*bez*' triggering verum focus is not restricted to last resort EPP environments. Kervella (1995: §742) mentions the use of preverbal '*Bez*' as a way to trigger focus on the inflected verb. However, I consider that this focus effect is suspect and I maintain my expletive hypothesis. Kervella's judgements on information packaging are subject to caution since he does not consider the very existence of out of the blue/wide focus sentences. I consider that focus on the lexical verb is obtained in Breton via VP fronting across a '*do*' auxiliary (-it is to read she does-). For previous mentions of the Breton preverbal expletive '*bez(añ)*', see Schafer (1997: 146) and Borsley and Kathol (2000) citing her. They remark that this preverbal expletive does not seem to be linked to any IP internal position. For a more fine-

grained view of the morphological variation of this element across dialects, see Leroux (1927) ALBB map 30 and Le Du (2001) NALBB, map 28.

8. The ungrammaticality of preverbal movement into FocP is accounted for by the stipulation that the incorporated C head is higher than FocP (Jouitteau 2005b: Chapter 2).

9. An anonymous reviewer points out that embedded sentences are not restricted to C-VSO orders with the particle *ha(g)*. The data raised is the following, illustrating verb-fronting in an embedded. This particle *ha(g)* is also used as a C head in assertive embedded, triggering the same optionality (Jouitteau 2005b: Chapter 2). The *ha(g)* particle is morphologically similar to a coordination particle. The *ha(g)* particle seem to either count as the first element of the linear V2, or to take a linear V2 clause as its internal argument.

> N'   ouzon   ket ha (lennet) en   deus (lennet) Yann al   levr.
> NEG know.1SG NEG Q   read   3SG.M have read   Yann the book
> 'I don't know whether Yann has read the book.'

10. I do not exclude that the expletive '*bet*' type also occurs in the postverbal position. Notice that in (42), the perfective value of the postverbal particle was already brought by the fronted past participle. The paradigms of '*bet*' expletive doubling should be analysed in a par with echoic pronouns in Wrong Subject Constructions, that instantiate similar postverbal doubling of the element that satisfies the EPP as in (x). Notice that the postverbal echoic pronoun [1sg] does not incorporate into the verbal head and seems invisible for agree.

> (x) Me 'zo me laouen ma c'hoar.
>   me ®is me happy my sister
>   'My sister is happy.'

11. An alternative assumption about adverbs is that they are freely inserted into the structure. Such an assumption could account for EPP satisfaction by the preverbal merge of an adverb. Breton still needs an investigation of adverb types, together with their respective behavior. Further research on the topic could for example check wether for any type of adverb, it can undergo fronting in wide focus sentences only when immediately postverbal. Counterexamples would advocate for the free-merge hypothesis of adverbs (Ernst 2002 *vs.* Cinque 1999 among others).

12. This tradition crucially ties the EPP effects to the inflected head. Bošković labels this EPP 'Final EPP', as it would be the latest EPP effect in a bottom-up derivation. Notice however that this does not mean that 'Final EPP' is site dependent. Final EPP targets indifferently SpecCP in V2 languages and SpecTP in SVO languages.

13. The Atomicity Thesis (Di Sciullo & Williams 1987): "Words are 'atomic' at the level of phrasal syntax and phrasal semantics. The words have 'features,' or properties, but these features have no structure, and the relation of these features to the internal composition of the word cannot be relevant in syntax." See Borer (1998) for discussion and overview.

14. A quick point about terminology: by the term 'trace', I mean an element of a chain which does not have a phonological matrix at any time in the derivation, namely the foot of the chain and intermediate positions, by contrast to the head of a chain whose phonological matrix I assume is present in syntax. My assumptions follow Holmberg (2000, 2005): abstract phonological matrices are manipulated in syntax, and intermediate copies lack such a phonological matrix. I also assume that the head of a chain has such an abstract phonological matrix, regardless of its eventual phonetic realization (see Section 4.2).

15. In Jouitteau (2004, 2005b: Chapter 6), I illustrate a paradigm of preverbal subject drop in Atlantic Spoken French, which independently shows that phonological matrices of preverbal elements must be present before undergoing topic-drop. In Atlantic French, as illustrated below, a weak pronoun subject can be dropped.

(i) a. (Ils) ont   joué   du   piano.   Atlantic French
         they have played of.the piano
         'They played piano.'
     b. /ilzɔƷwedupjano/
     c. /zɔƷwedupjano/
     d. */ɔƷwedupjano/

In (i)c, I show that the weak pronoun is erased at PF, but the /z/ liaison obligatory remains, showing that the liaison phonological process was prior to phonological erasure. In view of this, I assume that (59) and (60) can be derived by assuming that the fronted element that has satisfied the EPP had a phonological matrix at the relevant moment of the derivation, prior to phonological erasure.

16. In some examples, the preverbal particle is not itself realized but we can still determine which form is used: the form *zo* of the verb 'to be' for example signals the *a* realization of the preverbal particle. Infinitive heads trigger the nominal like realization of the preverbal particle. See Jouitteau (2005a, 2005b: Chapter 4) for the nominal behavior of verbal structures in Breton.

References

Anderson, Stephen R. 1981. "Topicalization in Breton". In *Proceedings of the Berkeley Linguistics Society*, 7, 27–39.

Anderson, Stephen R. and Sandra Chung. 1977. On Grammatical relations and clause structure in verb initial languages. In P.Cole and J.M.Sadock (eds.). *Syntax and semantics* 8, 1–25. New-York, Academic Press.

Awbery, Gwen. M. 2004. 'Clause-Initial Particles in Spoken Welsh', In G. R. Isaac (ed.), *Journal of Celtic Linguistics* vol. 8., School of Irish, National University of Ireland, Galway.

Bailyn, John F. 2004. 'Generalized Inversion', *Natural Language and Linguistic Theory* 22:1–44.

Boeckx, Cedric. 2000. *The EPP Eliminated*. ms, Uconn.

Borer, Hagit. 1998. 'Morphology and Syntax', In *The Handbook of Morphology*, Spencer, A. and Zwicky, A., Blackwell Publishers, 151–190.

Borsley, Bob M. Luisa Rivero and Janig Stephens. 1996. 'Long Head Movement in Breton'. In *The Syntax of Celtic languages: A comparative perspective*, ed. Robert D. Borsley and Ian Roberts, 53–74. Cambridge University Press.

Borsley, Tallerman and Willis (eds). 2007. *The Syntax of Walsh*. Cambridge University Press.

Borsley, Robert D. and Andreas Kathol. 2000. 'Breton as a V2 language', In *Linguistics* 38, 665–710.

Borsley, Robert D. and Janig Stephens. 1989. Agreement and the position of subjects in Breton. in *Natural Languages and Linguistic Theory* 7, 407–427.

Bošković, Zelko. 2002. 'A-Movement and the EPP', In *Syntax* 5:167–218.

Bošković, Zelko. 1997. *The Syntax of Non finite Complementation: An Economy Approach*. Cambridge, Mass.: MIT Press.

Bošković, Zelko. 1995. 'Participle Movement and second Position Cliticization in Serbo-Croatian', presentation at the Annual Meeting of the *Linguistic Society of America*, New Orleans.

Bury, Dirk. 2005. 'Preverbal Particles in Verb-Initial Languages', In *On the Syntax of Verb Initial Languages*, Carnie, A. and Harley, H. (eds.), Amsterdam/Philadelphia: John Benjamins Publishing Company.

Bury, Dirk. 2003. *Phrase Structure and Derived heads*. University College of London, PhD thesis.

Bury, Dirk. 2002. 'A reinterpretation of the loss of verb-second in Welsh', dans *Syntactic effects of Morphological Change*, D.W. Lightfooot (ed.), Oxford University Press, 215–231.

Burzio, Luigi 1986. *Italian Syntax: A Government and Binding Approach*. Dordrecht: Reidel.

Caink, Andrew. 1999. 'Against Long Head Movement', In M. Dimitrova-Vulchanova and L. Hellan (eds.), *Topics in South Slavic Syntax and Semantics*. Amsterdam: John Benjamins.

Chomsky, Noam. 2000. 'Minimalist Inquiries: The Framework', dans *Step by Step: Essays in Minimalist Syntax in Honor of Howard Lasnik*, R.Martin, D. Michaels and J. Uriagereka, 89–155. Cambridge, MA. MIT Press.

Chomsky, Noam. 1995. *The Minimalist program*, MIT Press, Cambridge, MA.

Chomsky, Noam. 1986. *Barriers*, Linguistic Inquiry Monograph 13. MIT Press, Cambridge, Mass.

Chomsky, Noam. 1982. Some concepts and Consequences of the Theory of Government and Binding. MIT Press, Cambridge, Mass.

Cinque, Guglielmo. 1999. *Adverbs and Functiuonal Heads. A cross-Linguistic Perspective*. New York and Oxford, OUP.

Diesing, Molly. 1990. 'Verb-movement and the subject position in Yiddish', in *Natural Languages and Linguistic Theory* 8: 41–79.

Dobrovie-Sorin, Carmen. 1995. 'Clitic Clusters in Rumanian: Deriving Linear Order from Hierarchical Structure', dans *Advances in Roumanian Linguistics*, Cinque, g. & G. Giusti (eds.). John Benjamins.

Embick David, Roumyana Izvorsky. 1994. 'On Long Head Movement in Bulgarian', *Proceedings of ESCOL 12*.

Ernst, Thomas. 2002. *The Syntax of Adjuncts*. Cambridge, Cambridge University Press.

Favereau, Francis. 1997. *Yezhadur ar brezhoneg a-vremañ. – Modern Breton grammar-* Skol Vreizh.

Gerven, Youenn. 2002. 'Eus ar Brezhoneg beleg d'ar brezhonegoù lennegel', presentation 17/02/2002 for UGB and KEAV in Planwour (ms. 28/04/2002).

Gros, Jules. 1996. *Le Tresor du Breton Parlé*. Première partie, 'Le langage figuré'. Emglev Breizh-Brud Nevez.

Guillevic and Le Goff. 1986. *Grammaire Bretonne du dialecte de Vannes*. Ar Skol Vrezoneg, Emgleo Breiz.

Halpern, Aaron. 1995. *On the Placement and Morphology of Clitics*, Stanford, CSLI Publications.

Halpern, Aaron. 1992. *Topics in the Placement and Morphology of Clitics*, ms. University of Stanford.

Harlow, Stephen.1981. 'Government and Relativisation in Celtic', in *Binding and Filtering*, F. Heny (ed.)Cambridge. Mass. MIT Press.

Hendrick, Randall. 1988. *Anaphora in Celtic and universal grammar*. Dordrecht: Kluwer.

Hendrick, Randall.1990. 'Breton pronominals, binding and barriers, in *The syntax of the modern Celtic languages*, Hendrick, R. (ed.), Syntax and semantics 23. San Diego: Academic Press.

Herrieu, Loeiz. 1994. *Kammdro an Ankou*, ed. Al Liamm.

Holmberg Anders. 2000. 'Scandinavian Stylistic Fronting: How Any Category Can Become an Expletive', *Linguistic Inquiry* vol. 31, n3, summer 2000, 445–483

Holmberg, Anders. forthcoming. 'Stylistic Fronting', In H. van Riemsdijk and M. Everaert (eds.), *The Syntactic Companion*. Oxford: Blackwell.

Jouitteau, Mélanie. 2004. 'Gestures as Expletives, Multichannel Syntax of Spoken Languages', *WCCFL 23 Proceedings*, Cascadilla Press.

Jouitteau, Mélanie. 2005a. 'Nominal Properties of *v*Ps in Breton, implications for the typology of VSO languages', in *On the Syntax of Verb Initial Languages*, Carnie, A. and Harley, H. (eds.), Amsterdam/Philadelphia: John Benjamins Publishing Company.

Jouitteau, Mélanie. 2005b. *La Syntaxe Comparée du Breton*. PhD ms.

Jouitteau, Mélanie. (forthcoming). 'What Breton can Tell Us About the EPP? Investigations on SpecTP'. In *International Journal of Basque Linguistics and Philology*, Irurtzun, A and Ormazabal, J. (eds.), University Press of the University of the Basque Country, Bilbao/Donostia-San Sebastian, Spain.

Kervella, Fransez. 1995. *Yezhadur Bras ar Brezhoneg. -(the great grammar of Breton)*-Al Liamm (ed.), First edition 1947.

Koeneman, Olaf. 1995. *Flexible Phrase Structure: On the Role of Verbal Projections in Dutch English and Yiddish*. MA dissertation, Utrecht University.

Koeneman, Olaf. 2000. *The Flexible Nature of Verb Movement*. Doctoral dissertation, Utrecht University.

Lambova, Mariana. 2002. 'Is Head Movement syntactic? Evidence from Bulgarian'. *MIT Working Papers in Linguistics* 43, 91–104.

Lapointe 1980. *A Theory of grammatical agreement*. PhD diss. University of Massachusetts, Amherst.

Lasnik, Howard. 2001. 'A note on the EPP'. In *Linguistic Inquiry* 32.2.

Le Du, Jean. 2001. *Nouvel Atlas Linguistique de Basse-Bretagne*, vol. I et II. CRBC, Brest.

Le Roux, Pierre. 1927. *Atlas Linguistique de la Basse Bretagne*, Plihon-Hommay Rennes Paris.

Le Roux, Pierre. 1957. *Le verbe breton (Morphologie, Syntaxe)*, Librairie J. Plihon 5, rue Motte Fablet, Rennes. first edition 1947.

Luzel, François-Marie. 1971. *Gwerziou Breiz-Izel* (-Songs of Low-Brittany), Maisonneuve et Larose (ed.), Paris. vol. I. First edition 1868.

Maling Joan. 1980. 'Inversion in embedded clauses in Modern Icelandic'. *Syntax and semantics* 24: Modern Icelandic Syntax, ed. Joan Maling and Annie Zaenen, 71–91, San Diego, Calif, Academic Press (1990).

Mantell, Olier. 2000. *Diazezoù ar yezhadur Gallaoueg* (-Basics of the Grammar of Gallo-), MA ms. University of Rennes/Roazhon II.

Manzini, Rita. 1992. *Locality. A Theory and Some of its Empirical Consequences*, Cambridge, MA. MIT Press.

Miyagawa, Shigeru. 2003. 'A-movement scrambling and options without optionality'. In *Word Order and Scrambling*. S. Karimi. (ed.), Blackwell Publishers.

Phillips, Colin. 1996. *Order and Structure*, MIT Working Papers in Linguistics. (mention of pages refer here to the pdf. version of PhD manuscript).

Rivero, Maria Luisa. 2000. 'Finiteness and Second Position in Long Verb Movement Languages: Breton and Slavic', Borsley (ed.), *The Nature and Function of Syntactic Categories*, 295–323. Academic Press.

Rivero, Maria Luisa. 1999. 'Stylistic Verb Movement in Yes-No questions in Bulgarian and Breton" Kenesei ed., Benjamins (ed.), *Crossing Boundaries*, 67–90.

Rivero, Maria Luisa. 1994. 'Clause structure and verb movement in the languages of the Balkans'. In *Natural Language and Linguistic Theory* 12: 63–120. Kluwer Academic Publishers, printed in the Netherlands.

Rezac, Milan. 2004. 'The EPP in Breton: An unvalued categorial feature.' In A. Breitbarth and H. van Riemdijk (Eds.), *Triggers*. Berlin, Mouton de Gruyter.

Roberts, Ian. 2005. *Principles and Parameters in a VSO language, a Case Study in Welsh*. Oxford Studies in Comparative Syntax, Oxford University Press.

Roberts, Ian. 1994. 'Two types of Head Movement in Romance', dans *Verb Movement*, Lightfoot & Hornstein (eds.), Cambrideg, Cambridge University Press, 207–242.

Roberts, Ian. 1992. *Verbs and Diachronic Syntax*. Kluwer, Dordrecht.

Roberts, Ian and Anna Roussou. 2002. 'The EPP as a condition on the Tense Dependency', in *Subjects, Expletives, and the EPP*, ed Svenonius, Oxford University Press.

Rouveret, Alain. 1996. *Bod* in the Present Tense and in Other Tenses. In Borsley, Robert D., and Ian Roberts (eds.), *The Syntax of the Celtic Languages: A Comparative Perspective*. Cambridge: Cambridge University Press. 125–171.

Rouveret, Alain. 1994. *Syntaxe du Gallois*, CNRS eds., Paris

Rouveret, Alain. 1990. 'X-bar theory, minimality and barrierhood in Welsh.' In *The syntax of the modern Celtic languages*, Hendrick, R. (ed.), Syntax and semantics 23. San Diego: Academic Press.

Sadler, Luisa. 1988. *Welsh Syntax: a Government-Binding Approach*. Croom Helm, London.

Sainz, Koldo. 2001. 'A Multi-causal approach to linguistic change: V2 to V1 and left-edge adjacency effects in Welsh', Abstract for Glow 2001.

Schafer, Robin. 1992. 'Negation and Verb Second in Breton.' Santa Cruz, UCSC unpublished manuscript.

Schafer, Robin. 1995. 'Negation and Verb Second in Breton.' In *Natural Languages and Linguistic Theory* 13, 135–172.

Schafer, Robin. 1997. 'Long Head Movement and Information Packaging in Breton'. In *Canadian Journal of Linguistics* 42(1–2): 169–203

Schapansky, Nathalie. 1999. 'Perspective nouvelle sur l'ordre V2 en Breton', dans *Proceedings of the 34th Linguistics Colloquium*, Germersheim, 189–197.

Schapansky, Nathalie. 1996. '*Negation, Referentiality and Boundedness in Breton, a case study in markedness and asymmetry.*' phD ms.

Schapansky, Nathalie.1992. 'The Preverbal Position in Breton and Relational Visibility.', dans *Working papers in Linguistics* 2, Burnaby SF

Sciullo, Anne-Marie and Williams, Edwin. 1987. 'On the Definition of Word', *Linguistic Inquiry Monograph* 14, Cambridge, Mass., MIT Press.

Stephens, Janig. 1990. 'Non-finite Clauses in Breton', dans *Celtic Linguistics*, Martin, Fife and Poppe, Amsterdam, john Benjamins.

Stephens, Janig.1983. 'Neutral Word Order in Breton.' présentation au *7th International Congress of Celtic Studies*.

Stephens, Janig.1982. *Word Order in Breton*. PhD Dissertation, London.

Stump, Gregory. 1984. 'Agreement versus incorporation in Breton'. In *Natural Languages and Linguistic Theory* 2, 289–348.

Spencer, Andrew. 1991. *Morphological Theory*, Oxford: Blackwell.

Tallerman, Maggie. 1998. *Understanding Syntax*. London: Arnold.

Timm, Lenora. 1989. 'Word Order in 20th century Breton'. *Natural Languages and Linguistic Theory* 7: 361–378.

Timm Lenora.1991. 'The discourse pragmatics of NP-initial sentences in Breton'. In J. Fife and E. Pope (eds.) *Studies in Brythonic word order*, 275–310. Amsterdam: Benjamins.

Tír na nÓg. 2000. (Breton Literature Magazine), Al Liam (ed.), Keltia Graphic. vol. 322.

Travis, Lisa. 1984. *Parameters and Effects of Word Order Variation*, PhD. dissertation, MIT.

Urien, Jean-Yves. 1999. 'Statut morphologique de la particule verbale.', In *Breizh ha pobloù Europa, Bretagne et Peuples d'Europe*, mélanges en l'honneur de Per Denez, Lesneven: Hor Yezh, Rennes : Presses Universitaires de Rennes.

Urien, Jean-Yves. 1989. *La trame d'une langue, Le Breton. Présentation d'une théorie de la syntaxe et application* Lesneven: Mouladurioù Hor Yezh. (first edition 1987).

Urien, Jean-Yves. 1982–5. *Le schème syntaxique et sa marque. Application au Breton contemporain*, Doctorat d'Etat, Rennes 2, ANRT de Lille III.

Wilder, Chris and Damir Cavar. 1994. 'Long Head Movement? Verb Movement and cliticization in Croatian'. In *Lingua* 93.1–58.

Willis, David. 1998. *Syntactic Change in Welsh, A study of the loss of verb-second*, Clarendon Press, Oxford.

Author's address:

CNRS, UMR 7110 LLF
Université Paris 7
Case 7031, 2 place Jussieu
F-75005 Paris Cedex 05
France

melanie.jouitteau@linguist.jussieu.fr

Evidentials as epistemic modals

Evidence from St'át'imcets*

Lisa Matthewson, Henry Davis and Hotze Rullmann
University of British Columbia

This paper argues that evidential clitics in St'át'imcets (a.k.a. Lillooet; Northern Interior Salish) must be analyzed as epistemic modals. We apply a range of tests which distinguish the modal analysis from the main alternative contender (an illocutionary operator analysis, as in Faller 2002), and show that the St'át'imcets evidentials obey the predictions of a modal analysis. Our results support the growing body of evidence that the functions of encoding information source and epistemic modality are not necessarily distinct. The St'át'imcets data further provide a novel argument against the claim that evidentiality and epistemic modality are separate categories. Many authors argue that evidentials differ from modals in that the former do not encode speaker certainty (see, e.g., de Haan 1999; Aikhenvald 2004). We argue that modals are also not required to encode speaker certainty; we provide evidence from St'át'imcets that marking quantificational strength is not an intrinsic property of modal elements.

Keywords: evidentiality, epistemic modality, Salish

1. Introduction

In this paper we argue that evidential markers in St'át'imcets (a.k.a. Lillooet; Northern Interior Salish) introduce quantification over possible worlds, and are restricted to epistemic conversational backgrounds. Thus, the St'át'imcets evidentials fall squarely into the category of epistemic modals. On the other hand, we also show that the St'át'imcets evidentials differ from English modal auxiliaries in two respects: the St'át'imcets evidentials explicitly encode the source of the evidence for the modal claim, and they do not encode differences in quantificational force. We further argue that these two differences are non-coincidental: an

Linguistic Variation Yearbook 7 (2007), **201–254**.
ISSN 1568–1483/E-ISSN 1569–9900 © John Benjamins Publishing Company

epistemic modal must choose either to distinguish source (information source) or force (quantificational strength).

Our proposals have consequences for a debate within current literature about the status of evidential markers, as well as for the theory of modals in general. Like Kratzer (1991), Izvorski (1997), Garrett (2001), Ehrich (2001), Rooryck (2001), McCready & Asher (2006), McCready & Ogata (2007) and Faller (to appear), we argue that at least some evidentials in some languages are epistemic modals. Thus, it cannot be right that evidentiality is fundamentally distinct from epistemic modality, as has been argued by, e.g., de Haan (1999), Lazard (2001) or Aikhenvald (2004). De Haan claims that evidentiality encodes the source of the information contained in the utterance, while epistemic modality encodes the degree of commitment on the part of the speaker to the truth of the information. He therefore proposes that an element which distinguishes only information-source is not a modal. In this paper we show that the St'át'imcets evidentials distinguish the source of the information, and do not encode distinctions of certainty / judgment / evaluation. They thus fall squarely into de Haan's evidential category. However, we also show that these elements must be analyzed as epistemic modals in the sense of being elements which quantify over epistemically accessible worlds. We thus reject the idea that it is an intrinsic requirement of a modal that it distinguish certainty or quantificational force. We therefore also reject Aikhenvald's (2004: 7) claim that evidentiality and modality are "fully distinct categories", with the latter category necessarily relating to the degree of certainty. As support for our claim that modals need not distinguish certainty level, we observe that not just the evidentials, but *all* modals in St'át'imcets (including deontics, circumstantials and futures) fail to encode distinctions of quantificational force (see Rullmann, Matthewson & Davis to appear; Davis, Matthewson & Rullmann to appear for detailed argumentation).

The St'át'imcets evidentials which are analyzed in this paper are listed in (1); an example of the use of each is given in (2)–(4).[1] Syntactically, the evidentials are all second-position clitics.[2]

(1)

evidential	gloss
ku7	reportative
k'a	inferential
-an'[3]	perceived evidence

(2) *wa7* **ku7** ku sts'éts'qwaz' l-ta stswáw'cw-a
     be REPORT DET trout in-DET creek-EXIS
     "[reportedly] There are trout in the creek."[4]

(3) *plan* **k'a** *tu7 wa7 tsu7c* *na máq7-a*
     already INFER then IMPF melt(INCH) DET snow-EXIS
     "The snow must have melted already."   (Davis 2006, Chapter 23)

(4) *pel'p-s-ácw-an'*   *nelh neklíh-sw-a*
     lost-CAUS-2SG.CONJ-PERC.EVID DET.PL key-2SG.POSS-EXIS
     "It looks like you've lost your keys."   (Davis 2006, Chapter 23)

The structure of the paper is as follows. In Section 2 we show that *ku7, k'a,* and *-an'* encode distinctions of information source: they are reportative, inferential, and perceived-evidence evidentials, respectively. In Section 3 we outline the major analyses of evidentials in the formal semantic literature: an epistemic modal analysis (following Izvorski 1997), an illocutionary operator analysis (Faller 2002; C. Davis, Potts & Speas 2007), and a spatio-temporal deictic analysis (Faller 2003; Chung 2005, 2007). In Section 4 we outline and test a set of predictions made by these approaches. We show that the St'át'imcets evidentials obey the predictions of the modal analysis in all respects. We conclude that *ku7, k'a* and *-an'* are epistemic modals. In Section 5 we show that the St'át'imcets evidentials differ from English modal auxiliaries in that the former do not encode distinctions of certainty / quantificational force. Section 6 provides a formal analysis which accounts for the generalizations presented in the paper. Section 7 concludes; we suggest there that many of the arguments in the literature for a separation between evidentials and epistemic modals rest on a mistaken assumption that epistemic modals must encode distinctions of quantificational force (= speaker certainty).

2. The St'át'imcets modals encode distinctions of information source

Each of the clitics in (1) above indicates something about the source of the information presented in the proposition. All the clitics therefore fall within the standard set of evidential meanings which are found cross-linguistically, and also within the definition of evidentiality assumed by e.g. de Haan (1999), Anderson (1986), Bybee (1985:184), Aikhenvald (2004:3), among many others.[5] Willett's (1988) categorization of evidentials (based on a study of 38 languages) is given in (5). Those categories which correspond to St'át'imcets clitics have been highlighted.

(5)   Types of Evidence (Willett 1988: 57)

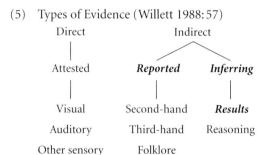

We will first show that according to Willett's categorization, *ku7* is an indirect reported evidential.

A sentence of the form [*ku7* p] is felicitous whenever the speaker came to believe the content of p by means of a report from some other person. *ku7* may be used regardless of whether the report is second-hand, third-hand, or folklore: this is illustrated in (6)–(9). Note that Willett's category 'third-hand' is not restricted literally to third-hand reports. Rather, any case where the speaker has heard about the situation from someone who did not themselves directly witness the situation is classified as third-hand. 'Folklore' cases are those where the speaker claims that the situation described is part of established oral history.[6]

(6)   *Second-hand context: Speaker is talking about a time during her childhood when a chicken attacked her. The speaker does not remember the occasion, but was told about it by her mother, who witnessed it.*
wá7-lhkan   **ku7**   nq'san'k
IMPF-1SG.SUBJ REPORT laugh
"[reportedly] I was laughing."   (Matthewson 2005: 380)

(7)   *Third-hand context: Speaker is talking about the birthplace of her grandmother's mother. She was told about this by one of her relatives, but not by anyone who witnessed the birth.*
l-ta   cácl'ep-a   **ku7**   lh-kwís-as   ku   skícza7-s
in-DET Fountain-EXIS REPORT HYP-fall-3CONJ DET mother-3POSS
"[reportedly] Her mother was born at Fountain."   (Matthewson 2005: 391)

(8)   *Third-hand context: Speaker is talking about when she heard bells ringing everywhere, and she was told that the bells were ringing because World War II had ended.*

nilh **ku7** *i* *tsúkw-as* *k-wa* *q'eltw'ácw kenkw7ú*
FOC REPORT when.PAST finish-3CONJ DET-IMPF wage.war DEIC
Europe-a
Europe-EXIS
"[reportedly] That was when they stopped fighting in Europe."

(Matthewson 2005:454)

(9)   *Folklore context: First line of a legend 'The Dog Children'.*
      wá7 **ku7** *láti7 ti* *pápel7-a* *smúlhats*
      be   REPORT DEIC DET one(HUMAN)-EXIS woman
      "[reportedly] There was this woman."

(van Eijk & Williams 1981:32; told by Martina LaRochelle)

The data in (6)–(9) confirm that *ku7* falls under Willett's definition of a general reported evidential.

Turning to *k'a* and *-an'*, we find that these are both indirect inferring evidentials. The distinction between the two sub-types of indirect inferring evidentials is given in (10) (from Willett 1988:96):

(10) i.   *Inference from results:* the speaker infers the situation described from the *observable evidence* (i.e. from perception of the results of the causing event or action.)

      ii. *Inference from reasoning:* the speaker infers the situation described on the basis of intuition, logic, a dream, previous experience, or some other *mental construct.*

The data reveal that *k'a* is a general indirect inferring evidential: it does not specify whether the inference is based on observable results or solely on mental reasoning. *-an'*, on the other hand, is restricted to cases where the inference is based on perceived results.[7] Thus, *-an'* is usable in a subset of cases in which *k'a* is. This is illustrated in (11)–(12) (adapted from data in Izvorski 1997). In (11), there is no observable evidence; the assertion is based only on reasoning, and only *k'a* is good. In (12), there *is* observable evidence, and both *k'a* and *-an'* are good.

(11) *Context: You had five pieces of ts'wan (wind-dried salmon) left when you checked yesterday. Today, you go to get some ts'wan to make soup and you notice they are all gone. You are not sure who took them, but you know that John is the person in your household who really loves ts'wan and usually eats lots whenever he gets a chance.*

      a.   *ts'aqw-an'-ás* **k'a** *i* *ts'wán-a* *kw s-John*
           eat-DIR-3ERG INFER DET.PL wind.dried.salmon-EXIS DET NOM-John
           "John must have eaten the *ts'wan*."

    b. *??ts'aqw-an'-ás-**an'***   *i*   *ts'wán-a*   *kw*   *s-John*

       eat-DIR-3ERG-PERC.EVID DET.PL wind.dr.salmon-EXIS DET NOM-John

       "John apparently ate the *ts'wan*."

    Consultant's comment re (b): "[Good] if he has bits of *ts'wan* on his shirt."

(12)   *Context: Same as above, except that this time, it's not just that you think it must be John because he's the one who likes ts'wan. This time, you see the ts'wan skins in his room.*

    a. *ts'aqw-an'-ás **k'a**   i*   *ts'wán-a*   *kw*   *s-John*

       eat-DIR-3ERG INFER DET.PL wind.dried.salmon-EXIS DET NOM-John

       "John must have eaten the *ts'wan*."

    b. *ts'aqw-an'-ás-**an'***   *i*   *ts'wán-a*   *kw*   *s-John*

       eat-DIR-3ERG-PERC.EVID DET.PL wind.dr.salmon-EXIS DET NOM-John

       "John apparently ate the *ts'wan*."

Another minimal pair is given in (13)–(14). We see that when the deduction is based on reasoning rather than any observable evidence, only *k'a* is felicitous (13); the presence of perceived evidence makes both *k'a* and *-an'* felicitous (14).

(13)   *Context: You are a teacher and you come into your classroom and find a caricature of you drawn on the blackboard. You know that Sylvia likes to draw caricatures.*

    a. *nilh **k'a**   s-Sylvia*   *ku*   *xílh-tal'i*

       FOC INFER NOM-Sylvia DET do(CAUS)-TOP

       "It must have been Sylvia who did it."

    b. *#nílh-as-**an'***   *s-Sylvia*   *ku*   *xílh-tal'i*

       FOC-3CONJ-PERC.EVID NOM-Sylvia DET do(CAUS)-TOP

       "Apparently it was Sylvia who did it."

    Consultant's comment for (b): "If you could see Sylvia hiding behind the door, you might say that."

(14)   *Context: You are a teacher and you come into your classroom and find a caricature of you drawn on the blackboard. You look around and you see that only one child is covered in chalk dust, Sylvia.*

    a. *nilh **k'a**   s-Sylvia*   *ku*   *xílh-tal'i*

       FOC INFER NOM-Sylvia DET do(CAUS)-TOP

       "It must have been Sylvia who did it."

    b. *nílh-as-**an'***   *s-Sylvia*   *ku*   *xílh-tal'i*

       FOC-3CONJ-PERC.EVID NOM-Sylvia DET do(CAUS)-TOP

       "Apparently it was Sylvia who did it."

Summarizing so far, we have established that all of the three clitics explicitly encode the source of the information presented in the utterance. Their primary semantics is thus evidential, and they are classifiable within Willett's typology as listed in (15).[8]

(15) *ku7* indirect reported evidential ('reportative')
       k'a   indirect inferring evidential ('inferential')
       -an' indirect inferring evidential of result ('perceived evidence')

3.   Formal approaches to evidentials

Within the formal semantic literature, there are three prominent classes of approach to evidentials. The first is to analyze evidentials as epistemic modals with an extra meaning component (see e.g., Izvorski 1997; Garrett 2001; Ehrich 2001; McCready & Asher 2006; McCready & Ogata 2007, among others). We outline the epistemic modal approach in Section 3.1. The second is to analyze evidentials as illocutionary operators which do not contribute to the content of the proposition expressed (see Faller 2002; C. Davis, Potts & Speas 2007); we discuss these approaches in Section 3.2. The third is a 'spatio-temporal operator' approach to deictic elements with evidential-like meanings; see Faller (2003) and Chung (2005, 2007). We briefly address the spatio-temporal analysis in Section 3.3. However, we will pay the least attention to this analysis, as it is obviously not applicable to the St'át'imcets evidential clitics we are examining.

   In Section 4 we will apply a range of tests which empirically distinguish the epistemic modal from the illocutionary operator type of analysis. The evidence will show that all three of the St'át'imcets evidentials are of the epistemic modal type. Our results therefore confirm the growing consensus in the literature that some natural-language evidentials are epistemic modals. However, we do not claim that *all* natural-language evidentials are epistemic modals. On the contrary, we believe that evidentials vary cross-linguistically in their semantics. See for example Faller (2006) for a comparison of reportatives in German and Quechua, arguing that the former are modals and the latter are illocutionary operators; see also Chung (2005) for the claim that Korean has both speech-act and non-speech act evidentials.

3.1   A modal analysis of evidentials

We adopt a standard view of the semantics of modals, according to which they introduce quantification over possible words. See Kratzer (1977, 1981, 1991) for the framework assumed.

Izvorski (1997) claims that in Bulgarian, the perfect is ambiguous between a perfect interpretation and an indirect evidential.[9]

(16)   *Az sâm   došal*
      I   be-1SG.PRES come-P.PART
      "I have come." (perfect)
      "I apparently came." (perfect of evidentiality)   (Izvorski 1997:222)

Izvorski argues that the perfect of evidentiality (PE) introduces a universal epistemic modal. However, she also observes that (16) under its evidential meaning does not simply mean "I must have come." Instead, the indirect evidential has an additional meaning component beyond the necessity modal. This is illustrated in (17).

(17)   Knowing how much John likes wine...

    a.   *toy **trjabva da** e izpil   vsičkoto vino včera*
        he must   is drunk all.the wine yesterday
        "...he must have drunk all the wine yesterday."
    b.   #*toy izpil   vsičkoto vino včera*
        he drunk-PE all.the   wine yesterday
        "...he apparently drank all the wine yesterday."   (Izvorski 1997:227)

Unlike the plain epistemic modal in (17a), the perfect of evidentiality in (17b) is only appropriate if there are observable results of John's having drunk the wine (e.g., one sees empty wine bottles). Izvorski accounts for this by analyzing the PE as asserting an epistemic modal meaning, and in addition presupposing that the speaker's evidence for the embedded proposition is indirect evidence. Note that the PE allows reportative as well as inferential interpretations. Thus, the presupposition is worded in terms of 'indirect evidence' generally. Izvorski's central idea is summarized in (18).

(18)   assertion: □p, in view of the speaker's knowledge state
      presupposition: the speaker has indirect evidence for p
                                        (Izvorski 1997:226)

According to Izvorski, the modal base is restricted by the indirect evidence presupposition; the modal base contains only those worlds in which the available indirect evidence for p holds. The PE contrasts with a plain epistemic modal in that with a plain modal, the modal base is merely restricted to worlds in which the available evidence (which may be of any kind) holds. Izvorski in addition utilizes a contextually-determined ordering source, which orders the worlds in the modal base according to how closely they correspond to certain beliefs about the indirect evidence.

Izvorski's analysis is informally illustrated in (19). Listed under 'modal base' and 'ordering source' are the propositions which narrow down or order the set of accessible worlds respectively.

(19)   *Ivan izpil   vsičkoto vino včera*
       Ivan drunk-PE all.the   wine yesterday
       "Ivan apparently drank all the wine yesterday."   (Izvorski 1997:228)

   a.   *Inferential interpretation:*
        Modal base: {*There are empty wine bottles in Ivan's office*}
        Ordering source: {*If there are empty wine bottles in someone's office,*
                            that person has drunk the wine}

   b.   *Reportative interpretation:*
        Modal base: {*Mary said that Ivan drank the wine*}
        Ordering source: {*Normally, Mary is reliable as a source of information*}

Just like ordinary epistemic modals, evidentials quantify over worlds which are compatible with some actual-world evidence. In the inferential case, this means that we quantify over worlds in which (for example) there are empty wine bottles in Ivan's office. The sentence asserts that in all worlds of this type in which also the proposition "If there are empty wine bottles in someone's office, that person has drunk the wine" is true, Ivan drank the wine. Since the actual world is presupposed to be a world in which there are empty wine bottles in Ivan's office, the sentence makes a strong claim about the actual world: unless the actual world is excluded by the ordering source, Ivan drank the wine in the actual world.[10]

Now let us turn to the reportative case. As with the inferential, the accessible worlds must be those in which some actual-world evidence holds. In a reportative case, the speaker's evidence for the assertion is the fact that a report was made which constitutes evidence for p. Therefore, the accessible worlds in the reportative case are all those worlds in which (for example) Mary said that Ivan drank the wine. The sentence asserts that in all worlds of this type in which Mary is reliable, Ivan drank the wine. Since the actual world is presupposed to be a world in which Mary said that Ivan drank the wine, the sentence makes a strong claim about the actual world: unless Mary is not reliable, Ivan drank the wine in the actual world.

A consequence of this analysis of reportatives is that a reportative sentence containing an embedded proposition p does not mean the same thing as "Somebody / Mary said that p." Under the modal analysis of reportatives, the sentence *presupposes* the existence of a report which constitutes evidence for p, and *asserts* that p must be true, given that report. In a sentence containing a verb of saying, the sentence *asserts* that a report was made, and does not commit the speaker to any claim about the truth or otherwise of p. We will see data below that confirm this difference between reportatives and verbs of saying in St'át'imcets.[11]

3.2 An illocutionary operator analysis of evidentials

A contrasting analysis of evidentials is provided by Faller (2002) on the basis of data from Cuzco Quechua. Faller argues that the Quechua direct and reportative evidentials are not epistemic modals; they are not analyzable in terms of necessity or possibility, and they do not contribute to the proposition expressed. She analyzes the direct and the reportative markers as illocutionary operators, which modify the sincerity conditions of the speech act. They may also change the illocutionary force of the sentence from plain 'assertion' to something else.

The idea is illustrated in (20) for the Quechua direct evidential *-mi*. The propositional content is p; the illocutionary force is assertion, and the sincerity condition states that the speaker believes that p and that that belief is justified by the speaker's having seen the event e described by p (Faller 2002: 25, 164). The sincerity condition results in an increase in illocutionary strength over an ordinary assertion.

(20)   *Para-sha-n-mi*
       rain-PROG-3-mi
       p = 'It is raining.'
       ILL = ASSERT$_s$ (p)
       SINC = {*Bel (s,p)*, EV = *See (s, e_p)*}
       STRENGTH = +1   (Faller 2002: 164)

Faller's analysis of the Quechua reportative *-si* is illustrated in (21). The illocutionary force is that of 'presentation', and the sincerity condition says that there is some other speaker, neither the current speaker nor hearer, who asserted p.

(21)   *Para-sha-n-si*
       rain PROG-3-si
       p = 'It is raining.'

ILL = PRESENT (p)

SINC = {∃s₂ [*Assert (s₂, p)* ∧ s₂ ∉ {h,s}]}   (Faller 2002: 199)

There is another evidential in Quechua, the conjectural, which Faller analyzes as involving epistemic modal semantics (as well as being an illocutionary operator, i.e. as well as introducing a sincerity condition).

C. Davis, Potts & Speas (2007) propose an alternative illocutionary operator analysis of evidentials, according to which an evidential changes the contextually determined standard for felicitous assertion of an utterance. Following Grice's (1975) Quality Maxim, C. Davis, Potts & Speas assume that a speaker is constrained to contributing only information about whose truth s/he is relatively certain; they model this as a requirement that the proposition fall above a certain 'quality threshold'. The quality threshold is contextually manipulable, and an evidential functions to change (usually lower) the quality threshold of an utterance. That is, a speaker who utters 'Ev p' asserts p, but does so in a context in which the standards for quality have been (usually) weakened.

Under this analysis, evidentials have a very similar effect to modals – hence their often-perceived similarities – but achieve the effect in different ways. An utterance of the form 'modal p' does not assert p itself; the entire proposition 'modal p' falls above the ordinary quality threshold. (This in fact implies that utterance of 'p' is infelicitous, presumably because p lies below the quality threshold.) An utterance 'Ev p', as noted above, does entail the asscrtion of p, but with a lowered threshold.[12]

3.3 A spatio-temporal analysis of evidentials

Before we begin applying tests to distinguish the modal from the illocutionary analysis, we will explain why we do not adopt the third potential analysis of the St'át'imcets evidentials. Faller (2003) and Chung (2005, 2007) have analyzed elements in Quechua and Korean respectively as being spatio-temporal operators which give rise indirectly to an evidential meaning. These elements are thus neither illocutionary operators, nor epistemic modals; instead, they operate at the event level and (roughly) locate an event with respect to the speaker's perceptual field at the reference time.

The St'át'imcets evidentials we are focusing on in this paper are not spatio-temporal operators. First, they have no relation to tense; *k'a, -an'* and *ku7* are compatible with past, present or future interpretations. This is shown in (22) for *k'a;* the data are replicable for all three evidentials.

(22) a.   *Context: You look in the fridge for cake and discover there is none left.*
           ts'aqw-an'-ás **k'a**   **tu7**   k   Lenny   ti   kíks-a
           eat-DIR-3ERG INFER then DET Lenny DET cake-EXIS
           "Lenny must have eaten the cake."

      b.   *Context: You saw cake in the fridge five minutes ago, and now it's gone. You*
           know Lenny is in his room.
           wa7   **k'a**   ts'áqw-an'-as   k   Lenny   ti   kíks-a
           IMPF INFER eat-DIR-3ERG DET Lenny DET cake-EXIS
           "Lenny must be eating the cake."

      c.   *Context: You put cake in the fridge and you know Lenny will be hungry for*
           something sweet when he gets home from work.
           cuz'   **k'a**   ts'áqw-an'-as   k   Lenny   ti   kíks-a
           going.to INFER eat-DIR-3ERG DET Lenny DET cake-EXIS
           "Lenny'll likely eat the cake."

Another important difference between the St'át'imcets evidentials being investigated here and the Quechua and Korean spatio-temporal markers discussed by
Faller and Chung is that the latter do not encode information source.[13] For example, Faller (2003) shows that many different types of information source are compatible with Quechua *sqa,* and she argues that *sqa* encodes no relation between the
speaker and the embedded proposition p. As was shown in Section 2 above, this is
not the case for the St'át'imcets evidentials, each of which specify the kind of information source the speaker makes use of. As noted in footnote 2, St'át'imcets does
possesses a spatio-temporal adverb *lákw7a* with evidential semantics. We leave
fuller analysis of that adverb for future work.

4.   The St'át'imcets evidentials are epistemic modals

Although there are several modal analyses of evidentials in the literature (Izvorski
1997; Garrett 2001; McCready & Ogata 2007, among others), the question of the
relationship between evidentials and modals is still under debate (see for example
the summary in Speas 2007). In this section we argue based on eight diagnostic
tests that the St'át'imcets evidentials cannot be illocutionary operators, but instead
obey the predictions of a modal analysis. The tests to be applied, most of which are
adopted from Faller (2002), are listed in (23).

(23) i.   (In)felicity if embedded proposition is known to be false
      ii. (In)felicity if embedded proposition is known to be true

iii. Indirect evidence requirement not cancelable
iv. Indirect evidence requirement not blocked by negation
v. Assent/dissent
vi. Embedding
vii. Readings in interrogatives
viii. (In)ability to raise assertive strength

We will see that a few of the tests do not actually distinguish between the rival analyses; nevertheless, the St'át'imcets evidentials obey the predictions of the modal analysis in every respect.

4.1 (In)felicity if embedded proposition is known to be false

An analysis of evidentials as epistemic modals predicts that they will be infelicitous in contexts where the speaker is sure that the embedded proposition is false. This is because the speaker is asserting that the embedded proposition is possibly or necessarily true. (24) illustrates this for English epistemic modals.

(24)   #It may/must be raining, but it is not (raining). (Faller 2002:191)

As predicted by the modal analysis, the St'át'imcets evidentials are infelicitous if the speaker is sure the embedded proposition is false. This is shown in (25)–(26) for the inferential evidentials.

(25) #wa7 **k'a**   kwis, t'u7 aoz t'u7 k-wa-s   kwis
     IMPF INFER rain but NEG just DET-IMPF-3POSS rain
     "It may/must be raining, but it's not raining."

(26) #wá7-as-**an'**   kwis, t'u7 aoz t'u7 k-wa-s   kwis
     IMPF-3CONJ-PERC.EVID rain but NEG just DET-IMPF-3POSS rain
     "It's apparently raining, but it's not raining."
     Consultant's comment: "It's contradictory."

This test applies to the reportative case as follows. A modal statement 'REPORT p' presupposes that there is reported evidence for p, and asserts that in some or all worlds in which such a report was made, p is true. We assume (following Faller 2002:105) that the modal base contains only worlds compatible with the speaker's knowledge. If the speaker knows that p is false, then the modal base contains only non-p-worlds, so the claim that some or all accessible worlds are p-worlds is not justified.

The data for the St'át'imcets reportative evidential are given in (27)–(28). These examples show that whether or not the source of the report is perceived to be reliable, reportative statements are always infelicitous if the speaker knows the embedded proposition to be false. (28) is adapted from similar data (with different results) given in Faller (2002); see (30) below.

(27)   *Context: Your husband always tells the truth; he is very reliable, and he also tries never to say things unless he knows for sure they are true. So when he says things, you always believe him. However, this time you know he was mistaken. Someone was injured at the Country Store and you know for sure it was Maria, because you were there when it happened and you saw it. You also know that Julia wasn't injured because you just saw Julia and she was not injured. But your husband misunderstood the story when he heard it, and he thinks it was Julia who was injured. Your husband comes home and tells you "xan' kw sJulia láku7 Country Storeha lhkúnsa ku sq'it" ('Julia was injured at the Country Store today'). Then, when you see me later that evening, you say:*

^#xan' **ku7**   kw   s-Julia   láku7 Country.Store-ha   lhkúnsa ku
hurt REPORT DET NOM-Julia DEIC Country.Store-EXIS now   DET
sq'it
day
"[reportedly] Julia was injured at the Country Store today."
Consultant's comment: "Okay if you add something like *tsut nkwtámtsa* [my husband said] at the end."

(28)   *Context: You had done some work for a company and they said they put your pay, $200, in your bank account. But actually, they didn't pay you at all.*

^#um'-en-tsal-itás   **ku7**   i   án'was-a xetspqíqen'kst táola,
give-DIR-1SG.OBJ-3PL.ERG REPORT DET.PL two-EXIS hundred   dollar
t'u7 aoz kw   s-7um'-en-tsál-itas   ku   stam'
but   NEG DET NOM-give-DIR-1SG.OBJ-3PL.ERG DET what
"[reportedly] They gave me $200, but they didn't give me anything."

Corrected to:
tsút-wit kw   s-7um'-en-tsal-itás   **ku7**   i   án'was-a
say-3PL   DET NOM-give-DIR-1SG.OBJ-3PL.ERG REPORT DET.PL two-EXIS
xetspqíqen'kst táola ...
hundred   dollar ...
"They SAID they gave me $200 ..."

In terms of their infelicity when the embedded proposition is known to be false, the St'át'imcets evidentials contrast with the Quechua evidentials. The latter *do* allow the speaker to know that the embedded proposition is false. This follows because, for example, a Quechua speech-act reportative merely *presents* the embedded proposition, and enforces a sincerity condition that a third person made the relevant report. This situation is compatible with the speaker being convinced that the embedded proposition is not true.[14] The Quechua data are shown in (29)–(30).

(29) *para-sha-n-si,   ichaqa mana crei-ni-chu*
rain-PROG-3-si but   not   believe-1-NEG
p = "It is raining, but I don't believe it."
EV = speaker is/was told that it is raining   (Faller 2002:194)

(30) *Pay-kuna-s ñoqa-man-qa qulqi-ta   muntu-ntin-pi saqiy-wa-n,*
(s)he-PL-si I-ILLA-TOP   money-ACC lot-INCL-LOC   leave-1o-3

mana-má riki   riku-sqa-yui ni   un   sol-ta   centavo-ta-pis
not-SURP right see-PP-2   not one sol-ACC cent-ACC-ADD

saqi-sha-wa-n-chu
leave-PROG-1o-3-NEG
"They left me a lot of money, but, as you have seen, they didn't leave me one *sol,* not one cent."
EV = It is said/They said that they left me a lot of money.   (Faller 2002:191)

The Quechua reportative patterns in terms of this test like an overt verb of saying: in both English and St'át'imcets, it is fine to say "They *said* it is raining, but I don't believe it" (cf. the consultant's comment for (27), and the correction for (28)). Recall that the modal analysis clearly differentiates a reportative from a verb of saying. A verb of saying asserts that a certain report was made, and makes no claim about the truth or falsity of that report. A modal reportative presupposes that a report was made, and asserts that the report was at least possibly true.

4.2 (In)felicity if embedded proposition is known to be true

The modal analysis predicts infelicity if the speaker knows that the embedded proposition is true. This is firstly because the evidentials presuppose that the evidence for p is only indirect; this implies that the speaker cannot know for certain that p is true. Moreover, there will be a violation of pragmatic principles (specifically, Grice's Quantity Maxim) if a speaker who knows that p is true asserts 'possibly p' (or even 'necessarily p'), since the modal statement makes a weaker claim than the simple assertion of p. The modal prediction contrasts with the facts for the Quechua direct evidential, which is as strong or stronger in its speaker-certainty level than a plain assertion.

The St'át'imcets evidentials behave like modals for the purposes of this test; they are not felicitous if the speaker is sure that the embedded proposition is true. This is shown in (31)–(36). The reportative data in (35)–(36) include a case where the source is reliable, and a case where the source is unreliable.

(31) #*ts'um'-qs-án'-as*   ***k'a***   *kw*   *s-Lémya7*   *kw*   *s-Roger;*
     lick-nose-DIR-3ERG INFER DET NOM-Lémya7 DET NOM-Roger
     ats'x-en-lhkán   *wi7*   *zam'*
     see-DIR-1SG.SUBJ EMPH after.all
     "Lémya7 must have kissed Roger; actually I saw it."
     Consultant's comment: "You're guessing but you're saying you saw it."

(32) #*nilh* ***k'a***   *k-Sylvia ku*   *xílh-tal'i;*   *wá7-lhkan*   *t'u7 áts'x-en*
     FOC INFER DET-S.   DET do(CAUS)-TOP IMPF-1SG.SUBJ just see-DIR
     "It must have been Sylvia who did it; I saw her."

(33) #*ts'um'-qs-án'-as-**an'***   *kw*   *s-Lémya7*   *kw*   *s-Roger;*
     lick-nose-DIR-3ERG-PERC.EVID DET NOM-Lémya7 DET NOM-Roger
     ats'x-en-lhkán   *wi7*   *zam'*
     see-DIR-1SG.SUBJ EMPH after.all
     "Lémya7 apparently kissed Roger; actually I saw it."

(34) #*nílh-as-**an'***   *k-Sylvia*   *ku*   *wa7 xílh-tal'i;*
     FOC-3CONJ-PERC.EVID DET-Sylvia DET IMPF do(CAUS)-TOP
     wá7-lhkan   *t'u7 áts'x-en*
     IMPF-1SG.SUBJ just see-DIR
     "It was apparently Sylvia who did it; I saw her."

(35) *Context: You were invited to Ted's wedding and you went there and watched him get married. Marilyn (Ted's sister) didn't see you at the wedding and didn't know you had been invited. She told you "Ted got married." Later, you see me and you tell me:*
     #*melyíh* ***ku7***   *kw*   *s-Ted*
     marry REPORT DET NOM-Ted
     "[reportedly] Ted got married."

(36) *Context: You were invited to Ted's wedding and you went there and watched him get married. Henrietta (Ted's other sister) didn't see you at the wedding and didn't know you had been invited. Henrietta has a reputation for being unreliable and often lying. She told you "Ted got married." Later, you see me and you tell me:*
     #*melyíh* ***ku7***   *kw*   *s-Ted*
     marry REPORT DET NOM-Ted
     "[reportedly] Ted got married."

4.3 Indirect evidence requirement not cancelable

According to the version of the modal analysis we adopt, the indirect evidence requirement is a presupposition.[15] As noted by Izvorski (1997), this predicts that the indirect evidence requirement is not cancelable (since it is not a conversational implicature). In fact, the predictions of the two theories converge here. Recall that for Faller, the indirect evidence requirement is contained within a sincerity condition. Faller observes (2002: 126) that "sincerity conditions are not implicatures, since they cannot be canceled."

Not surprisingly, the data reveal that the indirect evidence requirement cannot be canceled for St'át'imcets evidentials. This was already shown in (31)–(34) above for inferential *k'a* and for perceived-evidence *-an*. Parallel sentences are given in (37)–(38) for reportative *ku7*.

(37) #*ts'um'-qs-án'-as*   **ku7**   *kw   s-Lémya7*   *kw   s-Roger;*
lick-nose-DIR-3ERG REPORT DET NOM-Lémya7 DET NOM-Roger
ats'x-en-lhkán   *wi7   zam'*
see-DIR-1SG.SUBJ EMPH after.all
"[reportedly] Lémya7 kissed Roger; actually I saw it."

(38) #*nilh* **ku7**   *k-Sylvia   ku   wa7   xílh-tal'i;   wá7-lhkan   t'u7*
FOC REPORT DET-Sylvia DET IMPF do(CAUS)-TOP IMPF-1SB.SUBJ just
áts'x-en
see-DIR
"[reportedly] it was Sylvia who did it; I saw her."
Consultant's comment: "*ku7* means somebody told you, you didn't see it."

4.4 Indirect evidence requirement not blocked by negation

The modal analysis predicts that the indirect evidence requirement projects through negation, since it is a presupposition. Under an illocutionary operator analysis, the evidential may not take scope under any operator contained within the propositional content, including negation. The theories therefore converge in predicting that the requirement for indirect evidence will still obtain in negative contexts.[16] This is correct for the St'át'imcets evidentials. Before showing the data, though, we need to clarify the predicted readings.

An example from Izvorski involving scope interactions between evidentials and negation is given in (39).

(39)   *Ivan   ne   izkaral   izpita*
Ivan   not   passed-PE   the-exam
= "Ivan didn't pass the exam (it is said/I infer)."
≠ "It is not the case that {it is said/I infer} that Ivan passed the exam."
(Izvorski 1997: 228)

Izvorski uses (39) as an argument that the indirect evidence requirement of the PE does not disappear under negation and therefore is a presupposition. However, the modal analysis (unlike the illocutionary operator analysis) predicts that there is also *asserted* content to the evidential, which may potentially scope *under* negation. Thus, under an analysis of the PE as a necessity modal, (39) should still have two possible readings, depending on the scope of the modal with respect to negation. This is independent of, and consistent with, the inability of the indirect evidence requirement to be negated. We might expect both the readings informally summarized in (40a,b) to be available. We do not expect the reading in (40c).

(40)   a.   It is not the case that in all accessible worlds, Ivan passed the exam.
[allows Ivan to pass in some accessible worlds]
[presupposes speaker has indirect evidence for the modal claim]
   b.   In all accessible worlds, it is not the case that Ivan passed the exam.
[Ivan fails in all accessible worlds]
[presupposes speaker has indirect evidence for the modal claim]
   c.   It is not the case that I have indirect evidence that in all accessible worlds, Ivan passed the exam.
[can be understood as denying that speaker's evidence is indirect]

Based on the translations given by Izvorski in (39), it appears that the Bulgarian PE sentence has only reading (40b). This is consistent with the modal analysis, although an extra explanation needs to be offered for why (40a) is absent. However, such restrictions on available scope relations between modals and negation are well known from English and other languages; see for example Horn (1989: 259ff.).

The same results as in Bulgarian hold for the St'át'imcets evidentials, as shown in (41)–(43). The negation cannot be construed as negating the indirect status of the evidence, and the asserted content of the modal displays no ambiguity with respect to negation.[17]

(41)   *aoz   **k'a**   k-wa-s   Sylvia ku   xílh-tal'i*
NEG   INFER   DET-IMPF-3POSS   Sylvia   DET   do(CAUS)-TOP
= "It is necessarily not Sylvia who did it." [presupposition: indirect evidence]
≠ "It is not necessarily Sylvia who did it." [presupposition: indirect evidence]

≠ "It is not the case that I have indirect evidence that it was necessarily Sylvia who did it."

(42) *cw7áoz-as-**an'***   *kw*   *s-nilh-ts*   *s-Sylvia*   *ku*
NEG-3CONJ-PERC.EVID DET NOM-FOC-3POSS NOM-Sylvia DET
xílh-tal'i
do(CAUS)-TOP
= "It is necessarily not Sylvia who did it." [presupposition: indirect perceived evidence]
≠ "It is not necessarily Sylvia who did it." [presupposition: indirect perceived evidence]
≠ "I don't have indirect perceived evidence that it was necessarily Sylvia who did it."

(43) *cw7aoz **ku7***   *séna7*   *ku*   *qu7*   *láti7*
NEG   REPORT COUNTER DET water DEIC
= "There was necessarily no water there." [presupposition: reported evidence]
≠ "There was not necessarily water there."
[presupposition: reported evidence]
≠ "I do not have reported evidence that there was necessarily water there."
(Matthewson 2005: 389)

For the attempted third reading of (44), the consultant corrects the sentence to (45), which contains an explicit verb of saying.

(44) *cw7aoz kw sqwal'-en-tsál-em*   *kw*   *s-wá7*   *láti7 ku*   *qu7;*
NEG   DET tell-DIR-1SG.OBJ-PASS DET NOM-be DEIC DET water
pún-lhkan   *s7éntsa*
find(DIR)-1SG.SUBJ 1SG.EMPH
"I wasn't told that there was water there; I found it myself."

These data show that the requirement for indirect evidence is not blocked by negation; this is consistent with its status as a presupposition. With respect to the scope of the asserted content, we have translated (41)–(43) using wide-scope universal modals, and these sentences do not admit narrow-scope universal readings. However, as we will show in Section 5, the St'át'imcets evidentials, just like other modals in the language, have variable quantificational force in the sense that they allow existential as well as universal interpretations (see also Rullmann, Matthewson & Davis to appear). Given that, the single interpretation of (41)–(43) could just as well be rendered by an existential modal taking narrow scope with respect to negation. For current purposes, the relevant point is that the behaviour of the

St'át'imcets evidentials is consistent with their analysis as modals, which carry presuppositions which narrow down the information source.[18]

4.5 Assent/dissent[19]

The assent/dissent test as given by Faller (2002, 2006) says that if an element can be questioned, doubted, rejected or disagreed with, it contributes to the truth conditions of the proposition expressed. Otherwise, the element does not contribute to the truth conditions (Faller to appear: 10). Faller argues that the Quechua direct and reportative evidentials fail the assent/dissent test, and therefore are above the propositional level. As for epistemic modals, there is a debate in the literature about whether these pass the assent/dissent test; see Faller (2002, 2006), Papafragou (2000, 2006), and many references therein, for discussion. Faller and Papafragou both argue – convincingly, in our opinion – that epistemic modals, on at least some of their uses, do pass the assent/dissent test. We will see some examples below.

Before applying this test, we would like to first refine it slightly, to require that the assent or dissent take the form of an explicit agreement with, or denial of, the truth of the relevant aspect of meaning. The reason for this refinement – which actually merely makes explicit something which Faller already seems to assume when applying the test – is that even presuppositions, and even the sincerity conditions of speech acts, can be challenged or rejected, as shown in (45B) and (46B) (cf. also von Fintel's 2004 "Hey, wait a minute!" test for presupposition failure). Only the requirement that the challenge take the form of (the relevant language's equivalent of) "That is (not) true" ensures that the test distinguishes presuppositional material from material which contributes to the truth conditions of the utterance.

(45)   A: Harriet likes the sociolinguistics professor.
        B: What sociolinguistics professor? I didn't know we had one!
        B': ??That's not true. We don't have a sociolinguistics professor.
        B": That's not true. She hates him.

(46)   A: I promise I'll help you with the move.
        B: Yeah, right. Last time you promised you would help out but you never showed up.
        B': ??That's not true. Last time you promised you would help out but you never showed up.

Now, what about epistemic modals – do they pass the assent/dissent test? In (47), which contains an epistemic necessity modal, B's utterance does not deny the embedded proposition that Jo is the thief. Rather, B denies the modal claim that Jo *must* be the thief. This suggests that the modal is contributing to the propositional content.

(47)   A: Jo must be the thief.
       B: That's not true. There are some other plausible suspects. Jo may be entirely
           innocent.   (adapted from a similar example in Faller 2002:113)

In (47), B is challenging A's version of what the available evidence is. According to Faller (2002), this is the most common way to disagree with a modal statement: one denies one or more of the premises which narrow down the set of worlds in the modal base. The other way to dissent with a modal claim is to deny the logical relation that the speaker claims to hold between the premises and the embedded proposition.[20] We will see examples of the former type of dissent for St'át'imcets evidentials below.

Another example of assent/dissent applying to epistemic modals is given by von Fintel (2005) and von Fintel & Gillies (to appear). Following work by Simons (2006) on parentheticals, von Fintel & Gillies suggest that sentences containing epistemic modals may perform two speech acts simultaneously.[21] The first involves the standard truth-conditional semantics for epistemic modality. The second may consist of an assertion of p with a lack of conviction, or advice not to overlook the possibility that p holds. The claim is that hearers can respond to an epistemic modal claim by targeting either the epistemic claim *or* the embedded proposition. Their example is as follows (von Fintel & Gillies to appear: 13–14, adapted from an example in von Fintel 2005):

(48)   *Context: Pascal and Mordecai are playing Mastermind.[22] After some rounds where Mordecai gives Pascal some hints about the solution, Pascal says:*

      There might be some reds.

      Mordecai, knowing the solution, has a range of possible responses:

(49)   a. That's right. There might be.
      b. That's right. There are.
      c. That's wrong. There can't be.
      d. That's wrong. There aren't.

Responses (49a) and (49c) agree with or deny the modal claim, not the embedded proposition.

Turning to evidentials now, the modal analysis of these predicts that they should allow assent or dissent with the modal claim. As discussed above, this usually amounts to allowing assent or dissent with the premises which narrow down the modal base. The illocutionary operator analysis, on the other hand, predicts that evidentials do not contribute to the proposition expressed and therefore will fail the assent/dissent test.

The assent/dissent facts support a modal analysis of the St'át'imcets evidentials. Data for *k'a* and *-an'* are given in (50)–(53). In (50) and (51), we see that the hearer can challenge the premises used by the speaker in creating the modal base. B is crucially not denying the embedded proposition. Instead, B denies that A has the correct information about John's whereabouts in the worlds in which his lights are on.

(50)   *Context: A is driving past John's house with B and sees John's lights are on.*

   A: *wá7* **k'a** *l-ta* *tsítcw-s-a* *s-John;* *tákem* *i*
   be INFER in-DET house-3POSS-EXIS NOM-John all DET.PL

   sts'ák'w-s-a *wa7* *s-gwel*
   light-3POSS-EXIS IMPF STAT-burn
   "John must be home; all his lights are on."

   B: *aoz* *kw-a-s* *wenácw; papt* *wa7* *lháp-en-as*
   NEG DET-IMPF-3POSS true always IMPF forget-DIR-3ERG

   kw-a-s *lháp-an'-as* *i* *sts'ák'w-s-a*
   DET-IMPF-3POSS put.out-DIR-3ERG DET.PL light-3POSS-EXIS

   lh-as *úts'qa7*
   when-3CONJ go.out
   "That's not true. He always forgets to turn his lights off when he goes out."

   B's statement ≠ "John is not home."
   B's statement = "It is not true that John must be home."

(51)   *Context: A is driving past John's house with B and sees John's lights are on.*

   A: *wá7-as-**an'*** *l-ta* *tsítcw-s-a* *s-John;* *tákem*
   be-3CONJ-PERC.EVID in-DET house-3POSS-EXIS NOM-John all

   i *sts'ák'w-s-a* *wa7* *s-gwel*
   DET.PL light-3POSS-EXIS IMPF STAT-burn
   "Looks like John is home; all his lights are on."

   B: *Same answer as in (50b).*
   B's statement ≠ "John is not home."
   B's statement = "It is not true that John must be home."

The St'át'imcets Mastermind examples are given in (52)–(53); the results are almost the same as in English. The St'át'imcets speakers do not much like responses of the form "Yes, there might be" or "No, there can't be" in this context (see footnotes 23 and 24). However, this is not because they are unable to challenge the modal claim, but rather because in the Mastermind example, the responder is in possession of all the facts. Therefore, it is felt to be misleading to make a modal assertion instead of a plain assertion. However, once it is explained to the consultants that in this context, the responder is trying not to reveal the answer to the problem, the relevant sentences are accepted. These data therefore support the claim that the St'át'imcets evidentials pass the assent/dissent test, and therefore contribute to the proposition expressed.

(52) *Context: Imagine a game where someone places some different coloured pegs behind a screen and the other person has to guess the colours and the order after getting some clues. After some rounds where I give my son some hints about the solution, he says:*

    wá7 **k'a** *i   tseqwtsíqw-a*
    be   INFER DET.PL red-EXIS
    "There might be some reds."
    Possible responses include:

    a. *wenácw; wá7 k'a*
        true   be   INFER
        "That's right. There might be."[23]

    b. *wenácw; wá7*
        true   be
        "That's right. There are."

    c. *aoz kw-a-s   wenácw; aoz k'a   kw s-wá7*
        NEG DET-IMPF-3POSS true   NEG INFER DET NOM-be
        "That's wrong. There can't be."

    d. *aoz kw s-wenácw; aoz kw s-wá7*
        NEG DET NOM-true NEG DET NOM-be
        "That's wrong. There aren't."

(53) *Context: same as above.*

    *wá7-as-**an'**   i   tseqwtsíqw-a*
    be-3CONJ-PERC.EVID DET.PL red-EXIS
    "There might be some reds."
    Possible responses include:

    a. *wenácw; wá7-as-an'*
        true   be-3CONJ-PERC.EVID
        "That's true. There might be."[24]

b. *wenácw; wá7*
    true   be
    "That's true. There are."

c. *aoz kw s-wenácw; áoz-as-an'*   *kw s-wá7*
    NEG DET NOM-true NEG-3CONJ-PERC.EVID DET NOM-be
    "That's not true. There can't be."

d. *aoz kw s-wenácw; aoz kw s-wá7*
    NEG DET NOM-true NEG DET NOM-be
    "That's not true. There aren't."

Assent/dissent data for the reportative are given in (54). Here, the second speaker challenges the restriction on the ordering source that says the source of the report is reliable.

(54)   *Context: Bill is a liar; he always lies and never tells the truth. You never believe what he says. Yesterday, you heard Bill telling me that Buffy St. Marie is coming to Mt. Currie to give a concert. That was the first you had heard of it; you don't know whether it's true or not, but you usually don't believe what Bill says so you think he's probably lying. Then today, you hear me telling someone else:*
cuz' **ku7** *ts7as k* *Buffy St. Marie e-ts7á Líl'wat-a*
going.to REPORT come DET Buffy St. Marie to-DEIC Mt. Currie-EXIS
"[reportedly] Buffy St. Marie is coming to Mt. Currie."
You say to me:

aoz kw s-wenácw; kakez7-úlh k   Bill
NEG DET NOM-true lie-always DET Bill
"That's not true; Bill is a liar."[25]

To conclude this section, we can contrast the possibility of challenging the modal claim of the evidentials (as in (50)–(54)) with challenging the indirect evidence requirement. The latter can *not* be challenged using "That's not true", because it is a presupposition rather than part of the asserted content.

(55)   *Context: Your car was stolen.*

A: *nilh* **ku7** *s-Bill*   *ta* *naq'w-ens-táli-ha* *n-káoh-a*
    FOC REPORT NOM-Bill DET steal-DIR-TOP-EXIS 1SG.POSS-car-EXIS
    "[reportedly] It was Bill who stole my car."

B: #*aoz   kw   s-wenácw;   plan-lhkacw   lháp-en   kw*
   NEG DET NOM-true already-2s.SUBJ forget-DIR DET

   s-7áts'x-en-acw   ta   káoh-sw-a   láku7
   NOM-see-DIR-2s.CONJ DET car-2SG.POSS-EXIS DEIC

   tsítcw-s-a   s-Bill
   house-3POSS-EXIS NOM-Bill
   "That's not true. You forgot you already SAW your car at Bill's house."

   Consultant's comment (looks confused): "He didn't take it, but the car was
   over at his house?!"

The consultant's response to (55) demonstrates that she understands B's statement
"That's not true" as denying A's claim that Bill must/might have stolen the car. Crucially, the consultant is unable to understand B as denying the indirect evidence
requirement of A's evidential. A similar example is given in (56).

(56) *Context: Your car was stolen.*

A: *nilh **ku7**   s-Bill   ti   naq'w-ens-táli-ha   n-káoh-a*
     FOC REPORT NOM-Bill DET steal-DIR-TOP-EXIS 1SG.POSS-car-EXIS
     "[reportedly] It was Bill who stole my car."

B: #*aoz   kw   s-wenácw;   plan-lhkacw   lháp-en   kw*
   NEG DET NOM-true already-2s.SUBJ forget-DIR DET

   s-7áts'x-en-acw   s-Bill   i   naq'w-ens-as   ti
   NOM-see-DIR-2s.CONJ NOM-Bill when.PAST steal-DIR-3ERG DET

   káoh-sw-a
   car-2SG.POSS-EXIS
   That's not true. You forgot you SAW Bill steal your car."

   Consultant's comment (looks confused): "I don't know! Bill DID steal the car,
   didn't he? So why is that other person denying it?"

The comparison between the data in (54) and that in (55)–(56) is worth empha-
sizing, because there has been some confusion in the literature about exactly how
to test assent/dissent with evidentials. For example, Faller (2002: 157–158) tests
assent/dissent for the Quechua direct evidential *-mi* by testing whether the requirement that the speaker have the best possible grounds for the statement can
be challenged. Faller shows that if a speaker says (57a) using the direct evidential, the hearer may not reply with (57b'), which denies the speaker's having best
possible grounds.

(57)   a.   *Ines-qa   qaynunchay ñaña-n-ta-n   watuku-rqa-n*
             Ines-TOP yesterday   sister-3-ACC-*mi* visit-PST1-3
             p = "Inés visited her sister yesterday."
             EV = speaker saw that p
       b.   *Mana-n chiqaq-chu*
             not-mi   true-NEG
             "That's not true."
       b'. *Mana-n chiqaq-chu.* #*Mana-n chay-ta   riku-rqa-nki-chu*
             not-mi   true-NEG   not-*mi* this-ACC see-PST1-2-NEG
             "That's not true. You didn't see this."   (Faller 2002:157–158)

However, the inability to deny the source of the evidence using "That's not true" is predicted under *either* the modal approach *or* the illocutionary operator approach. Under an Izvorski-type modal approach, it is predicted because the (in)direct evidence requirement is modeled as a presupposition. The data in (57) therefore do not actually distinguish the two analyses. Similarly, although Faller shows (2002:195–196; to appear: 11) that the Quechua reportative -*si* does not allow cancellation of the requirement that the source of the information was a report – one cannot reply to (58a) with (58b) –, she does not show whether the modal claim itself can be canceled.

(58)   a.   *Ines-qa   qaynunchay ñaña-n-ta-s   watuku-sqa*
             Ines-TOP yesterday   sister-3-ACC-*si* visit-PST2
             p = "Ines visited her sister yesterday."
             EV = speaker was told that p
       b.   *Mana-n chiqaq-chu.* #*Mana-n   chay-ta   willa-rqa-sunki-chu*
             not-BPG true-NEG   not-BPG this-ACC tell-PST1-3s2o-NEG
             "That's not true. You were not told this."   (Faller to appear: 11)

To really show whether the Quechua reportative passes the assent/dissent test, we would need data more like that schematized in (59) (cf. the St'át'imcets example in (54)). In this case, the hearer challenges the premises the speaker used to narrow down the modal base (i.e., the premise that the source was reliable).[26]

(59)   A: Inés visited her sister yesterday [reportative]
       B: That's not true. You heard that from a totally unreliable source, so it could easily be false that she visited her sister yesterday.

Such data will be difficult to come by in spontaneous discourse, because usually, the hearer will not know exactly who the report was heard from. However, we saw

above that when the right context is created, the St'át'imcets reportative passes the
assent/dissent test.

4.6 Embedding

Another test for whether evidentials contribute to the truth of the proposition
expressed involves embedding. The idea is that an element which can be embedded
within the antecedent of a conditional or under a factive attitude verb or a verb of
saying must be contributing to the propositional content, and is therefore not an
illocutionary operator. For example, (60) shows that illocutionary adverbials such
as *frankly* are not embeddable, while *reportedly* and *obviously* are.

(60) a. If John's book has *frankly* sold very little, you shouldn't be surprised.
      b. If the ball was *reportedly* over the line, the matter should be investigated
          further.
      c. If the cook *obviously* won't poison the soup, we can eat the meal without
          worrying.   (Faller 2002: 216; data from Ifantidou-Trouki 1993)

In (60a), the addressee is instructed not to be surprised if John's book has sold very
little – not if the speaker is frank when saying the sentence. The meaning of *frankly*
is not embeddable (and the sentence is, in our judgement, degraded). In (60b), on
the other hand, the matter should be investigated if the ball is *reported* to be over
the line; the requirement is not that the ball *be* over the line before an investigation
is warranted. Similar results obtain for (60c) with *obviously*.

It is important to note that this test provides a one-way implication only, for
reasons discussed in detail in Faller (2002, to appear), and Papafragou (2006).
An element which contributes to propositional content – such as, by hypothesis,
epistemic modals – may be embeddable, *or may not* be embeddable, due to independent reasons. For instance, Papafragou (2006) and Faller (2002, to appear)
discuss how the embeddability of epistemic modals may depend upon whether
they are interpreted 'objectively' or 'subjectively' (Papafragou's terms), or 'descriptively' or 'm-performatively' (Faller's terms). We will show in this section that
the St'át'imcets evidentials are freely embeddable under verbs of saying, but not
under the St'át'imcets equivalent of *if*. In this respect they behave like the Tibetan evidentials discussed by Garrett (2001), and like subjectively-interpreted
epistemic modals in English. As just discussed, the failure to embed under *if* does
not require us to conclude that the St'át'imcets evidentials are not contributing to
propositional content.[27]

We begin with reportative *ku7*. This has two readings when it is embedded under verbs of saying. It may either merely reinforce the matrix verb of saying (cf. Portner's 1997 'mood-indicating' modals in English), or it may be semantically embedded (in which case it was the embedded subject who heard about the proposition from someone else). Examples of each are given in (61) and (62) respectively. Note that the issue here is not one of relative scope between the evidential and the attitude verb. The contrast here is between an essentially meaningless (or reinforcing) use of the modal (61), as opposed to a true embedded reading (62). It is the latter reading which provides evidence against an illocutionary operator analysis.

(61)   a.   *Context: Lémya7 saw Mary at the bank and Mary was obviously pregnant. Later, Lémya7 told you that Mary was pregnant. You yourself haven't seen Mary yet. Then you tell me:*

   tsut   kw   s-Lémya7   kw   sqwemémn'ek   **ku7**   s-Mary
   say   DET   NOM-Lémya7   DET   pregnant   REPORT   NOM-Mary
   "Lémya7 said that Mary is pregnant."
   [speaker was told by Lémya7; Lémya7 witnessed it; *ku7* merely reinforces the matrix verb of Lémya7's saying]

   b.   wa7   tu7   tsun-tumúl-itas   kw   s-wá7   **ku7**   cw7it
   IMPF   then   say(DIR)-1PL.OBJ-3PL.ERG   DET   NOM-be   REPORT   many
   láti7   i   ámh-a   melk
   DEIC   DET.PL   good-EXIS   milk
   "They told us that there was lots of good milk there."
   [We were told by them; they witnessed it; *ku7* merely reinforces matrix verb of telling]   (Matthewson 2005:204)

   c.   tsut   kw   s-ats'x-en-ás   **ku7**   ku   wa7   'sasquatch'
   say   DET   NOM-see-DIR-3ERG   REPORT   DET   IMPF   sasquatch
   "He said he saw a sasquatch."
   [Speaker was told by him; he witnessed it; *ku7* merely reinforces matrix verb of saying]   (adapted from Matthewson 2005:416)

(62)   a.   tsut   kw   s-Lémya7   kw   s-melyíh   **ku7**   ta
   say   DET   NOM-L.   DET   NOM-marry   REPORT   DET
   í7mats-s-a   s-Rose
   grandchild-3POSS-EXIS   NOM-R.
   "Lémya7 said that [she was told that] Rose's grandchild got married."
   [Lémya7 was told; Lémya7 did not witness it; *ku7* relates to the report given to Lémya7]
   Consultant's comment: "Lémya7 was saying that and she wasn't there either."

b. *tsut s-Lémya7 kw sqwemémn'ek **ku7*** *s-Mary, t'u7*
say NOM-L. DET pregnant REPORT NOM-M. but
plán-lhkan ti7 zwát-en – áts'x-en-lhkan s-Mary áta7
already-1SG.SUBJ DEM know-DIR see-DIR-1SG.SUBJ NOM-M. DEIC
tecwp-álhcw-a inátcwas
buy-place-EXIS yesterday
"Lémya7 said that [she was told that] Mary is pregnant, but I already knew
that; I had seen Mary at the store."
[Lémya7 was told; Lémya7 did not witness it; *ku7* relates to the report given
to Lémya7]

St'át'imcets *ku7* contrasts in its ability to be embedded with the Quechua reportative *-si*, which cannot scope under a verb of saying, as shown in (63). (63ii) corresponds to the 'mood-indicating' reading, and (63iii) to the embedded reading.[28]
-si also cannot appear in the antecedent of a conditional; see Faller (2002:221; to
appear: 8).

(63) *Marya ni-wa-rqa-n Pilar-(*si) chayamu-sqa-n-ta-s*
Marya say-1o-PAST1-3 Pilar arrive-PP-3-ACC-si
"Marya told me that Pilar arrived."
i. speaker was told by someone else that Marya told the speaker that Pilar
arrived
ii. speaker was told by Marya that Pilar arrived
iii. ≠ Marya was told that Pilar arrived (Faller 2002:222)

The St'át'imcets inferential *k'a*, like *ku7*, also has not only reinforcing (or 'mood-
indicating') readings, as in (64), but crucially also embedded readings, as in (65)
which contains the attitude verb "believe".

(64) *Context: Your small nephew comes running up to you and tells you that his sister
punched him in the face. He has a red mark on his face, and you notice that the
sister is looking guilty. You tell the kids' mother what happened and she says she
doesn't believe it, because her daughter never punches people. You say:*
*wenácw-nun'-lhkan kw s-tup-un'-ás **k'a** ta*
true-DIR-1SG.SUBJ DET NOM-punch-DIR-3ERG INFER DET
n-sqwsés7-a, ka-kíilus-a ta smém'lhats-a
1SG.POSS-nephew-EXIS CIRC-embarrassed-CIRC DET girl-EXIS
"I believe she must have hit my nephew, the girl looks guilty."
[*k'a* relates to speaker's belief; speaker has inferential evidence]

(65)   *Context: Lémya7 was babysitting your nephew and niece and she noticed at one point that the boy had a red mark on his face and his sister was looking guilty. She tells you when you get home what she noticed. Then you tell the mother of the kids:*

tsut s-Lémya7   kw   s-tup-un'-ás   **k'a**   s-Maria   ta
say   NOM-Lémya7   DET   NOM-punch-DIR-3ERG   INFER   NOM-Maria   DET
sésq'wez'-s-a
younger.sibling-3POSS-EXIS
"Lémya7 said that Maria must have hit her younger brother."
[*k'a* relates to Lémya7's belief; Lémya7 has evidence]

Finally, the same is true of *-an'*, as shown in (66)–(67), where (67) is the semantically embedded reading.

(66)   *Context: Same as for (64).*

wenácw-nun'-lhkan kw   s-tup-un'-ás-**an'**   ti
true-TR-1SG.SUBJ   DET NOM-punch-DIR-3ERG-PERC.EVID   DET
n-sqwsés7-a,   ka-kíilus-a   ti   smém'lhats-a
1SG.POSS-nephew-EXIS   CIRC-embarrassed-CIRC   DET   girl-EXIS
"I believe she must have hit my nephew, the girl looks guilty."
[*-an'* relates to speaker's belief; speaker has inferential evidence]

(67)   *Context: Same as for (65).*

tsut k-Lémya7   kw   s-tup-un'-ás-**an'**   s-Maria   ti
say   DET-Lémya7   DET NOM-punch-DIR-3ERG-PERC.EVID   NOM-Maria   DET
sésq'wez'-s-a
younger.sibling-3POSS-EXIS
"Lémya7 said that Maria must have hit her younger brother."
[*-an'* relates to Lémya7's belief; Lémya7 has evidence]

We conclude based on these data that the St'át'imcets evidentials can be embedded in the scope of an attitude verb and therefore cannot be accounted for by an illocutionary operator analysis.

We now provide the conditionals data, noting as above, however, that the results for this sub-test are inconclusive with respect to whether the St'át'imcets evidentials contribute to propositional content. Our findings are that none of the St'át'imcets evidentials can take scope inside a conditional antecedent. Examples are given in (68); these are translations of examples given by McCready & Ogata (2007:167–168) (who obtain opposite results for some Japanese evidentials). The consultant's comments for (68c) indicate that she can only understand the evidential as taking scope *outside* the *if*-clause.

(68)   a.   *lh-t'íq-as   **ku7**   k   Sonja, sqwal'-en-ts-kál'ap
             HYP-arrive-3CONJ   REPORT   DET   Sonja   tell-DIR-1SG.OBJ-2PL.SUBJ
             "If [reportedly] Sonja arrives, tell me."

       b.   *lh-t'íq-as   **k'a**   k   Sonja, sqwal'-en-ts-kál'ap
             HYP-arrive-3CONJ   INFER   DET   Sonja   tell-DIR-1SG.OBJ-2PL.SUBJ
             "If Sonja has apparently arrived, please tell me."

       c.   *lh-t'íq-as-**an'**   k   Sonja, sqwal'-en-ts-kál'ap
             HYP-arrive-3CONJ-PERC.EVID   DET   Sonja   tell-DIR-1SG.OBJ-2PL.SUBJ
             "If it looks like Sonja has arrived, please tell me."

Consultant's comment: "No! … You wouldn't say *sqwal'entskál'ap*, because you already think you know, you said *lht'íqasan'*. So nobody needs to tell you."

In conclusion, the embedding data are consistent with – and in the case of the subordinate clauses in (62, 65, 67), force – an analysis whereby they contribute to propositional content.[29,30]

4.7 Readings in interrogatives

Faller (2002:229ff.; to appear) argues that only an illocutionary analysis can account for Quechua discourses such as (69), where the reportative is used to ask a question on someone else's behalf. The situation here is that MF's question to the mother-in-law is not heard, so the consultant repeats the question on MF's behalf.

(69)   *MF to mother-in-law:*
       Imayna-n ka-sha-nki
       how-BPG   be-PROG-2
       "How are you?"
       Consultant to mother-in-law:

       Imayna-s ka-sha-nki
       how-REP   be-PROG-2
       "(She says) How are you?"   (Faller to appear: 14–15)

Faller argues that a question is a speech act of requesting the hearer to assert one proposition contained in the set of answers. In (70), q is an element of the answerset:

(70)   QUEST = REQUEST(ASSERT$_h$(q))
       SINC = {*Des* (s, ASSERT$_h$(q))}   (Faller 2002:237)

In the consultant's question in (69), the reportative takes the entire question act in its scope, as in (71). This means that the speaker presents the information that a third party requested the hearer to assert a proposition from the answer set.

(71)   EVI(REQUEST(ASSERT_h(q)))   (Faller 2002:237)

We have not been able to replicate examples like (69) in St'át'imcets despite extensive elicitation. However, St'át'imcets reportative *ku7* does allow the 'interrogative flip' reading which appears to be cross-linguistically quite common. On this reading, the hearer is asked to base their answer on reportative evidence. An example is given in (72), adapted from data in Faller (to appear: 14).

(72)   *Context: Your husband is out of town, and there was a big party last night. You wake up groggy the next morning and your friend tells you that people have been saying you were dancing with some guy at the party last night. You ask your friend:*
        swat **ku7**   k-wa   táns-ts-an
        who   REPORT   DET-IMPF   dance-CAUS-1SG.ERG
        "Who did they say I was dancing with?"

Interrogative flip with evidentials has received both illocutionary and modal analyses; see Faller (2002), C. Davis, Potts & Speas (2007), Garrett (2001).[31] These readings therefore do not distinguish the two analyses (see Faller to appear for arguments to this effect). The test cases are instead those like (69). In the absence of cases like in (69) in St'át'imcets, we conclude that the interrogative data are consistent with a modal analysis of the St'át'imcets evidentials.[32]

4.8 (In)ability to strengthen assertive strength

It is occasionally argued that evidentials and ordinary epistemic modals differ in that the former, but not the latter, can strengthen the force of an assertion rather than weaken it; see for example Faller (2002:155–156), Speas (2007:18). Faller argues that Quechua statements containing the direct evidential are understood as stronger than their plain counterparts; she further argues that their ability to strengthen the assertion is not predicted by a modal analysis, but is easy to deal with under an illocutionary operator analysis. According to her analysis (2002:25, 165ff.), the direct evidential *-mi* enforces a sincerity condition that the speaker has the best possible grounds for making the assertion. As a side-effect of the best possible grounds sincerity condition, the assertive strength of the utterance is increased. The framework of C. Davis, Potts & Speas (2007) also predicts the existence of evidentials which strengthen the assertion, as they observe (2007: 13) that raising the quality threshold is as easy as lowering it.

We have several reasons to be skeptical of the use of assertive strength as a diagnostic to distinguish an illocutionary operator from a modal analysis. First, the postulated increase in assertive strength is not easy to test in a fieldwork situation. Faller (2002: 156) states that when Quechua consultants are asked about the difference between assertions containing -*mi* and those without, the consultants are "vague", but often describe the former as "more emphatic" than the latter. It seems that there is no truly reliable way of independently testing the increase in assertive strength which is predicted by Faller's best possible grounds analysis.

Our second ground for skepticism is that it is not clear that a modal analysis predicts only weakening of assertive strength. According to von Fintel & Gillies (to appear), statements involving epistemic necessity modals are not necessarily weaker than ordinary assertions.[33] They note, for example, that English *must* is perfectly felicitous in a logical inference drawn from premises, where there is no uncertainty whatsoever.[34]

The final thing to note about the 'strengthening' diagnostic is that it is inapplicable to all indirect evidentials, since these are never claimed to increase assertive strength. The argument thus reduces to the claim that direct evidentials are not subject to a modal analysis. This may be correct, but would affect our proposals only if we wished to claim that all evidentials in all languages are epistemic modals. Since we do not claim this, all we need to show here is that the St'át'imcets evidentials which we *are* claiming to be modals are not direct evidentials. This was argued for in Section 2.[35]

4.9 Summary

We have tested the St'át'imcets evidentials against eight diagnostics, most of which have been presented in the literature as ways to distinguish an illocutionary operator analysis from a modal analysis (or at least from an analysis involving contribution to propositional content). We have argued that a few of the diagnostics are inconclusive, as they do not, in fact, distinguish the analyses. However, the results are still quite striking: the St'át'imcets evidentials obey the predictions of the modal analysis in every respect. Our findings are summarized in (73).

(73)

	illoc. op. analysis	modal analysis	St'át'imcets evidentials
1. felicitous if p is known to be false?	yes	no	no
2. felicitous if p is known to be true?	yes	no	no
3. indirect evidence requirement cancelable?	no	no	no
4. indirect evidence requirement blocked by negation?	no	no	no
5. pass assent/dissent test?	no	yes	yes
6. embeddable?	no	yes	yes
7. allow speech-act readings in interrogatives?	yes	no	no
8. can strengthen assertion?	unknown	unknown	unknown

The St'át'imcets evidentials are clearly not illocutionary operators, and we conclude that they are epistemic modals. The latter conclusion is further supported in the next section, where we will see that the evidentials share an important property with all other modals in the language, namely that they allow variability in quantificational force.

5. The St'át'imcets evidentials do not encode distinctions of speaker certainty

According to de Haan (1999), evidentials are distinguishable from epistemic modals in that the former encode the source of information, while the latter encode the speaker's certainty level about the proposition expressed. For example, de Haan argues that Dutch *moeten* (cognate with English *must)* is ambiguously either an epistemic modal or an evidential.[36] He argues that under its epistemic reading, *moeten* "denotes a high degree of confidence in the truth of the statement on the part of the speaker." However, on its evidential interpretation, *moeten* allows continuations that express either confidence or doubt. The evidential uses are illustrated in (74).

(74) a. *het **moet** een goede film   zijn, en   ik ben daar zeker van*
       it   must a   good movie be   and I   am there sure of
       "It is said to be a good film, and I am convinced of it."(de Haan 1997: 16)

b. *het **moet** een goede film   zijn, maar ik heb er   mijn twijfels*
   it   must a   good movie be   but   I have there my   doubts
   over
   about
   "It is said to be a good movie, but I have my doubts about that."
                                                              (de Haan 1997:17)

De Haan uses the *moeten* data to argue that epistemic modals necessarily encode speaker certainty distinctions. We reject this idea, and will provide evidence in the rest of this section that modal elements do not always encode certainty.[37]

Within the possible worlds semantics for modals, variation in certainty levels equates with variation in the strength of the quantification over possible worlds. Thus, a speaker who uses an existential modal is less certain about the truth of the embedded proposition than a speaker who uses a universal modal: the speaker of (75b) is less certain about the truth of (75a) than the speaker of (75c) is.

(75) a. Michl is the murderer.
      b. Michl *might* be the murderer.
      c. Michl *must* be the murderer.

In Rullmann, Matthewson & Davis (to appear) and in Davis, Matthewson & Rullmann (to appear), we argue against de Haan's contention that modals necessarily encode distinctions of quantificational strength. We show there that a wide range of modals in St'át'imcets – including epistemics, deontics, circumstantials and futures – display variability in quantificational force. In fact, we have not discovered any modal element in St'át'imcets which encodes a particular quantificational strength. Examples are given in (76)–(77) for deontic *ka*, with universal and existential interpretations respectively; see the references above for many more examples, involving a range of modals in St'át'imcets.

(76) *cúy'-lhkacw   ká   t'u7 nas áts'x-en ta   kwtámts-sw-a*
      going.to-2SG.SUBJ DEON just go   see-DIR DET husband-2SG.POSS-EXIS
      "You must go to see your husband."
                                        (Rullmann, Matthewson & Davis to appear)

(77) *lán-lhkacw   ka   áts'x-en ti   kwtámts-sw-a,   t'u7*
      already-2SG.SUBJ DEON see-DIR DET husband-2SG.POSS-EXIS but
      áoz-as   k-wá-su   xát'-min' k-wá-su
      NEG-3CONJ DET-IMPF-2SG.POSS want-RED DET-IMPF-2SG.POSS
      nás-al'men, t'u7 áma
      go-want   just good

"You may go see your husband, but if you don't want to go, that's okay."
(Rullmann, Matthewson & Davis to appear)

Given the general variability of modals in St'át'imcets in terms of certainty/quanti-ficational force, and given the evidence presented in the previous section that the St'át'imcets evidential clitics are epistemic modals, we predict that the eviden-tials do not lexically encode the level of the speaker's certainty. This prediction is correct.

The examples in (78)–(80) are all drawn from spontaneously-produced oral narratives. (78a) presents a universal epistemic claim using *k'a*. The continuation in (78b) shows that the speaker perceives the anger to be a result of the loud-ness. This context supports a universal rather than an existential interpretation of the modal.

(78)   *Context: Speaker is telling about when she was a child and she used to play in the evenings with her friends.*

a.   *na   s-pála7-s-a,   wá7-lhkalh   **k'a**   wenácw-ts-am'*
DET NOM-one-3POSS-EXIS IMPF-1PL.SUBJ INFER true-mouth-MID
"One time, we must have been loud."

b.   *ni…lh s-zaw't-min-tumúlh-as   **k'a**   láti7 nu   wa7   wá7,*
FOC   NOM-fed.up-RED-1PL.OBJ-3ERG INFER DEIC DET IMPF be
s-Ernest Jacob
NOM-Ernest Jacob
"And Ernest Jacob, who was living there, got fed up with us."
(Matthewson 2005:410)

In (79), there is strong evidence in the context that Jim Hoffmann is frightened. The context thus involves a high degree of certainty on the part of the speaker and thus supports a universal epistemic modal claim.

(79)   *Context: Jim Hoffmann thought he saw a sasquatch and came running back with huge terrified eyes.*
*ka-qus-tum'-á   **k'a**   wi7*
CIRC-frighten-PASS-CIRC INFER EMPH
"It really must have frightened him!"   (Matthewson 2005:418)

(80) seems to involve existential force. The first sentence explicitly states that the speaker is unsure about the truth of the proposition embedded under *k'a* in the second sentence. Note that we cannot conclude in this context that the speaker's mother *must* have put the fish away for eating later. She could have given it to relatives instead.

(80) *cw7aoz kw-en-wá   stexw lexláx-s   lh-as*
      NEG   DET-1SG.POSS-IMPF very   remember-CAUS HYP-3CONJ

      kás-tum'   i   sk'wílh-a   ts'úqwaz'
      what-1PL.ERG DET.PL leftover-EXIS fish

      "I don't remember what we did with the leftover fish."

      *wa7 **k'a** qelh-n-ás   nilh kw s-ts'áqw-an'-em*
      IMPF INFER put.away-DIR-3ERG FOC DET NOM-eat-DIR-1PL.ERG

      lh-kalál-as
      HYP-soon-3CONJ

      "Maybe she put it away and we ate it later."   (Matthewson 2005: 58)

An elicited example involving existential force is given in (81). Here, a continuation asserting that perhaps the embedded proposition is false is accepted by consultants.

(81) *Context: There is some evidence that John has left, e.g. his bag has gone, but maybe he just took his bag to the bathroom.*

      *qwatsáts **k'a**   tu7   k   John, t'u7 wa7 k'a   sxek*
      leave   INFER then DET John but IMPF INFER maybe

      k-wa-s   cw7aoz t'u7 k-wa-s   qwatsáts
      DET-IMPF-3POSS NEG   just DET-IMPF-3POSS leave

      "John may (#must) have left, but maybe he hasn't left."

A final (volunteered) example which forces existential quantification is given in (82).

(82) *Context: There is some evidence that John has left, e.g. his bag has gone, but maybe he just took his bag to the bathroom.*

      *qwatsáts **k'a**   tu7   k   John, t'u7 sxek   cw7aoz k'a   kw*
      leave   INFER then DET John but maybe NEG   INFER DET

      s-qwatsáts
      NOM-leave

      "John may have left, but he may not have left."

These data show that *k'a*, which is lexically specified for indirect inferential evidence, is not lexically restricted in terms of its quantificational force / certainty level.

   Next we turn to the perceived-evidence clitic *-an'*. This seems to prefer universal interpretations. As shown in (83)–(84), *-an'* is usually rejected if it is made explicit that only an existential claim is being made.

(83) #*qwatsats-as-án'*   *tu7   kw   s-John, t'u7 wa7   k'a   sxek*
      leave-3CONJ-PERC.EVID then DET NOM-J. but IMPF INFER maybe
      k-wa-s   *cw7aoz t'u7 k-wa-s*   *qwatsáts*
      DET-IMPF-3POSS NEG   just DET-IMPF-3POSS leave
      "John apparently left, but maybe he hasn't left."
      [Attempted meaning: There is some evidence that John has left, e.g. his bag
      has gone, but maybe he just took his bag to the bathroom.]

(84) #*qwatsats-as-án'*   *tu7   kw   s-John, t'u7 aoz   t'u7*
      leave-3CONJ-PERC.EVID then DET NOM-J. but NEG   just
      kw-en-s-wá   *zwát-en   lh-qwatsáts-as*
      DET-1SG.POSS-NOM-IMPF know-DIR COMP-leave-3CONJ
      "John may have left, but I don't know whether he did leave."

However, *-an'* is sometimes accepted and even volunteered in contexts which seem
to support existential interpretations. This suggests that the universal effect with
-an' is only a preference.

(85) *Context: You're not sure it was Dave who stole your ts'wan, but maybe it was.*
      nílh-as-an'   *kw   s-Dave   ta   naq'w-ens-táli-ha   i*
      FOC-3CONJ-PERC.EVID DET NOM-Dave DET steal-DIR-TOP-EXIS DET.PL
      n-ts'wán-a
      1SG.POSS-wind.dried.salmon-EXIS
      "It looks like it was Dave who stole my ts'wan."

With reportative *ku7*, the difference between universal and existential force would
correspond to a difference between "[Given what I've been told], p *must* be true"
and "[Given what I've been told], p *may* be true".[38] Like *-an'*, *ku7* seems to prefer
a high level of certainty. The reportative is always felicitous when the speaker is
strongly convinced of the truth of p, because the source of the report is very reliable. This is the case in (86), where the speaker may not have ever witnessed her
father driving a cab, but surely heard about it from very reliable sources.

(86) *wa7 ku7   aylh múta7 tq-álk'-en-as   ta   taxicab-a*
      IMPF REPORT then and   touch-string-DIR-3ERG DET taxicab-EXIS
      knáti7 táown-a
      DEIC   town-EXIS
      "[reportedly] He [my father] also drove a taxicab around town."
                                                        (Matthewson 2005: 378)

When the speaker is less certain about the truth of the embedded proposition,
there is speaker variation in acceptability judgments. This is the case for example

in (87), a context which is designed to force an existential interpretation ("in some possible worlds in which I was told that p, p is true").

(87)   *Context: There is a rumour going around that Roger was elected chief. Some-*
       times that kind of rumour is right, sometimes it's wrong. You really have no idea
       whether it's likely to be right or wrong. You tell me:
       %*aw-an-ém*   **ku7**   *kw   s-Roger   ku   cuz'   kúkwpi7*
       choose-DIR-PASS   REPORT   DET   NOM-Roger   DET   going.to   chief
       "[reportedly] Roger was elected to be chief."

Situations similar to (87) are described by Faller (2002) as test cases for the quan-tificational force of a reportative modal. Faller observes (2002:109) that if the reli-ability of the source is unknown, only an existential analysis predicts a reportative sentence to be true. This is because if the reliability of a source is unknown, then the set of worlds in which that report is heard will include both worlds where the report is true, and worlds where it is false. Correspondingly, a universal quan-tification over the report worlds will be false. The fact that some speakers accept (87) therefore provides some support for the claim that *ku7* allows an existential interpretation.

So far in this section we have shown that all three evidentials under discus-sion show variable quantificational force, being possible both in contexts where the speaker is fairly certain about the truth of the embedded proposition, and in contexts where the speaker is less certain. We have also noted that while existential readings are relatively easy to find and elicit for *ka'*, they are less easy to obtain for *-an'* and *ku7*. In the remainder of this section we propose that this latter fact does not affect our main claim that St'át'imcets evidentials fail to encode certainty distinctions.

The first thing to note is that even though *-an'* and *ku7* prefer universal in-terpretations, they clearly do not *encode* universal force. We know this because there are no contrasting elements in the system: there is only one perceived-evidence evidential, and only one reportative. If existential force is appropriate in a perceived-evidence or reportative context, *-an'* or *ku7* will be used.

The second thing to note is that the difference between *k'a* and *-an'/ku7* with respect to speaker certainty tendencies actually falls out from the differences in their respective information sources. As discussed by Faller (2001, 2002), many people have argued that distinctions in information source are automatically also distinctions in certainty. Thus, for example, a visual information source leads to greater certainty than an indirect inferential information source (see e.g., By-bee 1985; and also Willett 1988 for an evidential hierarchy organized along these lines). However, Faller (2001, 2002:96–98) argues that such correlations are indirect and context-dependent, and similarly Fitneva (2001) and C. Davis, Potts & Speas (2007) claim that there is no strict or cross-linguistically consistent correlation between the source of information and the degree of speaker certainty. Assuming this is right, we expect that individual evidentials can exhibit tendencies towards greater or lesser levels of speaker certainty, based on the type of information source they encode, but that these tendencies can be overridden in context. This accords with the St'át'imcets situation, since an evidential which requires perceived evidence, such as -an', will naturally tend towards higher levels of certainty than one which does not, such as k'a.

Let us summarize what we have established so far. We saw in Section 2 that the St'át'imcets evidentials encode differences in information source, and in Section 4 we argued that they should be analyzed as epistemic modals. We gave further support for that conclusion in this section, where we showed that the St'át'imcets evidentials pattern with other modals in the language in failing to encode quantificational force (which for epistemic modals/evidentials corresponds to speaker certainty).[39] The obvious conclusion to be drawn from this is that (contra de Haan) it is not an intrinsic requirement of a modal that it distinguish certainty level. In Section 7, we will draw an even stronger conclusion. We will claim that cross-linguistically, modals must choose between either encoding *source* (as the St'át'imcets evidentials do) or *force* (as English modals do).

6.   A modal analysis of St'át'imcets evidentials[40]

In this section we present our formal analysis of the St'át'imcets evidentials. The basic idea is inspired by Klinedinst's (2005) work on possibility modals in English. Klinedinst argues that possibility modals are analogous to plural indefinite DPs. In the same way that plural indefinites existentially quantify over pluralities of entities, possibility modals existentially quantify over pluralities of possible worlds. The individual worlds that are members of the plurality of worlds introduced by the existential quantifier are then universally quantified over. The logical structure of possibility modals can be represented as in (88):

(88)   MODAL(p) is true with respect to a modal base B and a possible world w iff:
$$\exists W[W \subseteq B(w) \wedge W \neq \varnothing \wedge \forall w'[w' \in W \rightarrow p(w')]]$$

The modal is interpreted with respect to a given modal base B and a possible world w (the evaluation world). B(w) is the set of worlds that are accessible from the evaluation world w given the modal base B. (88) can therefore be paraphrased as "there is a set of worlds W that are accessible from w, such that p is true in every world in W", or more concisely, "in some set of accessible worlds W, p is true".

We adopt Klinedinst's proposal as the basis for our analysis of *all* modals in St'át'imcets, including evidentials. We add a twist, however. Within Klinedinst's analysis, assuming W is non-empty, (88) is truth-conditionally equivalent to the traditional existential interpretation of possibility modals. We propose that St'át'imcets modals are analogous to *specific* plural indefinites ("there is a *specific* set of worlds W...."). We adopt a particular formal interpretation of specific indefinites involving choice functions (Reinhart 1997; Winter 1997; Kratzer 1998; Matthewson 1999, among others). In the same way that a choice function representing a specific indefinite determiner picks out an individual from the set denoted by the common noun (or NP), the modal choice function f will pick out a subset of the possible worlds that are accessible from the actual world. The universal quantifier then quantifies over the individual worlds that are members of the set picked out by f.

According to our analysis, St'át'imcets modals thus involve *two* contextually determined parameters, the modal base B and the choice function f. The modal base B functions in the same way as it does in Kratzer's analysis of English modals: it is a function (of type $<s,st>$) which maps the evaluation world w onto the set of possible worlds that are accessible from it.[41] The choice function f picks out a subset of B(w). The semantic type of f is therefore $<st,st>$. f is moreover restricted in such a way that, for any set of worlds W, $f(W) \subseteq W$. Following Kratzer's (1998) analysis of specific indefinites, we propose that f is a free variable whose value is determined by context.[42] We also assume that the choice function is present in the LF representation of the sentence; see Rullmann, Matthewson & Davis (to appear) for discussion.

The general interpretation schema for St'át'imcets modals, interpreted with respect to an utterance context c and a world w, is given in (89). Particular modals impose lexical restrictions on the modal base; we return to this below.

(89) $[[\text{MODAL}]]^{c,w}$ is only defined if c provides a modal base B.
       If defined, $[[\text{MODAL}]]^{c,w} = \lambda f_{<st,st>}. \lambda p_{<s,t>} . \forall w'[w' \in f(B(w)) \rightarrow p(w')]]$

This analysis accounts for the apparent variability in quantificational force of St'át'imcets evidentials as follows. The quantifier is uniformly universal, but variation in the choice functions affects the interpretation. The larger the subset of B(w) which f selects, the stronger the proposition that is expressed. At one extreme, f may simply be the identity function. This results in a reading that is equivalent to the standard analysis of strong modals like English *must*. However, if f selects a proper subset of B(w), the resulting reading is weaker, although it still involves universal quantification.[43]

Let's look at an example of how different choices of f explain the apparent quantificational variability of St'át'imcets evidentials. Consider (90):

(90)   *t'cum*   ***k'a***   *kw*   *s-John*
       win(MID)   INFER   DET   NOM-John
       "John must/may have won."   (Rullmann, Matthewson & Davis to appear)

(90) means approximately "for a specific subset of epistemically accessible worlds W, John won in all worlds that are members of W". Now, one possible scenario is that the speaker knows that John had played bingo last night and is spending lots of money today. The modal base therefore contains all the worlds in which John played bingo last night and is spending lots of money today, and the choice function picks out a subset of these worlds. If f is the identity function, the reading is that of a standard necessity modal: "(Given his bingo-playing and money-spending), John must have won." However, suppose that f instead picks out a proper subset of the accessible worlds, say those worlds in which John not only played bingo last night and is spending lots of money today, but also is unemployed. In that case, the sentence asserts that in all of the bingo-playing-money-spending-unemployed worlds, John must have won. But now, the sentence no longer makes a universal modal claim based on the known facts (since perhaps there are worlds compatible with the speaker's knowledge in which John is not unemployed; these are the accessible worlds which failed to be selected by the choice function). Instead, the utterance reduces to an existential claim: in some proper subset of the worlds compatible with the known facts, John won.

According to this proposal, there is no ambiguity or under-specification in the semantics of the modals; they are uniformly universal quantifiers over worlds. Their apparent quantificational variability simply depends on the size of the subset of B(w) that is selected by f. There is no dichotomy between a strong and a weak reading, but instead there is a continuity of different degrees of strengths. The smaller f(B(w)) is, the more restricted the universal quantifier is, and the more likely it is to be translated as English *may, could,* or *might* rather than *must*. However, this apparent ambiguity is only an artifact of using English as the translation medium.

The analysis of the inferential evidential is given in (91).

(91) *Semantics of k'a (inferential)*

$[[k'a]]^{c,w}$ is only defined if c provides a modal base B such that for all worlds w', w' ∈ B(w) iff the inferential evidence in w holds in w'.

If defined, $[[k'a]]^{c,w} = \lambda f_{<st,st>}. \lambda p_{<s,t>} . \forall w'[w' \in f(B(w)) \rightarrow p(w')]]$

The analyses of *-an'* and *ku7* are exactly parallel; the only difference resides in the definedness condition, which for *-an'* requires that the modal base contain all those worlds in which the perceived evidence in w holds, and for *ku7* requires that it contain all worlds in which the reported evidence in w holds.

We should note that the idea that modals can lexically encode restrictions on the modal base goes back to Kratzer's original analysis. Kratzer notes (1991:650), for example, that German *darf* is unambiguously circumstantial (with a deontic ordering source), while *wird* is unambiguously epistemic. Another similarity between the St'át'imcets evidential modals and modals in more familiar languages is that in both systems, restrictions on the modal base can be explicitly spelled out. This is illustrated for *k'a* in (92).[44]

(92) *Context: You are driving past John's house, and wondering if he might be home. You notice his lights are on. You say:*

wa7 lhap-an'-ítas   i   ucwalmícw-a i

IMPF extinguish-DIR-3PL.ERG DET.PL person-EXIS   DET.PL

ts'ák'w-i-ha   lh-as   nás-wit kenká7, t'u7 wa7 **k'a**   t'u7

light-3PL.POSS-EXIS HYP-3CONJ go-3PL DEIC   but IMPF INFER just

zam'   s-t'al,   wa7 s-gwel   ti ts'ák'w-s-a

after.all STAT-stop IMPF STAT-burn DET light-3POSS-EXIS

"People usually turn their lights off when they go out, so given that John's lights are on, he must be home."

7. Conclusion

In this paper we have provided an analysis of three St'át'imcets evidentials as epistemic modals. Here we summarize our findings and briefly discuss the implications for the analysis of evidentials cross-linguistically.

We began by showing that the three elements *k'a, -an'* and *ku7* encode distinctions of information source: *k'a* requires indirect inferring evidence, *-an'* requires indirect perceived evidence, and *ku7* requires reported evidence. We then argued, on the basis of eight diagnostics, that the St'át'imcets evidentials are not analyzable as illocutionary operators, but instead are epistemic modals with a presupposition which restricts the modal base. We further showed that the evidentials, just like all other modals in the language, display apparent variability in quantificational force. Our formal analysis adapts proposals by Klinedinst (2005) to account for this apparent variability in quantificational force. We analyze the quantification as unambiguously universal, but utilize a choice function which narrows down the modal base, by selecting a (possibly proper) subset of the accessible worlds as the domain of the quantifier.

There is one potential counter-argument to our claim that *k'a, -an'* and *ku7* are modal evidentials. This would be to say that these St'át'imcets elements may indeed be epistemic modals, but they are not really evidentials. Semantically, *k'a, -an'* and *ku7* clearly count as evidentials: according to Aikhenvald (2004: 3), "[t]o be considered as an evidential, a morpheme has to have 'source of information' as its core meaning." This is certainly the case for *k'a, -an'* and *ku7*, as was shown in Section 2. However, Aikhenvald also imposes a stronger requirement on 'grammatical evidentiality': "[i]n languages with grammatical evidentiality, marking how one knows something is a must" (2004: 6). This obligatoriness requirement is *not* met in St'át'imcets: we show in Matthewson & Davis (in prep.) that evidential marking in this language is optional (though strongly preferred). Does the optionality of *k'a, -an'* and *ku7* therefore render irrelevant all our efforts to prove they are epistemic modals?

We maintain that it does not. First, the St'át'imcets elements differ from the weaker 'evidential strategies' discussed by Aikhenvald (e.g., 2004: 365) in that they have information source as their primary, not a secondary, meaning. Second, *k'a, -an'* and *ku7* are much more common than lexicalized evidential strategies in English. Their use is so pervasive, and their absence when their conditions are satisfied is so dispreferred by consultants, that Matthewson (1998) (incorrectly) claimed that their use was obligatory. Finally, we agree with McCready & Ogata (2007: 152) that

> Empirically, the statement that 'true evidentials' are obligatory is not accurate. Although it is true that many languages that have evidentials strongly prefer their use, such use is almost never – and possibly simply *never* – obligatory.

McCready & Ogata correctly observe that although Quechua is very frequently cited as an obligatory-evidential language, Faller (2002) has clearly shown that evidentials are not in fact obligatory in this language. There is no reason not to believe that other claims about obligatory evidential use may be just as mistaken. We therefore share McCready & Ogata's (2007) skepticism about the usefulness of the obligatory/non-obligatory opposition with respect to evidentials. Like Mc-

Cready & Ogata for Japanese, we reject any notion that the non-obligatoriness of the St'át'imcets elements disqualifies them from being 'true evidentials'.

Given, then, that the St'át'imcets *k'a, -an'* and *ku7* are evidentials and also modals, our findings have several implications for the analysis of evidentials cross-linguistically. The first is that the two categories of evidentiality and epistemic modality cannot be entirely distinct, as has been claimed by de Haan (1999) and Aikhenvald (2004). We are certainly not the first to provide a modal analysis of evidentials; see Izvorski (1997), Garrett (2001), Ehrich (2001), McCready & Asher (2006), McCready & Ogata (2007), among others. However, the St'át'imcets data contribute something novel to the debate, which we believe allows us to effectively negate many of the arguments which have been made against modal analyses of evidentials.

The critical property of St'át'imcets is that in this language, *modals do not encode the level of speaker certainty* (or in other words, they do not encode distinctions of quantificational force). It is striking that many of the arguments in the literature against modal analyses of evidentials reduce to the claim that evidentials do not encode certainty distinctions. This is true of arguments presented by de Haan (1999) and Aikhenvald (2004), as well as by Lazard (2001). For example, Aikhenvald (2004:7) cites Lazard (2001) as having providing "highly convincing arguments" that evidentiality is not a subcategory of modality. However, what Lazard actually argues is that (contrary to claims by Plungian 2001) there is no class of 'modalized evidentials' which "imply a judgment about the reliability of the information" (Lazard 2001:366). What Lazard claims is therefore that evidentials do not directly encode notions such as reliability or doubt. His argument – like those of de Haan and Aikhenvald – is thus not against *modality* (a category whose essence, for us, is that it involves reference to or quantification over possible words), but rather against *certainty distinctions*.

Bearing this in mind, recall that all St'át'imcets modals – not just epistemic, but deontic, circumstantial and future modals – fail to encode certainty distinctions. This provides strong evidence for uncoupling the two notions of 'modality' and 'certainty distinctions', thereby automatically negating all Lazard-style arguments against modal analyses of evidentials.[45]

There is one respect in which we agree with de Haan, Aikhenvald and others, however. We believe it to be true that elements which distinguish information source usually or always fail to distinguish certainty distinctions (and vice versa). We thus predict that epistemic modals must choose to encode either 'source or force'. Chung (2005:185–186) makes a similar suggestion; she observes that regular modals focus on the difference in probability, while evidential modals focus on the difference in the modal base and the ordering source. We thus predict that there will be no language which is like St'át'imcets, but which possesses two reportative morphemes, one which involves universal quantification and one which involves existential quantification.[46]

Finally, we hope that this paper has contributed to the growing evidence for the semantic heterogeneity of evidentials. As argued by Faller (2002, 2006), there is no reason to expect the core function of evidentials – the encoding of information source – to be restricted to one grammatical domain or to manifest itself in identical semantics from language to language. Empirically also, we see ample evidence that evidentials are sometimes epistemic modals, but sometimes are not. The question of whether the semantics of evidentials is predictable from independent properties (such as syntactic position, as claimed by Blain & Déchaine 2007) is an interesting question which deserves further investigation.

Notes

* We are very grateful to St'át'imcets consultants Gertrude Ned, Laura Thevarge, Rose Agnes Whitley and the late Beverley Frank. We are also very grateful to Seth Cable, Rose-Marie Déchaine, Martina Faller, Angelika Kratzer, Tamina Stephenson, Martina Wiltschko and an anonymous reviewer for helpful feedback and suggestions, as well as to the UBC pragmatics readings group and audiences at the University of British Columbia, the Paris Conference on Time and Modality, and the 41st International Conference on Salish and Neighbouring Languages. Errors are our own. This research is supported by SSHRC grants #410-2002-1715, #410-2203-1138, and #410-2005-0875.

1. All data come from original fieldwork unless otherwise stated. Data are presented in the official St'át'imcets orthography, developed by Jan van Eijk (see van Eijk 1997). Abbreviations used are: CAUS = causative, CIRC = circumstantial modal, COLL = collective, CONJ = conjunctive (subjunctive) subject, COUNTER = counter to expectations, DEIC = deictic, DEM = demonstrative, DET = determiner, DIR = directive transitivizer, EMPH = emphatic, ERG = ergative, EXIS = wide-scope existential, FOC = focus, HYP = hypothetical complementizer, IMPF = imperfective, INCH = inchoative, INFER = inferential evidential, MID = middle intransitivizer, NEG = negative, NOM = nominalizer, OBJ = object, PERC.EVID = perceived evidence evidential, PL = plural, POSS = possessive, RED = redirective transitivizer, REPORT = reportative evidential, SG = singular, STAT = stative, SUBJ = indicative subject, TOP = non-topical subject marker, TR = transitive.

2. In addition, the demonstrative adverb *lákw7a*, which is discussed in Matthewson and Davis (in prep.), has an evidential meaning, involving knowledge based on non-visual perception (hearing, smell, taste).

3. *-an'* differs morphosyntactically from the other two evidentials in several ways. First, it obligatorily induces conjunctive subject morphology; second, it precedes rather than follows the enclitic *-a* which occurs with existence-asserting determiners, as well as the suffix *-a* which forms

part of the discontinuous circumstantial modal. Finally, in its phonological shape *-an'* resembles an affix rather than a clitic, since (aside from *-a*) vowel-initial clitics are disallowed. The last two features account for the orthographic convention whereby *-an'* is written together with the preceding word, whereas *k'a* and *ku7* are not.

4. *ku7* is sometimes not expressed in the English translations given by consultants, and is sometimes rendered with 'I was told' or 'somebody told me'. However, these glosses are misleading, since they express an aspect of meaning truth-conditionally which we show in Section 4.4 to be only a presupposition. We have translated sentences containing *ku7* uniformly with '[reportedly]'.

5. Aikhenvald (2004) distinguishes 'grammatical evidentials' from 'evidential strategies'; in Section 7 we argue that the St'át'imcets evidentials cannot be relegated to the latter category.

6. Aikhenvald (2004:59) casts doubt on Willett's distinction between second- and third-hand information, since she has been unable to find good evidence for a distinction between these two kinds of information sources. We include data for Willett's full range of cases here for completeness.

7. According to van Eijk (1997:200), *-an'* "indicates that the speaker concludes something from circumstantial evidence." Davis (2006: Chapter 23) observes that *-an'* "refers to a situation where the speaker has come to a conclusion about the truth of an event on the basis of appearances."

8. A reviewer asks whether speakers prefer *-an'* in cases where there is perceived evidence. Since the requirements for *-an'* are stronger than for *ka'*, Gricean reasoning might lead us to expect that using *k'a* would implicate that the requirements for felicitous use of *-an'* are not met. We have not been able to detect a preference for *-an'* in cases like (12) or (14). However, this is consistent with other parallel cases elsewhere in the language. For example, the St'át'imcets determiner system contrasts a general singular determiner with one which specifies that the referent of the DP is absent at the time of speech. Here we see no strong requirement to use the latter determiner if the referent is absent. Rather, the absent determiner is used only if the speaker wishes to emphasize the absence; the general determiner is the default. The same may be true of the evidentials: *k'a* may be the default indirect evidential. Potential evidence for this comes from (i), where the English translation was volunteered by the consultant, suggesting that *k'a* may even be licit in reportative contexts. Further research is required into whether this is generally possible.

(i)   *kwis* **k'a**   *kelh lh-nátcw-as*
      rain INFER FUT HYP-tomorrow-3CONJ
      "They say it's going to rain maybe tomorrow."

9. Izvorski also discusses Turkish and to a lesser extent Norwegian, which appear to have very similar constructions.

10. See Garrett (2001), McCready & Ogata (2007) for differing versions of a general epistemic modal approach to evidentials in Tibetan and Japanese respectively.

11. It is an interesting question how one restricts the content of the report which is presupposed to have been made. On the one hand, the report does not have to have exactly the same form or truth conditions as the embedded proposition in the reportative evidential utterance. On the other hand, the content of the two cannot be too disparate, as shown in (i) for St'át'imcets. Even though John's statement constitutes evidence for what you later express to me, your utterance cannot contain a reportative. We leave the precise characterization of the content of the report for future research.

(i)   *Context: You are sitting with John and there is one cup of coffee on the table. John says*:

áts'x-en-lhkan   i   án'was-a   zew'áksten
see-DIR-1SG.SUBJ   DET.PL   two-EXIS   cup
"I see two cups."
Later, you tell me:

#*qyax*   ***ku7***   *k*   *John*
drunk   REPORT   DET   John
"[reportedly] John is/was drunk."

12. A direct evidential (such as the Quechua 'best possible grounds' evidential) is claimed to be able to raise the quality threshold. We return to this issue in Section 4.8.

13. In Korean, the spatio-temporal element co-occurs with true evidentials; see Chung (2005, 2007) for details.

14. The framework of C. Davis, Potts & Speas (2007) seems to also predict that the speaker can know that the embedded proposition is false: they argue that the use of an indirect evidential implies that the embedded proposition is below the quality threshold.

15. See McCready & Ogata (2007) for arguments against a presuppositional modal analysis of some evidentials in Japanese.

16. Faller (2002:227) advances the negation test as support for her illocutionary analysis of the Quechua evidentials, none of which scope under negation. Appropriately, however, she does not argue that the negation facts mitigate *against* a modal analysis. In fact, all the negation data provided by Faller are equally well accounted for under an Izvorski-style analysis. In de Haan's (1999) discussion of interactions with negation, he argues that evidentials differ from epistemic modals in taking obligatory wide scope. However, he fails to distinguish between the restriction on the source of the information (which is predicted to take wide scope by both the modal and the non-modal analysis) and the asserted content.

17. The translations given for (41)–(43) are not natural ones. We have attempted to disambiguate the readings, while avoiding interference from restrictions on scopal interactions between modals and negation in English. See also below in the text, where we point out that the St'át'imcets modals do not even necessarily have the interpretation of a universal quantifier.

18. The Bulgarian perfect of evidentiality also involves variable quantificational strength, in spite of the translations in (39) above; see Izvorski (1997:226) for discussion.

19. This test was called 'challengeability' by Faller (2002); it is called 'assent/dissent' by Papafragou (2006) and Faller (to appear).

20. Papafragou (2006) also argues that dissenting with an epistemic modal involves claiming either that the specification of the modal base is incorrect, or that there has been a logical mistake such that the modal assertion does not follow from the available evidence. See also Garrett (2001:29–31). In our formal analysis to be given below, challenges to the modal base can be viewed in the same light as challenges to (premises which help set) the value of other free variables in discourse, such as pronouns, tenses, or quantifier domain restrictors.

21. Note that von Fintel & Gillies do not actually commit themselves to this analysis of the data; see their paper for details.

22. Mastermind is a game in which one player places coloured pegs behind a screen and the other must work out the colours and the order of the pegs after eliciting some clues.

23. The consultant's initial response to (52a) was "You know, so you can't really say *k'a.*" Once the context was more fully explained, she commented "It's okay, if you don't want to let him know."

24. One consultant freely accepted (53a). A second consultant's initial response to (53a) was "You wouldn't say *wá7asan'* because then *you* would be guessing." When asked whether it would it be okay if the responder is trying not to let the son know the facts, but merely wants to say "You're right, there might be," the consultant accepted the sentence. This second consultant also displayed the same initial reluctance to accept (53c).

25. It may seem as if the response in (54) denies the embedded proposition "Buffy St. Marie is coming to Mt. Currie", rather than the modal claim. However, the continuation of the response indicates that what is being denied is the premise that Bill is reliable. The responder thus challenges the first speaker's assumption that the set of worlds in which Bill reported that Buffy is coming contains some/only worlds in which the report is true. (See discussion in Faller 2002: 102ff. on how the reliability of the source affects the modal base with a reportative modal evidential.) Similar issues arise with an example provided by Faller (2002: 113); see her discussion in fn. 18. Faller observes that if the challenger does not know for sure whether the embedded proposition is true (as in (55)), challenges as in (55) can be reasonably assumed to involve denial of the modal claim.

26. Faller does apply the assent/dissent test in the way we suggest here to one of the Quechua evidentials, the conjectural *-chá* (Faller 2002: 181). This evidential passes the assent/dissent test, which is consistent with Faller's analysis of it as containing a modal component.

27. See Garrett (2001) for detailed discussion of embedded evidentials in Tibetan, and Sauerland & Schenner (2007) on embedded evidentials in Bulgarian. See McCready & Asher (2006), McCready & Ogata (2007) for discussion of Japanese evidentials and modals in conditionals.

28. *-si* also cannot appear in the antecedent of a conditional; see Faller (2002: 221; to appear: 8).

29. A reviewer asks whether the St'át'imcets evidentials scope over or under quantified subjects. Preliminary results suggests that both scope relations may be possible, but there are many interfering factors to control for and we have to leave discussion of this issue for future research.

30. There is another issue with respect to conditionals, namely whether the presupposition restricting the evidence source projects. As is well-known, presuppositions are blocked if the trigger appears in the consequent of a conditional whose antecedent asserts the presupposition. For example, (ia) presupposes (ib), but (ic) does not presuppose (ib).

(i) a.   John will stop smoking when he reads this.
     b.   John currently smokes.
     c.   If John smokes, he will stop smoking when he reads this.   (Faller 2002: 118)

Given this, Faller (2002) argues that an element whose evidential meaning is a presupposition should lose its evidential meaning in cases parallel to (ic). Faller then offers (ii) as evidence that this prediction is not born out for the Quechua reportative. She observes (2002:118) that "[i]n as much as the statement in [ii] makes any sense at all, it is clear that the evidential meaning of -si in the consequent is not cancelled by expressing it explicitly in the antecedent." In other words, the requirement that the speaker of (ii) has reported evidence that Juan will come is not canceled by the fact that this information is contained within the antecedent.

(ii)   *sichus ni-wa-rqa-n   Juan hamu-na-n-ta   chay-qa, Juan-qa   hamu-nqa-s*
       if   say-1o-pst1-3 Juan come-NMLZ-3-ACC this-TOP, Juan-TOP come-3FUT-si
       p = "If I was told that John will come, then John will come."
       EV = speaker was told that Juan will come.   (Faller 2002:118)

Corresponding data have been difficult to elicit in St'át'imcets, since the sentences sound bizarre to consultants. However, we argue that even if the evidential meaning is preserved in the consequent of examples such as (ii), this does not necessarily constitute evidence against the presuppositional analysis of the evidential requirement. Notice that other grammatical elements which are frequently analyzed as inducing presuppositions also retain their presuppositions in parallel contexts. This is illustrated in (iii) for the gender features of pronouns. The pronoun in the second clause is still interpreted with its usual gender restrictions.

(iii)   If the teacher is female, then she can coach the girls' basketball team.

31. Garrett (2001) argues that evidentials in Tibetan interrogatives allow *only* the reading whereby the hearer is expected to use a certain type of evidence in their reply.

32. There is further work to be done on evidentials in St'át'imcets questions. Consistent judgments are difficult to obtain, and evidentials in questions often appear to be simply treated as vacuous, a fact for which we have no explanation at this time.

33. C. Davis, Potts & Speas (2007) admit this point as well; thus, they do not present the strengthening evidentials as evidence against a modal analysis.

34. Interestingly, von Fintel & Gillies argue that the apparent weakness of epistemic necessity modals in many contexts arises because epistemic modals incorporate evidential meaning. That is, they "signal the presence of an indirect inference or deduction rather than of a direct observation" (von Fintel & Gillies to appear: 8).

35. We can actually go further and say that there is no direct evidential in the language, neither overt nor null; see Matthewson & Davis (in prep.) for argumentation. Of course, there *could* be a language which possessed evidentials exactly like the St'át'imcets *k'a, -an'* and *ku7*, and also possessed a direct evidential. There is no reason why all evidentials in a single language should be of the same type. See Blain & Déchaine (2007) for arguments that there are several different types of evidentials in Cree, for example.

36. *Moeten* also allows a deontic modal interpretation, which is not relevant here.

37. However, in Section 7 we will agree with de Haan that elements choose *either* to encode information source, *or* to encode speaker certainty. We can thus (like de Haan) account for the data in (74) by means of an ambiguity analysis. We differ from de Haan in not assuming that *moeten* on its information source-reading is non-modal.

38. Recall that the existence of the report is presupposed, not asserted. Thus, the truth conditions of reportative sentences depend not on whether there was a report, but on whether the report was true. The speaker asserts that it is at least possible that the report was true.

39. The parallel between the evidentials and other modals in the language also further reinforces the conclusion of Section 3.3 that the evidentials should not be analyzed as spatio-temporal operators.

40. The material in this section draws heavily on parts of Rullmann, Matthewson & Davis (to appear), where we adopt the same general analysis for a number of different St'át'imcets modals, including deontics and futures. See also Davis, Matthewson & Rullmann (to appear), where we apply the same basic idea to circumstantial modals in St'át'imcets.

41. We are simplifying things slightly here. According to Kratzer, the modal base maps the evaluation world onto a set of *propositions*; it is therefore a function of type $<s,<st,t>>$.

42. In Rullmann, Matthewson & Davis (to appear), we argue that the choice function variable can be existentially bound as well, but we abstract away from that here as it is not relevant to the main point.

43. A similar suggestion is made by von Fintel & Heim (2005:76, fn. 3) in order to distinguish English *likely* from *must*: perhaps both involve universal quantification over worlds, but the domain of quantification is smaller for *likely* than for *must*, giving rise to a weaker interpretation for the former.

44. Thanks to a reviewer for asking us to include these data.

45. Incidentally, Aikhenvald also asserts that modal analyses of evidentials reflect a euro-centric bias:

> Scholars tends to assume that evidentials are modals largely because of their absence in most major European languages, thus trying to explain an unusual category in terms of some other, more conventional, notion. There is simply no other place in Standard Average European grammar where they could be assigned.   (Aikhenvald 2004:7)

We trust that Section 4 of the present paper provides enough empirical evidence to exempt us from membership in the putative set of euro-centric researchers.

46. Note that we do not claim that elements which distinguish force can never narrow down the modal base in any respect; the German modals *darf* and *wird* discussed by Kratzer (1991) would be counter-examples to that claim (see Section 6 above).

References

Aikhenvald, Alexandra Y. 2004. *Evidentiality*. Oxford: Oxford University Press.

Anderson, Lloyd B. 1986. "Evidentials, paths of change and mental maps: Typologically regular asymmetries". *Evidentiality: The Linguistic Coding of Epistemology* ed. by Wallace Chafe & Johanna Nichols, 273–312. Norwood: Ablex Publishing Corporation.

Blain, Eleanor & Rose-Marie Déchaine. 2007. "Evidential types: Evidence from Cree dialects". *International Journal of American Linguistics* 73:257–291.

Bybee, Joan. 1985. *Morphology: A Study of the Relation Between Meaning and Form.* Amsterdam: John Benjamins.

Chung, Kyungsook 2005. *Space in Tense: The Interaction of Tense, Aspect, Evidentiality and Speech Act in Korean.* Ph.D. dissertation, Simon Fraser University.

Chung, Kyungsook 2007. "Spatial deictic tense and evidentials in Korean". *Natural Language Semantics* 15:187–219.

Davis, Christopher, Christopher Potts & Margaret Speas. 2007. "The pragmatic values of evidential sentences". *Proceedings of SALT 17* ed. by Masayuki Gibson & Tova Friedman. Ithaca, New York: CLC Publication.

Davis, Henry. 2006. *A Teacher's Grammar of Upper St'át'imcets.* Ms., University of British Columbia.

———, Lisa Matthewson & Hotze Rullmann. to appear. 'Out of control' marking as circumstantial modality in St'át'imcets". *Cross-Linguistic Semantics of Tense, Aspect and Modality* ed. by Lotte Hogeweg, Helen de Hoop & Andrey Malchukov. Oxford: John Benjamins.

Ehrich, Veronika. 2001. "Was *nicht müssen* und *nicht können* (nicht) bedeuten können: Zum Skopus der Negation bei den Modalverben des Deutschen". *Modalität und Modalverben im Deutschen,* Vol. 9 of *Linguistische Berichte Sonderhefte* ed. by R. Müller und M. Reis, 149–176. Hamburg: Buske.

van Eijk, Jan. 1997. *The Lillooet Language: Phonology, Morphology, Syntax.* Vancouver: UBC Press.

——— & L. Williams 1981. *Lillooet Legends and Stories.* Mount Currie, BC: Ts'zil Publishing House.

Faller, Martina. 2001. "Remarks on evidential hierarchies". *Proceedings of the "Semfest"* ed. by David Beaver, Stefan Kaufmann, Brady Clark & Luis Casillar, 37–59. Standford, California: CSLI Publications.

——— 2002. *Semantics and Pragmatics of Evidentials in Cuzco Quechua.* Ph.D. dissertation, Stanford.

——— 2003. "Propositional- and illocutionary-level evidentiality in Cuzco Quechua". *Proceedings of SULA* 2, 19–33. Amherst, Mass.: GLSA.

——— 2006. "Evidentiality above and below speech acts". *Functions of Language,* ed. by C. Paradis & L. Egberg.

von Fintel, Kai. 2004. "Would you believe it? The king of France is back! Presuppositions and truth-value intuitions". *Descriptions and Beyond* ed. by M. Reimer & A. Bezuidenhout, 269–296. Oxford: Oxford University Press.

——— 2005. "Epistemic modals: A linguistic perspective". Paper presented at the APA Eastern Division, New York.

——— & Anthony S. Gillies. to appear. "An opinionated guide to epistemic modality". *Oxford Studies in Epistemology, Volume 2* ed. by T.S. Gendler & J. Hawthorne.

——— & Irene Heim. 2005. "Intensional semantics lecture notes". Ms., MIT.

Fitneva, Stanka A. 2001. "Epistemic marking and reliability judgements: Evidence from Bulgarian. *Journal of Pragmatics* 33(3):401–420.

Garrett, Edward. 2001. *Evidentiality and Assertion in Tibetan.* Ph.D. dissertation, UCLA.

Grice, H. Paul. 1975. "Logic and conversation". *Syntax and Semantics, Vol. 3: Speech Acts* ed. by P. Cole & J. Morgan (eds.), 43–58. New York: Academic Press.

de Haan, Ferdinand. 1999. "Evidentiality and epistemic modality: Setting the boundaries". *Southwest Journal of Linguistics* 18:83–101.

Horn, Laurence R. 1989. *A Natural History of Negation.* Chicago: University of Chicago Press.

Ifantidou-Trouki, Elly. 1993. "Sentential adverbs and relevance". *Lingua 90*: 69–90.

Izvorski, Roumyana. 1997. "The present perfect as an epistemic modal". *Proceedings of SALT* VII: 222–239.

Klinedinst, Nathan. 2005. "Plurals, possibilities, and conjunctive disjunction". Paper presented at *Sinn und Bedeutung 10.*

Kratzer, Angelika. 1977. "What "must" and "can" must and can mean". *Linguistics and Philosophy* 1: 337–355.

——— 1981. "The notional category of modality". *Words, Worlds, and Contexts* ed. by H.-J. Eikemeyer & H. Rieser, 38–74. Berlin: de Gruyter.

——— 1991. "Modality". *Semantics: An International Handbook of Contemporary Research* ed. by Dieter Wunderlich & Arnim von Stechow, 639–650. Berlin: de Gruyter.

——— 1998. "Scope or pseudo-scope? Are there wide-scope indefinites?". *Events in Grammar* ed. by Susan Rothstein, 163–196. Dordrecht: Kluwer.

Lazard, Gilbert. 2001. "On the grammaticalization of evidentiality". *Journal of Pragmatics* 33:359–367.

McCready, Eric & Nicholas Asher. 2006. "Modal subordination in Japanese: Dynamics and evidentiality". *U. Penn. Working Papers in Linguistics* 12 ed. by A. Eilam, T. Scheffler & J. Tauberer, 237–249.

McCready, Eric & Norry Ogata 2007. "Evidentiality, modality and probability". *Linguistics and Philosophy* 30:147–206.

Matthewson, Lisa. 1998. *Determiner systems and quantificational strategies: Evidence from Salish.* The Hague: Holland Academic Graphics.

——— 1999. "On the interpretation of wide-scope indefinites". *Natural Language Semantics* 7:79–134.

——— 2005. *When I was Small – I Wan Kwikws: Grammatical Analyis of St'át'imc Oral Narratives.* Vancouver, BC: UBC Press.

——— & Henry Davis. in prep. Deictic evidentials in St'át'imcets. Ms., University of British Columbia.

Papafragou, Anna. 2000. *Modality: Issues in the Semantics-Pragmatics Interface.* Amsterdam: Elsevier.

——— 2006. "Epistemic modality and truth conditions". *Lingua* 116:1688–1702.

Plungian, Vladimir A. 2001. "The place of evidentiality with the universal grammatical space". *Journal of Pragmatics* 33:349–357.

Portner, Paul. 1997. "The semantics of mood, complementation, and conversational force". *Natural Language Semantics* 5:167–212.

Reinhart, Tanya. 1997. "Quantifier scope: How labor is divided between QR and choice functions". *Linguistics and Philosophy* 20:335–397.

Rooryck, Johan. 2001. "Evidentiality, Part I". *GLOT International* 5:125–133.

Rullmann, Hotze, Lisa Matthewson & Henry Davis. to appear. "Modals as distributive indefinites". *Natural Language Semantics.*

Sauerland, Uli. & Mathias Schenner. 2007. "Embedded evidentials in Bulgarian". *Proceedings of Sinn und Bedeutung 11* ed. by E. Puig-Waldmüller, 525–539. Barcelona: Universitat Pompeu Fabra.

Simons, Mandy. 2006. "Observations on embedding verbs, evidentiality, and presupposition". *Lingua* 117:1034–1056.

Speas, Margaret. 2007. "On the syntax and semantics of evidentials". Ms., University of Massachusetts, Amherst.

Willett, Thomas. 1988. "A cross-linguistic survey of the grammaticization of evidentiality". *Studies in Language* 12:51–97.

Winter, Yoad. 1997. "Choice functions and the scopal semantics of indefinites". *Linguistics and Philosophy* 20:399–467.

Author's address:

University of British Columbia
Department of Linguistics
Totem Field Studies
Vancouver, BC V6T 1Z4
Canada

lisamatt@interchange.ubc.ca

Language index

A

Arabic   VI, 121, 141, 144, 147,
    153, 157
    Moroccan Arabic   157
    Lebanese Arabic   157
    Palestinian Arabic   122
    Standard Arabic   144–145,
        147–148, 155, 157

B

Breton   VII, 163–178, 180, 183,
    185–196
    Standard Breton   169–171,
        189
Brythonic   VII, 163–166, 168,
    172, 182, 183, 190–194

C

Celtic   VII, 163, 165, 183, 192

D

Dutch   VI, 85, 88–90, 97–98,
    108, 111, 113, 121–125, 127,
    129–133, 135–139, 143,
    145–146, 148–151,
    154–156, 158, 234
    Lapscheure Dutch
        122–124, 132, 137, 150–151,
        155, 158
    Tegelen Dutch   122,
        124–125, 127, 129–133,
        135–139, 148–150

Tielt Dutch   123, 125, 127,
    129, 131–133, 137–138, 150,
    155

E

English   1, 4, 7, 11–13, 16, 18–19,
    21, 34, 47, 59, 75, 78, 82,
    85, 110, 170, 201, 203, 213,
    215, 218, 222, 227–228,
    233–234, 240–242, 244,
    247–248, 251
    African American English
        (AAE)   1, 4, 7–16, 18, 24
    Anglo-Saxon   16, 18
    Mainstream American
        English (MAE)   7–8, 12,
        14–16, 18, 24

F

French   82, 83, 196
    Atlantic French   196

G

German   VI, 13, 16–18, 21, 30,
    40, 47, 57, 59, 62, 70,
    72–75, 77–80, 85, 89, 90,
    97, 98, 108, 110–111, 129,
    132, 139, 207, 243, 251
    Bavarian   VI, 129, 132–134,
        138, 139, 151–152, 155
    Swiss German   85, 89–90,
        97–98, 108, 111

Germanic   VI, 13, 17, 85, 112,
    153

I

Icelandic   82, 163–164, 183,
    185–186, 190–191, 193
Irish   VI, 121, 144–148, 153,
    156–157, 165

K

Kiitharaka   83

L

Latinate   16–18

N

Norwegian   88–89, 94, 97–98,
    105, 112–113, 247

P

Polish   141

S

Salish   VII, 201, 246
St'át'imcets   VII, 201–203,
    207–223, 226–227, 229–230,
    232–236, 239–251

W

Welsh   VII, 163–172, 183, 187,
    192, 194

Subject index

Access to online full text   ɪngenta *connect*

John Benjamins Publishing Company's journals are available in online full-text format as of the volume published in 2000. Some of our journals have additional (multi-media) information available that is referred to in the articles.

Access to the electronic edition of a volume is included in your subscription. We offer a pay-per-view service per article for those journals and volumes to which you did not subscribe.

Full text is provided in PDF. In order to read these documents you will need Adobe Acrobat Reader, which is freely available from **www.adobe.com/products/ acrobat/readstep2.html**

You can access the electronic edition through the gateways of major subscription agents (SwetsWise, EBSCO EJS, Maruzen) or directly through IngentaConnect.

If you currently use **www.ingenta.com** or **www.ingentaselect.com** (formely, Catchword) to access your subscriptions, these rights have been carried over to **www. ingentaconnect.com**, the new, fully merged service. All bookmarked pages will also be diverted to the relevant pages on **www.ingentaconnect.com**.

If you have not yet set up access to the electronic version of the journal at IngentaConnect, please follow these instructions:

If you are a personal subscriber:
- Register free at **www.ingentaconnect.com**. This is a one-time process, that provides IngentaConnect with the information they need to be able to match your data with the subscription data provide by the publisher. Your registration also allows you to use the e-mail alerting services.
- Select *Personal subscriptions*.
- Select the publication title and enter your subscription number. Your subscription number can be found on the shipping label with the print journal, and on the invoice/renewal invitation.
- You will be notified by email once your online access has been activated.

If you are an institutional subscriber:
- Register free at **www.ingentaconnect.com** by selecting the registration link and following the link to institutional registration.
- Select *Set up subscriptions*.
- Select the publication title and enter your subscription number. Your subscription number can be found on the shipping label with the print journal, and on the invoice/renewal invitation.
- You will be notified by email once your online access has been activated.
  If you purchase subscriptions via a subscription agent they will be able to set up subscriptions on IngentaConnect on your behalf – simply pass them your IngentaConnect ID, sent to you at registration.

If you would like further information or assistance with your registration, please contact **help@ingentaconnect.com**.

For information on our journals, please visit **www.benjamins.com**